From the Hudson to the Yalu

TEXAS A&M UNIVERSITY MILITARY HISTORY SERIES

31

From the Hudson to the Yalu

WEST POINT '49 IN THE KOREAN WAR

Harry J. Maihafer

TEXAS A&M UNIVERSITY PRESS

COLLEGE STATION

Library of Congress Cataloging-in-Publication Data

Maihafer, Harry J., 1924–
    From the Hudson to the Yalu : West Point '49
in the Korean War / Harry J. Maihafer.
        p.   cm. — (Texas A&M University
military series ; 31)
    Includes index.
    ISBN 0-89096-554-4
    1. Korean War, 1950–1953—Personal narra-
tives, American.   2. United States Military
Academy. Class of 1949.   I. Title.   II. Series:
Texas A&M University military history series ; 31.
DS921.6.M35   1993
951.904'2—dc20   93-12948
                                   CIP

Contents

Illustrations

Maps

Preface

In July of 1945, shortly before the end of World War II, 1,200 nervous, hopeful young men joined the US Corps of Cadets. Four years later, at graduation, our number had dwindled to 574. In the interim, we had undergone the finest military training our country had to offer.

Together, we had suffered through the rigors of plebe year; had cheered for some of the greatest teams in the history of college football; had struggled through academics; and had finally been rewarded, both with diplomas and with class rings marking us forever as West Point '49ers. Along the way, the Academy motto, "Duty, Honor, Country," had become part of our value system. The term "classmate" had also acquired a special meaning, but its full significance was, at graduation, yet to be appreciated.

It would be difficult to say exactly why this story was written. One reason, of course, was to remember those '49ers who fought in Korea, many of whom gave their lives in what was to become a "forgotten war." Then too, there was a desire to thank the magnificent noncoms, our friends and teachers, who helped us to cope with the awesome challenges of combat. Finally, recalling the mountaineer who attempted Mt. Everest "because it was there," there was a need to describe certain things just because they happened, and because, if they weren't recorded, certain deeds might be forgotten and the sacrifices unappreciated.

Did things happen just this way? The best I can say now, years later, is I *believe* so. At least the stories which follow, including my own, have been told honestly, and if this account is not precisely the way things happened, it's the way they were perceived by a group of green and often scared lieutenants.

From the Hudson to the Yalu

1. School Is Out

JUNE–JULY 1950

On 7 June 1949, when our class graduated from West Point, Doug Bush was already something of a legend. During World War II, he had left Vanderbilt to enter the army as an 18-year-old private, had completed Officer Candidate School (OCS) and paratrooper school, then gone overseas with the 82nd Airborne Division. As commander of an airborne pathfinder unit, he had jumped into Normandy before H-Hour of D-Day and had later fought through the Battle of the Bulge. Then, as a first lieutenant with a chest full of ribbons, he had returned to the States to prepare for the West Point entrance exams.

At the Military Academy, Doug had at one time or another participated in six varsity sports—football, track, soccer, lacrosse, boxing, and gymnastics. His leadership ability was also well recognized, and in his final year he was a cadet captain and company commander.

The day after graduation, Doug married the lovely Carolyn Thomas. He seemed to have everything, but there was one exception: he had been commissioned in the infantry, and his heart was set on flying. So a week later, Doug, along with Carolyn, set out for Washington to change things. For the next few days he prowled the corridors of the Pentagon, filling out applications and requests for transfer to the Air Force—all to no avail.

No one had ever questioned Doug's courage, but his next act, which made even his best friends gasp, required more audacity than even his deeds in combat.

The doorbell rang at Quarters 1, Fort Myer, Virginia, home of Omar Bradley, the Army Chief of Staff. An orderly, opening the door, saw a six-foot-one, two-hundred-pound, strikingly handsome officer with coal-black hair.

"I'm Lieutenant Bush, and I'd like to see General Bradley," said

Doug. After considerable difficulty, he was ushered in to see the general. Bradley was at first astounded by Doug's brashness, but as they talked, the man they called the "soldier's general" became not only amused but also remarkably understanding. When Doug left, he had the general's verbal order for a transfer to the Air Force, not only for Doug, but for six classmates who also wanted to switch.

Now, a year later, in June of 1950, Doug had been one of the few from his flight class selected for jet fighter training (having somehow, to no one's surprise, overcome the regulation prohibiting six-foot-one fighter pilots).

By this time, of course, the rest of our West Point class was dispersed throughout the country in a variety of situations. Ralph "Buff" Buffington, for example, having completed the engineer course at Fort Belvoir, was driving to Fort Mason, California, with his wife Barbara, en route to an assignment with the 14th Engineer Battalion in Japan. Ralph had graduated fifth in his class at the Engineer School. This was no surprise; he had always excelled scholastically, not only during his time at the Military Academy, but also during three earlier semesters at Stanford. Buff would undoubtedly have graduated even higher in the class had he not spent so much time coaching those less gifted. Many men owed their remaining at the Academy to Ralph's unselfishness, and among those he helped along was All-American quarterback Arnold Galiffa.

As for me, I was playing tennis that month at Fort Eustis, Virginia, representing Fort Knox in a Second Army tournament. It seemed a fitting and enjoyable way to end the preparatory phase of my army career.

Earlier in the day, I had won my second-round singles match, but since my opponent was a lieutenant colonel, I'd been careful not to gloat. Prudent second lieutenants did *not* gloat at colonels. After our match, the colonel had congratulated me and invited me to join him later at the Officers' Club.

After four years at the Military Academy, plus an additional year at service schools, the army members of West Point '49, to our great relief, were finally finished with school and games and ready to enter the "real" army. The Air Force Academy was not yet in existence, and some 40 percent of our class (supplemented by the audacious Doug Bush) had entered the Air Force. The rest of us, however, for the first six months after graduation, had attended the Ground General course at Fort Riley, Kansas. After Riley, and as 1950 began, we had separated for our branch training. Infantrymen had gone to Fort Benning; artillerymen to Sill; engineers to Belvoir. Personally, having been commissioned as a tanker (although, with a bow to tradition, the branch was still called the Cavalry), I had attended the Armored School at Fort Knox.

As branch training ended at the various schools, our assignment orders were published. Some would be going to stateside posts, but after a thirty-day leave, most would be headed overseas, to Germany, Panama, Hawaii, or even, like me, to the Far East.

That evening at the Officers' Club, while drinking a beer graciously provided by my erstwhile opponent, I heard startling news on the radio: Communist forces had crossed the 38th Parallel and invaded South Korea. I told the colonel about my orders to Japan.

"What do you think?" I asked him. "Do you suppose this Korean thing means I'll be going into combat?"

"Not a chance, Harry."

"Why is that, Colonel?"

"Figure it out for yourself. Combat is for reserve officers like myself. It'd be stupid to send West Point second lieutenants into combat—the attrition is too great. Don't get me wrong; I admire West Point; wish I'd gone there myself—but you fellows are too much of an asset to squander as platoon leaders. No, Harry, you'll no doubt end up in some cushy headquarters job."

Was he trying to reassure me, or was this some deep resentment coming out? In any case, I didn't think he was right. I'd heard of too many West Pointers who had become casualties in World War II. Also, in a way I hoped he *wasn't* right. The thought of getting shot at was not a happy one, but on the other hand, what had I been getting trained for at West Point, at Fort Riley, at Knox?

By 28 June Seoul, South Korea's capital city, had fallen. Two days later, President Truman, with the consent of the United Nations Security Council, had authorized General MacArthur to use American troops to repel the assault. Wherever we were, members of West Point '49 with orders to the Far East felt excitement blended with apprehension. Although many '49ers had pre-Academy service during World War II, only a handful had seen combat. Now, as Civil War soldiers used to say, we were about to "see the elephant."

Task Force Smith, a battalion from the 21st Infantry Regiment plus an artillery battery from the 52nd Field, landed in Korea on 1 July. Four days later, near Suwon, they came under attack and were forced to retreat. It became clear a mere American "show of force" would not do the trick. In the following days, other American troops

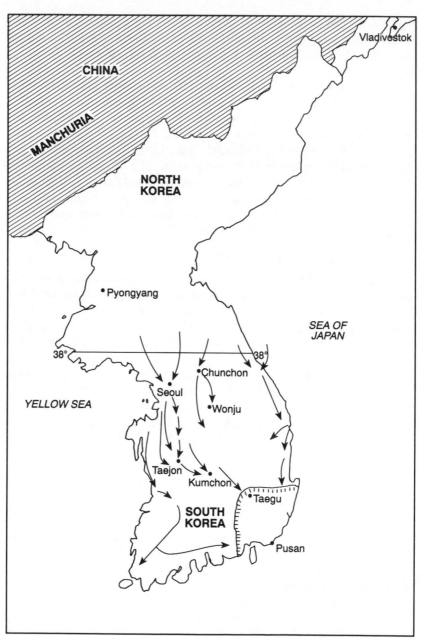

The North Korean Invasion of South Korea, June–July 1950

were committed, including the remainder of the 24th Division. Unfortunately, however, these were "occupation" troops, understrength, underequipped, and poorly trained. The build-up continued, but the situation worsened. Smith's task force was being overwhelmed by Communist tanks and swarming Red infantry. Positions were abandoned; losses mounted; the term "bug out" entered the GI vocabulary.

After losing my quarterfinal match in the tennis tournament, I went on to New Jersey. The leave, spent with my wife Jeanne and our two-month-old baby daughter, was all too short. One evening Jeanne and I treated ourselves by going to a Broadway show—Carol Channing in *Gentlemen Prefer Blondes*. As we left the theater, newspapers on the street had headlines saying Major General Dean of the US 24th Division, the senior American officer in Korea, was missing at a place called Taejon.

Soon it was time to leave for Fort Lawton, near Seattle, first stop on my way to Japan. Jeanne and some of her family took me to the airport, and as the plane prepared to leave the gate, we waved goodbye, sad and apprehensive, wondering what lay ahead and how long it would be before we were together again. From the plane's window, I saw Jeanne in the terminal doorway. She was starting to cry.

Similar scenes were being duplicated around the country. Bill Moore, with orders to the same engineer battalion as Ralph Buffington, was on leave in Springfield, Illinois, when he heard about the North Korean invasion. Thinking, like many of us, that the war would be a short one, he loaded his car with fishing tackle and golf clubs and started out for California. Bill Marslender left North Carolina for Wisconsin, where he joined his West Point roommate, Roger Kuhlman. The two of them then traveled together to Seattle. Ralph and Barbara Buffington, meanwhile, had gone on ahead, arriving in Yokohama on 8 July.

At Fort Benning about this time, infantry classmates with orders to Hawaii or Japan were also heading for the West Coast. Cecil Newman, a short, slender Texan who had won a Combat Infantry Badge in World War II, was the proud owner of a 16-mm movie camera and a roll of colored film. His orders called for him to proceed to San Francisco en route to his assignment in Hawaii. After he posed holding his tiny baby daughter, Cec's wife Wes insisted Cec take the camera with him so as to make a record of his trip. Many of our infantry classmates, including Kenny Miller, had volunteered to give up part of their leave so as to attend airborne school. Before jump school, however, Kenny, along with Barney Cummings, Court Davis, and Dick Stauffer, went to Kenny's home in Concord, North Carolina, to usher at classmate Chuck Spettel's wedding. Soon after jump school, Stauffer and Spettel were on their way to Europe and the other three were headed for the Far East.

Fellow infantrymen Ernie Denham and Mike Wadsworth, whose wives were about to give birth, learned their orders to the Far East were being deferred. They'd be staying at Benning for a while as instructors.

Jack Madison, having finished airborne school, spent the first part of his leave at the Citadel, in Charleston, where his father was commandant of cadets. Then, en route to the West Coast, he ran into Bill Wilbur in Chicago, and the two of them traveled together to Seattle. Jack reported in to Fort Lawton, and while he was waiting for shipment, managed a side-trip to nearby Fort Lewis to see a girl he knew, Arden Hennig. Arden's father, Colonel Hennig, had already left for the Far East with his artillery group.

Hayes Metzger was at Fort Hamilton, in Brooklyn, and on a bus which would take him to a plane heading for Germany. At the last minute, Hayes was pulled from the bus and told his orders had been changed. He was to report to a newly activated airborne unit in North Carolina. Although it would take a while, he'd eventually end up in Korea.

When the war started, Clay Buckingham had written the War Department asking that his orders be changed from Germany to Korea. Receiving no response, Clay proceeded to Fort Dix, New Jersey, golf clubs and tennis racket in hand. He had already turned in his hold baggage when new orders arrived telling him to report to Travis Air Force Base in California for further shipment to the Far East.

Meanwhile, '49er Lew Baumann had just transferred from the Air Force to the Army. Upon graduation, Lew had chosen the Air Force so he could become a pilot. When he was eliminated from flight school, he asked to return to the Army. When the Korean War started, his request was granted. Soon he was made a second lieutenant of infantry and placed on orders for Japan.

At Fort Lawton, classmates from various service schools were being reunited, not only West Pointers, but also many who'd received their Regular Army commissions through ROTC. We were all just a year out of college, and there was still room for the campus prankster, one of whom, an ROTC graduate, picked on a young dentist who had just been called to active duty.

"What's that, doc? You say you were issued *two* dogtags? Why that's terrible!"

"It is?"

"Well, of course! This probably means there are duplicate records on you. One place will show you to be present, and the other will have you listed as AWOL. You'd better go talk to the supply people about this!" He did and was solemnly referred from office to office before realizing he'd been had.

My name appeared on orders to fly out, and I was just as happy to be leaving Lawton's hurry-up-and-wait confusion. The order showed me on a flight with thirty-five enlisted men and two other officers, and for some reason I'd been designated officer in charge, even though each of the other officers outranked me.

Beecher "Beech" Brian, who on his mother's side was related to Harriet Beecher Stowe, author of *Uncle Tom's Cabin*, was shipping out about the same time. He wrote his parents he'd be on the same plane as George Tow. Beech and George had known each other since grade school, when their fathers were stationed together in the Philippines, and over the years the families had kept in touch.

I packed my bags and reported as directed. A warrant officer was calling roll. Behind him, a young corporal, due to ship out for someplace in the States, interrupted to ask a question. The warrant officer turned on him with mock ferocity, saying, "Look, fella, these men are all on their way to Korea. Did you want to get in with them?"

"No sir!" The corporal grinned and jumped back. There was no way *he* wanted to get caught up with this group of unfortunates! We looked at each other and grinned too, but somehow we weren't sure it was all that funny.

At the airfield, Air Force C-54s, tired but sturdy veterans of World War II, were waiting for us. Our group climbed aboard the first plane, each man carrying his own duffel bag and placing it along the center axis of the cabin. Then we sat, with our backs to the windows, in canvas bucket seats which ran the length of the plane along each side. Next stop: Alaska.

Hour after hour, our flight droned over forests stretching to the horizon in monotonous grandeur. It was still broad daylight when we landed in late evening at Elmendorf Air Force Base outside Anchorage.

Next morning we flew west over the Aleutians, but after two or three hours we returned to Elmendorf. "We're having a problem with the hydraulic system," the crew chief told me. "It looks as though we'll have to spend another night in Anchorage."

Next morning, with a different plane, we took off again for a long dull flight over gray, icy waters. The crew included a lieutenant colonel pilot, two captains, a lieutenant, and a pair of sergeants. The lieutenant, West Point '48, said we'd be staying overnight on the island of Kiska, then leave early the next day for the long final leg into Japan.

The Navy base at Kiska was windswept, treeless, and bleak. One couldn't help feeling sorry for the men stationed there. That night I shared the quarters of a Navy lieutenant (jg), whose copy of the *Stars and Stripes*, already a few days old, told how the Americans' Kum River defensive line had been overrun and how the North Koreans, with their Russian-built T-34 tanks, were continuing to flow south.

We took off in the early dawn. The Navy lieutenant, from the snugness of his bunk, wished me "good-bye and good luck," looking somewhat embarrassed about staying behind while others were going off to war. In a way I envied him his safety, but I didn't envy him Kiska at all.

Once we were airborne, the lieutenant on the flight crew explained that we'd be having a long day of flying. Four or five hours would take us to Shemya, near the end of the Aleutian chain. We'd make a quick refueling stop, then fly another ten hours on into Tokyo.

"Will there be time for the men to eat lunch?" I asked.

"No," he said, "we won't be on the ground that long."

"Then can you radio ahead and see if they can prepare some box lunches?"

"I'll check with the pilot," he said. Finally we landed at Shemya, a barren hump rising ungracefully from the Arctic Ocean. We climbed out of the plane, which was parked well away from the nearest buildings. The flight crew said they were going in to Base Operations while the plane was being refueled and told me to keep all the men near the plane. I again asked about lunch, but they said there wouldn't be time for the men to eat, and no, they hadn't called ahead about box lunches. Somehow it sounded as though my request had been of little importance to them.

The men were asking about chow when a jeep drove alongside the plane. It was the base mess officer, a personable first lieutenant. "Are the men coming in to eat? We're all ready to serve them."

"No," I answered, "they tell me that would take a couple of hours, and we won't be on the ground that long."

"Well, if you want we can do it faster than that. How much time do you have?"

"Could I borrow your jeep, Lieutenant? I'll try to find out." His driver took me to Base Ops, a low, gray Quonset. Inside, there was no sign of the flight crew.

"Does anyone know when we'll be leaving?" I asked.

The operations sergeant said, "As soon as the crew finishes eating, I suppose. They went over to the cafeteria."

Next door, in the cafeteria, the crew had just placed their orders. "Colonel," I asked the pilot, "is it all right to bring my men into the mess hall? The people there are all set to serve them."

"No, that won't be possible. We'll be taking off in a few minutes."

"Then how about having some box lunches made up? It's going to be a long, hungry day otherwise."

"No, we don't have time for that either. Relax, Lieutenant."

The captain at the table, in a not unkindly manner, said, "Of course there's no point in *your* going hungry, Lieutenant. Pull up a chair and join us."

I just glared at him. Then I glared at the West Point lieutenant on their crew. Surely *he* knew better than this. He kept his eyes on his plate.

Back at the plane, I asked the mess officer how long it would take to prepare some box lunches.

"I'll have them here in forty-five minutes!" he said. I told the other two officers what had happened, and felt annoyed that they weren't as upset as I was. Taking care of the troops, especially when they were *my* troops (and my first ones at that) had become terribly important.

About thirty minutes later, a carryall arrived with the flight crew.

"Okay, Lieutenant. Have the men load back up now." The crew climbed into the aircraft. I didn't say anything to the troops.

Everett, one of the other army officers, said, "Shouldn't we have the men start mounting up?"

"Let's stall a few minutes," I said. The copilot climbed down from the cockpit and told some of the men to start getting aboard.

"Just a minute, Captain," I said, "we're waiting for box lunches. They'll be here any moment."

"I'm sorry, Lieutenant. We have to leave now in order to avoid some weather in Japan. The colonel wants everyone back on board."

Butterflies were gathering in my stomach. The men were standing nearby in small groups, well aware of what was happening. "Captain, I think we should wait until the lunches arrive."

A master sergeant called out, "You tell him, Lieutenant!" The captain, looking confused, went back inside to confer with the pilot.

Everett asked, "What'll you do if he comes back with a direct order to load them up?"

"Maybe I should remind him that the pilot, regardless of rank, is in command while we're in the air, but when troops are on the ground, the senior ground force officer is in command." Even as I said it, I realized how ridiculous it sounded to refer to a second lieutenant as a "senior ground force officer."

Suddenly the mess truck arrived, well loaded with box lunches. The men cheered. To me, that truck looked like the cavalry to the rescue in the nick of time. Lunches were distributed; we quickly climbed aboard, and away we went. As it turned out, Tokyo was weathered in and we couldn't have gotten that far anyhow.

We landed at Misawa Air Base in northern Honshu, spent the night, and next day flew on to Haneda Airport outside Tokyo. From Haneda, trucks took us to Camp Drake, former home of the 1st Cavalry Division, which had left shortly before for Korea.

At Camp Drake the transient officers were billeted in a large gym. Steel cots were crowded row upon row, our bags piled under them or alongside. The gym became a reunion hall for West Point '49, with twenty-five or more of our class on hand. A leading topic of conversation was the Officers' Club, where the liquor supply of the recently departed 1st Cavalry Division was being disposed of at bargain rates: five cents for a bottle of beer, ten cents for a mixed drink or highball.

That afternoon we turned in our civilian luggage, together with any items for storage. (In my case that included a tennis racket. I had felt very self-conscious carrying it all the way across the Pacific.) We then went to a warehouse and drew our field gear—helmets, ponchos, canteens, weapons, etc.

Later that day, the first of our group prepared to ship out. I said so long to Beecher Brian, Roger Fife, and Cec Newman, all of whom were going to the 1st Cavalry Division. Cec had sent his camera home, along with its film, which began with pictures of Cec holding his baby daughter, and now included scenic shots of San Francisco and Hawaii. Cec said, "Just think. It looks as though I'll be the first in our class to hear a shot fired in anger."

The "shot fired in anger" cliché came out quite naturally. It was still hard to accept that this was really happening, and in conversation, one had to make an effort not to sound dramatic. Leslie "Kirk" Kirkpatrick and I even joked about it, with Kirk proposing we write our wives, "Darling, my regiment sails at dawn!"

Kirk was another friend of long standing; we'd been in the army together as fellow sergeants in the West Point preparatory course at Lafayette College in Easton, Pennsylvania. He and I had shared many happy times, beginning with the weekends at Lafayette, when paratrooper Kirk, just back from Italy, had been the ringleader as our group left campus to drink some beer and court the girls of Easton.

Leaving at the same time was Bill Moore, who was headed for the 14th Engineer Battalion. Bill's orders had called for him to join his unit in Japan, but when he arrived, he found the entire battalion, including Ralph Buffington, had left for Korea three weeks earlier, on 12 July.

One evening Capt. Tom Parr and two others invited me to join them on an excursion into Tokyo. "But we're supposed to be restricted to Camp Drake," I protested.

"Look," Tom said, "you're a second lieutenant, and you're about to go into combat, just what are they going to do to you?" It was a compelling argument. We sneaked off post, and once in town, decided to crash the palatial General Headquarters (GHQ) Officers' Club, only to be stopped by a polite but firm Japanese majordomo, who made it clear this was a place reserved for senior officers. At this point the club manager, a courtly retired officer, West Point '17, came to our rescue. Not only did he admit us, but when he learned we were on our way to Korea, he insisted on acting as our special host. It was a balmy summer evening, and tables had been set outside in a magnificent terraced garden. A Japanese dance band played Glenn Miller arrangements to perfection. There were steaks, wine, a waiter hovering behind each chair. Our host made certain we had an evening to remember. Then, back to Camp Drake, the spell of the evening somewhat marred by a charcoal-burning taxicab, which coughed to a stop at every incline.

Next day we boarded a train for Sasebo, a seaport on the western shore of Kyushu. The scenes from the train window were full of charm and fascination for someone new to the Orient. However, our trip would have been more enjoyable if we hadn't seen the latest *Stars and Stripes.*

"Stand or Die, Says Gen. Walker," the headline screamed. The lead article told how US troops had fallen back to the Naktong River, the last line of defense. If this line crumbles, General Walker had said, "we'll see the worst bloodbath Americans have ever known." It was a message with very little sales appeal for those of us hurrying forward to join the team.

We traveled overnight on the train, passed through the tunnel connecting Honshu and Kyushu, and next morning at Sasebo learned we'd be sailing that very evening. Along with some others, I went to the Legal Assistance Office and made out a last will and testament. Under the circumstances the idea seemed rather practical. Next I inquired at the Service Club if there was a Catholic chaplain nearby who could hear confession.

"There's no Army chaplain here," they said. "However, there's a European missionary priest in Sasebo. We'll try to locate him." Around 5:00 P.M., some four or five hundred of us boarded the *Yoshiba Maru*, an ancient, weatherbeaten Japanese freighter.

The missionary, riding a bicycle, his threadbare cassock flapping wildly in the breeze, appeared just as I was about to climb the gangplank. The good father came on board, heard confessions, chatted with me a while in a warm and understanding manner, even promised to write a letter to my wife.

Somewhat behind schedule, the ship cast off. We steamed northward along the shoreline for a time, then headed west, across the Strait of Tsushima toward Korea.

A call came over the loudspeaker, and we learned that a Protestant chaplain would be holding services in the main cabin at 7:30 P.M. I went to the meeting a few minutes early, and the chaplain assured me that I as a Catholic would be most welcome at his service, but he also suggested I hold a meeting myself for the Catholics. But what could we do without a priest? In any case, I talked to one of the crew, who said he would have an announcement made inviting Catholics to assemble at 8:30 P.M.

At the Protestant service, we prayed and sang hymns, after which the chaplain gave a low-keyed talk, which to my mind was right on target. He began by acknowledging that most of us were scared.

"But look around you," he said. "Imagine yourself going into combat this week not as an American but as a Communist North Korean. How would you like to be going up against the men you see in this room — men with training and courage, who have all the wealth and power of America backing them up! Consider the position of that North Korean, if you will, and then think who it is that should be feeling afraid. . . ." It was a good theme and, for me at least, gave a certain measure of reassurance.

As soon as the Protestant meeting broke up, Catholics began assembling, nearly fifty of them. Self-consciously, I acted as group leader, said a few words, trying to repeat the theme of the chaplain as well as I could. At my suggestion, we then said the rosary. Our impromptu service seemed to strike the right chord. That phrase about "no atheists in foxholes" was more than applicable aboard the *Yoshiba Maru* that night.

When I awoke the next morning, I looked through a porthole and saw for the first time the Land of the Morning Calm.

2. Seeing the Elephant

1–12 AUGUST

The Pusan Perimeter, a thin line of weary South Koreans and Americans, was established during the first week of August. Using the Naktong River as a barrier, it extended about a hundred miles north to south, about fifty miles east to west, and was anchored on the port city of Pusan. Soon the North Koreans, hoping for an early breakthrough, were attacking at several points.

The ship shuddered and came to rest alongside the Pusan dock. On deck, lined up alphabetically, we waited patiently as someone chalked a number on each helmet. I mentioned to artillery classmate Earl Lochhead that today, 8 August, was my twenty-sixth birthday. Soon the word spread among friends who delighted in mixing black humor with their congratulations. George Tow said, "Well, Harry, and how old *would* you have been next year?" Very funny, George. Other jokes were made about the ignorance of tankers, who went to war in iron coffins, while I responded with a line I'd learned at Knox, that at least a tank's armor plate was better protection than an infantry-man's OD shirt!

My name was called. I picked up my duffel bag and weapon, walked down the gangplank, and climbed into a waiting truck. We came to a school building, which had been pressed into service as a processing center. When my turn came, I learned I'd be going to the 78th Medium Tank Battalion of the 24th Infantry Division, and that I'd be shipping out by train that afternoon.

Trucks brought us to the Pusan railstation, where I climbed aboard the train and found a seat next to a man I'd known at Fort Knox, a World War II veteran whose service included several months in a German prison camp. Just then another train, carrying wounded South Korean soldiers, pulled in on an adjacent track. Amid much shout-

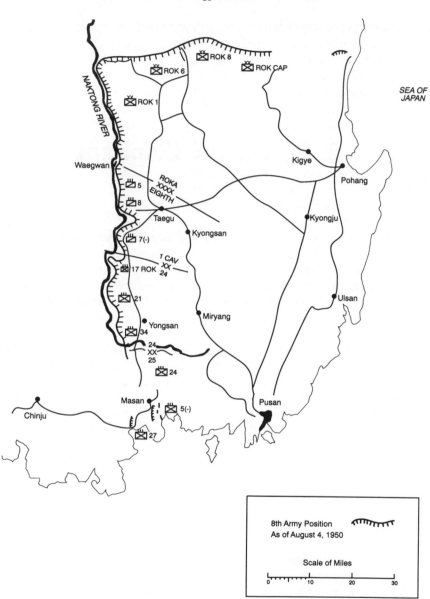

The Pusan Perimeter, 4 August 1950

ing, Korean corpsmen began unloading litters from the hospital train.

Suddenly my seat companion spoke, "Lucky devils!"

"Who?" I asked.

"Those guys on the litters."

"Maybe *not* so lucky," I said. "Don't forget, some of them may be losing an arm or a leg."

"I *still* say lucky. I'd give an arm to get out of this." I was too surprised to say anything more. My friend from Fort Knox, a man I'd been envying for his poise and background, was evidently even more apprehensive than I was. Maybe combat experience wasn't necessarily all positive. My "ignorance" wasn't exactly "bliss," but at least I was able to feel, along with my fear, a certain measure of excitement and optimism. Most of my classmates probably felt the same—we were young, felt personally invulnerable, and though we wouldn't have admitted it, we also felt a certain sense of adventure.

Finally our train jolted underway. Slowly we headed north, winding through valleys terraced with rice paddies and past an occasional village of mud houses with thatched roofs. There were many stops and starts, and it wasn't until dusk that we came to Miryang, campsite of the 24th Infantry Division Replacement Company. We were given something to eat and told to bed down for the night. I presumed there were sentries posted; at least I hoped so.

In the morning, we realized the Replacement Company was actually in a rather attractive spot. Nearby was a river and a grove of trees. After breakfast, and as the temperature climbed, we moved under the trees, stripped, and went swimming. I didn't know what was coming next, but this day at least was starting out well.

From time to time a sergeant from the Replacement Company appeared and read a list of names, whereupon those whose names had been called loaded aboard trucks and headed out to their respective units. In midafternoon, a list was read of those going to the 78th Medium Tank Battalion.

"Lieutenant Maihafer, Harry J." As usual, my last name was mispronounced, but there it was. The butterflies, which had flown away for a time, once more reassembled in my stomach.

All of us going to the 78th Battalion, replacement officers plus a few men returning from the hospital, fitted easily into one truck. The driver told us we were headed for Yongsan, where the 78th Battalion was located. I threw my gear into the back of the truck and climbed aboard, finding a seat next to a talkative corporal who seemed eager to impress the new lieutenant with war stories, the bloodier the better. He told of the fearsome accuracy of North Korean gunners, who adjusted their mortar fire not by yards or tens of yards, but by *feet;* of the enemy antitank rifle with a shell which easily penetrated the thin skin of the M-24, of the hopelessness of pitting our light M-24s against the heavy Russian-made T-34s. At Taejon, he said, the 78th Battalion had lost eleven of its seventeen tanks in a single day.

My corporal friend kept talking steadily, playing the role of combat veteran to the hilt. I asked where he'd been wounded, and learned he'd been hospitalized not for a wound but for a stomach disorder. Somehow that put the rest of his stories in perspective. I was also starting to object a bit to his buddy-buddy manner, especially his deliberate failure to sprinkle even an occasional "sir" into the conversation. After all, I was going to my first outfit and wanted to discover a few of the ground rules myself, not just rely on someone who sounded too much like a know-it-all.

Next he explained that once you got into combat, all rank distinctions were forgotten. All the officers and men, for example, called each other by their first name. "What's yours?" he asked.

"Maihafer."

"No, I mean your first name."

"Why don't you just call me Lieutenant Maihafer or simply Lieutenant," I answered. Somehow that seemed to inhibit his conversation, but only momentarily. Soon he shifted his attention to one of the other replacement officers.

Eventually, in early evening, we came to Yongsan, a fair-sized village with a dusty "main street" and some shops, all of which appeared to be empty. The truck dropped us on the far edge of town, in the courtyard of a one-room masonry building; probably it had been some sort of town office. A first sergeant collected copies of our orders and brought us inside.

Capt. Tom Parr, a man I'd met earlier, acted as spokesman for our group. "Who's in charge here?" Tom asked.

A fortyish, rather seedy-looking captain answered, "I guess I am."

He then gave us what was apparently all the welcoming and orientation we were going to get. "Look, I've only been here a couple of weeks myself, so I can't tell you much. The 78th is no battalion, it isn't even a platoon. The outfit came to Korea with seventeen light tanks; now it has two. To tell the truth, I don't know why in hell they sent you guys up here. Maybe it means they're going to give us some tanks. Have you heard anything?"

Parr, taking the initiative, asked some rather obvious questions.

Q: "What mission do we have?"

A: "None really. Except we send our two tanks to maintain a roadblock outside town. We take turns manning it."

Q: "Where are the front lines?"

A: "Hell, fella, don't you know this war doesn't *have* any front lines? Those North Korean gooks just bypass the poor infantry slobs whenever they decide to. There are probably some of them right now with that group of 'civilians' you see. [A column of refugees was trudging down the street outside the building.] All I know is that the infantry is supposed to be somewhere up on those mountains outside town."

Q: "But how do you keep in touch?"

A: "You see that field telephone? We call in to regiment on a regular schedule. Whenever those guys decide to bug out, they're supposed to call us so we can haul ass too! When the time comes, I just hope to God someone remembers."

A: "What do you want *us* to do?"

A: "Hell, I don't know. For now you might as well go to sleep; just sprawl out anyplace."

This was pretty sad, and the most depressing part was the defeatist attitude of the captain, our nominal leader, who obviously wanted no part of command responsibility. He had, in fact, asked Tom Parr his date of rank as a captain, and had seemed disappointed that Tom was junior to him, which meant he himself would continue to have responsibility for our group. In short, his attitude seemed to be "everything is so messed up—what's the use"?

Next morning we had a substantial breakfast at the field kitchen, across the road from our building and near the small motor pool containing the unit's remaining trucks and jeeps. For a while we sat around, talked, wrote letters. Someone said the one-room headquarters was getting too crowded, and several of us moved outside to the courtyard. We listened to a shortwave radio, hoping to get some news. No news, but we picked up an Armed Forces Network station from Japan, relaying the broadcast of a baseball game between the New York Yankees and the Cleveland Indians.

In the early twilight, we heard the roar of engines and a clatter of tank tracks. Two M-24s, followed by two jeeps mounting machine guns, raced past our building. Their bumper markings showed they were from the 24th Division Reconnaissance Company. As they passed our building, they swung left and headed north along a trail which led to a narrow stream, about a half-mile away. There they stopped and began firing their tank cannons and machine guns, spraying the slope on the far side of the stream.

What was going on? Had there been a breakthrough? Were there actually enemy soldiers that close? If so, what if anything should *we* be doing about it?

Evidently just watch; at least that's all we did. We weren't able to make out what they were shooting at, and somehow the whole scene seemed remote and unreal. After a while the firing stopped. The tanks and jeeps backed up, turned around, and drove quickly back the way they had come. We were very much in the dark about what was happening. Our phone to the regiment was no help; only word was that the infantry up on the mountain were under attack and we should be ready to move out on short notice.

Another man and I agreed to buddy-up and take turns staying awake during the night. After all, if the infantry were still on that mountain, why had those recon people been firing at something on *this* side of the ridgeline?

Nearby, although I didn't realize it, was the headquarters of the 14th Engineer Battalion, which Bill Moore had joined a few days earlier, and where Ralph Buffington had been named the assistant communications officer. By this time, the Naktong Perimeter was stretched so thin that every available Eighth Army unit was up on line. Consequently, when Bill reported in to his battalion headquarters, he found it was just that—a headquarters, and *only* a headquarters. All the unit's line companies were up forward, manning their own defensive sectors alongside the infantry.

So far, the North Koreans had been not only successful, but also remarkably consistent with their tactics. Whenever they encountered opposition, they would send units to encircle and to get behind either the Americans or the South Koreans opposing them. Time after time those on line had found themselves surrounded and forced to retreat in disorder.

On the night of 11 August, based on a report that enemy patrols had again gotten into the rear, the 14th Engineers were told to send outposts to four critical road junctions. Hastily, four squads of a dozen men each were constituted from the only troops available, the clerks, cooks, and miscellaneous drivers and mechanics around the headquarters. Moore was put in charge of the third of these unorthodox squads, and about midnight, he and his men, in pitch darkness, were dropped off at a lonely road junction. They crawled into ditches alongside the road and waited.

Bill tried to call battalion on his radio, but could get no response. As it began to get light, he moved his men from the ditches, onto a nearby knoll, and told them to dig in. Soon a patrol, sent to check on the outposts, arrived at Moore's location. At the first two squad locations, they had found only dead bodies. The lieutenants with those squads had been found with their hands tied behind their back and a bullet hole in the back of their heads.

A short time later, Ralph Buffington, in his role of commo officer, arrived to try and get Bill's radio working. Moore was crouching down, digging a hole for himself, and Buffington was standing erect, when an enemy machine gun opened up. Ralph was hit three times; two others nearby were also hit. The squad was pinned down, but about then an armored reconnaissance platoon, possibly the one I'd seen in Yongsan a few hours earlier, appeared and took the enemy under fire.

Thanks to the covering fire, Bill and another man were able to carry Ralph down the hill. They put him into a jeep, which immediately headed for an aid station. However, Ralph Buffington, the brilliant, unselfish young scholar, was already dead.

For me, the night had passed uneventfully. A good breakfast made the morning seem almost normal, and I was standing in the courtyard behind our building, cleaning my mess kit, when there was an explosion on the hillside behind us.

What was *that?* A short round from some erratic American howitzer? There was another explosion near the same spot, then a third, this time on the other side of us. Tom Parr was first to realize what was happening.

"Those rounds are incoming," he yelled. "Someone just got a bracket on us!"

Why hadn't it occurred to the rest of us that those explosions were *enemy* shells? For me, I suppose, it was because this had never happened before, and the very idea that someone was actually shooting at *me* was one my brain tried to reject.

There was another crash. Then another, which hit our headquarters building. I threw myself on the ground. More explosions until I lost count. Now each one was preceded by a ripping sound. That meant, I guessed, that the projectiles were coming with a low trajectory and high velocity, quite possibly from a tank gun. Did that mean the North Koreans were in the town itself?

The explosions stopped, then started again a distance away. I heard yelling, looked around, and realized three or four men had been wounded. Nearby someone was crying: "Oh mother, mother, someone help me. It *hurts.* Oh, mother . . ."

On the ground near one corner of the building, a soldier was ly-

Ralph Maurice Buffington. Courtesy US Military Academy Archives.

ing with a bloody pant leg. Two of us helped him into a sitting position. He kept screaming, and as we tried to calm him, I realized it was the garrulous corporal I'd met on the truck. We loosened his belt, eased his trousers down, and found where a shrapnel fragment had gone in just above the knee. I took the first-aid packet from his cartridge belt (remembering the injunction to use the wounded man's packet, not my own), unwrapped the compress from the packet, and tied it over the wound.

By this time his cries had changed to a whimper. I hoped he wouldn't go into shock but realized it was a possibility. Two of us helped him to his feet, then half carried, half supported him out to the street and to a litter jeep. The medics put him on board and pulled away, just as another round landed nearby.

Lying on the street was a shapeless white bundle, an old Korean man who must have been one of the refugees. For the first time, I was seeing violent death up close. There was another explosion nearby and we hit the ground.

"Let's get the hell out of here!" someone yelled. Along with several others, I started down the street, in a direction we hoped was away from the enemy. A few had gotten onto the available trucks and jeeps, but the rest of us were on foot. Ahead of me was a tall, thin sergeant who looked like a veteran. He staggered, and I saw his right arm was shattered.

I ran up and put an arm around him. We walked on together, slow and unsteady. It appeared we were the only Americans left, that all the others had gone on ahead. A Korean with a wispy white beard came from his shop out onto the street, holding out a piece of cloth. He made a gesture offering to apply the cloth as a sort of bandage. I motioned him away, at the same time nodding in a way I hoped showed my appreciation.

Haltingly, the sergeant and I continued walking. Were we going to be left behind? He looked at me and said, "Begging the lieutenant's pardon, I think the lieutenant had better go on without me."

His old-Army mannerism of addressing an officer in the third person seemed truly incongruous. Maybe, in his condition, he felt a need to prove himself capable of functioning as a professional. In any case, this was a man to be admired.

"We'll be okay, Sarge," I said. "Let's just keep going." We stumbled on. Miraculously, a litter jeep carrying a driver and a first-aid man appeared from a side street, and I called for it to stop. We loaded the sergeant onto one of the litters, covered him with a blanket, and they drove off.

Up ahead I saw some Americans running. I ran and caught up with them. "Where're you going?" I asked.

"Just someplace to get out of the way until that shelling stops." I tagged along, followed the group down an alley and crawled after them through a doorway. It turned out to be a low-ceilinged, one-room building, about five feet in height, perhaps a place to store grain. I sat by myself, feeling sheepish, realizing I'd been running aimlessly. There were eight or ten of us in the room, including one or two other officers, but no one I recognized. The room was dim and the only light came from the open doorway. In the distance we could hear more shelling. I listened for rifle or machine-gun fire, which might mean enemy foot soldiers were in the town. What would we do if we were suddenly confronted by Communist infantrymen? Shoot? Surrender? Run?

I felt guilty, but in an undefined sort of way—guilty for having run, for feeling so afraid, for not knowing what to do. Somehow it seemed I had done something wrong, but I didn't know just what it was.

After a while I realized I was bleeding from a cut near my left wrist. Had it been made by a sliver from one of the exploding shells? In a way I almost hoped so; that would prove something, wouldn't it? More likely, though, the cut was just from banging against my weapon when I dove to the ground. I tied a handkerchief around my wrist and the bleeding stopped.

We stayed in the room about an hour. It seemed longer, since each moment we were dreading what might be happening outside. After a while, we realized there had been no firing for some time. Cautiously I peeked out the doorway and saw a Korean woman with a small child. She was ambling along as though this were just a normal day.

Those of us from the 78th Battalion decided to head back to our original location. In single file, we walked warily down the main street, not knowing what to expect. Shortly we came to a wide intersection, probably the town square or marketplace. Since I still didn't know if any enemy were around, I ran in short dashes from one point of cover to another, thinking it might be unnecessary, but feeling better safe than sorry. I was secretly pleased when the others followed my example. Until then they had been strolling almost casually, perhaps wanting to advance in a more tactical fashion, yet afraid of looking melodramatic.

We proceeded another block and met the tank company captain.

He assured us, in a rather condescending manner, that it was all clear. Once back at our headquarters, though, the captain lost his composure and began a nervous monologue about the damned messed-up situation, the damned Koreans, the damned everything. He was noticeably shaken by the old Korean man who lay dead in the street, and by the senselessness of it all. He also complained because one of the men at the motor pool had destroyed two vehicles with grenades before pulling out that morning. Personally, I thought the man had used good initiative, especially since his "leaders" had left without providing any guidance.

A message arrived saying the new replacement officers were to be reassigned. I assumed those making the decisions at division headquarters had abandoned, at least for the moment, any thought of rebuilding the shattered 78th Battalion. Along with two others, I would be going to the 21st Infantry Regiment.

No one at the 78th Battalion seemed particularly concerned about how we would get to our new unit. However, the three of us managed to borrow a jeep, and together with our driver, set out to find the 21st Infantry.

The rest of the day is a blur. We headed out of Yongsan, not only ignorant as to the location of the 21st Infantry, but also wondering if the roads had been cut by enemy infiltrators. After a time, we came abreast of an artillery battery whose six howitzers were firing over our heads toward some distant hills. Suddenly two of the gun crews stopped, turned their guns a full 180 degrees, and began shooting point-blank into a hillside only seventy-five yards to their immediate rear. We tore on down the road, wanting to get clear, hoping we weren't heading into an ambush. We bumped along, scanning the rice paddies on either side of the road, feeling vulnerable, wondering if people might at any moment appear and start shooting.

Farther on we came to an intersection where an MP stopped us. "Where're you heading?" he asked.

"We're trying to get to the 21st Infantry Regiment. Is this the way?"

"It's the right direction, but you can't go this way. This road has been cut. Take the other fork; it'll get you to the command post of the 34th Infantry. Maybe somebody there has more information and can show you an alternate route to the 21st."

We headed in the new direction, looking for the command post (or CP) of the 34th Infantry, but at first we succeeded only in finding their regimental aid station. Someone said about thirty-five casualties had been brought to their station that day. A harassed, tired-looking medic provided some vague directions for getting to the 34th Infantry's CP. His listless voice sounded negative and defeatist, and I began to believe the rumor someone had whispered, that the wounded included a number of people with self-inflicted wounds. From the haunted look on most of the faces, it seemed possible.

It was early evening before we found the schoolhouse housing the 34th Infantry CP. By this time I'd learned that the 24th Division had three regiments—the 19th, the 21st, and the 34th. Each of them, in turn, had two battalions, numbered the 1st and the 3rd, since the second battalion of each regiment had been dispensed with as a peacetime economy measure.

At the CP, we figured either the S-2 intelligence officer or the S-3 operations officer would know about roads to the 21st Regiment. Two of us went to the room labelled "S-2," were shown on a map the road to the 21st Regiment, and were told it was still open. Our companion, however, who had been with the S-3, said he'd heard the road to the 21st Regiment had been cut. In other words, staff members in adjacent rooms were dealing with conflicting information. Prudently, we decided to call it a day and to stay put until things became clearer.

We were invited to bed down for the night in a room next to the S-3 section. Tired after our long, frantic day, we were thankful to spread our sleeping bags and stretch out on the bare floor. Before going to sleep, however, we extracted assurances from *both* the S-2 and S-3 sections that we'd be awakened if they had to leave in a hurry.

"Hey, you guys, wake up!" It was about 4:00 A.M. People were rushing about, grabbing weapons, folding maps, putting on their steel helmets. The other two "transients" and I went outside. In the darkness, a jeep driver invited us to climb in with him. Vehicles were pulling out; we got in column and followed slowly, creeping along with only blackout lights.

We had gone two or three miles when the first rays of morning softened the night. In the dim light, I saw for the first time that our driver, wearing the eagles of a full colonel, was the 34th Infantry's regimental commander. On down the road, we pulled into the yard of another schoolhouse. Radios were crackling out messages; there was an air of nervous urgency. Apparently, though, whatever had triggered the predawn move had been a false alarm. An hour later, after having had breakfast, we loaded up and returned to the place we had just left. We then thanked the people of the 34th Infantry, and equipped with new directions, we set out again for the 21st Regiment.

Before the month was out, the 34th Infantry, after suffering further heavy losses, was finally disbanded. Normally, breaking up a unit would have caused a severe problem with unit loyalty. In this case, however, there weren't enough people left to be disturbed; of the 2,000 who had come from Japan, only 184 remained. The others were either killed, wounded, or missing.

3. The Pusan Perimeter

13–23 AUGUST

As the August fighting continued, the North Koreans kept pressing their attacks, hoping to break through and to drive on to Pusan. Some of the heaviest fighting was north of Taegu, along the Sangju-Tabudong road, in an area defended by the 27th Infantry Regiment and known as the Bowling Alley. Other points from Pohang on the east coast to Masan in the south, were also threatened.

West Point '49er lieutenants on the ground, denied a glimpse of the big picture, saw only the fighting in their own particular sector. All of it was confusing, and much of it was bloody.

We arrived without incident at the command post of the 21st Infantry Regiment, a schoolhouse with a sign saying "Diamond CP." Evidently the 21st Infantry was "Diamond," and all 24th Division names were "D"; the Division itself was "Danger," and to find the Division's advance element, one followed rather aptly named signs to "Danger Forward."

The staff people at the CP looked worn out, but nevertheless businesslike. They said the regimental commander, Colonel Stephens, would want to talk to us personally. Stephens had been up most of the night, but was now awake and would see us in a few minutes. Meanwhile, the adjutant said I'd be assigned to the Regimental Tank Company.

"However," he said, "for now the Tank Company is only on paper. There's a first sergeant assigned, and now you, but that's it. We'll probably arrange a temporary job of some sort for you until we get enough men and tanks to justify activating the company."

The regimental commander appeared, wearing a faded old bathrobe. He was Richard W. Stephens, West Point '24, known to his staff as "Big Six": short, compact, leathery, exuding an air of tough professionalism. Somehow that bathrobe was reassuring. Wearing a robe, or merely having one available, was only a minor amenity, but it made one feel Stephens was a man who moved with confidence and who planned on staying around awhile. I found him not only impressive, but more than a little intimidating.

Stephens asked what we had been doing and we described our brief adventures, no doubt trying to impress him with the fact that we had been under fire and weren't just fresh off the boat. At one point, I mentioned the shelling we'd received at Yongsan, saying it was "when the 78th got all shot up."

Immediately he challenged me, saying, "What do you mean? How many casualties did you take?"

"I don't know, sir. Not too many, I guess."

"Didn't you fellows have any holes to get into?"

"No sir."

"Well, you've learned a valuable lesson. If men have dug in, they can get through a shelling okay. If they're exposed, they're bound to take casualties. More than likely they'll get scared as hell, and no telling what they'll do. Always dig in when you have a chance."

He was right, of course, and while he said it with emphasis, he also said it in a way which didn't embarrass us. He then brought us to his situation map, showed us the regimental dispositions, and described the actions of the past few days. His two under-strength battalions were covering a frontage along the Naktong which would have been more appropriate for a full-strength division, and he'd been forced to convert nearly all his supporting units into infantry. Even his Heavy Mortar Company was up on line, as was an attached company from the 3rd Engineer Battalion. His only reserve was a single rifle platoon.

I was impressed by the way Colonel Stephens took time to explain all this to three lowly lieutenants. It was comforting to feel someone knew what he was doing, and I felt lucky to be in his outfit.

To the south, near Masan, Trevor "Ted" Swett, another '49er who'd graduated from "Benning's School for Boys," was reporting in to the 24th Infantry Regiment of the 25th Division, a unit which, except for 60 percent of its officers, was made up entirely of African Americans. His battalion commander was Lt. Col. John Corley, one of the most decorated Americans of World War II (a Distinguished Service Cross, 5 Silver Stars, 4 Bronze Stars, and a Purple Heart) and who'd been a highly regarded tactical officer of ours at West Point.

Ted found Corley seated on a makeshift bench, a plank stretched between two ammunition boxes, near the foot of Battle Mountain, a hill mass which for several days had been the scene of heavy fighting. Corley retrieved two cans of beer which had been cooling in a nearby stream, gave one to Ted, and made room for him on the bench.

With a wry smile, Corley raised his beer in a toast, saying, "Welcome to the 3rd Battalion." Next he asked Ted if he remembered Stan Crosby.

Ted said he remembered Crosby, West Point '47, quite well, and he was shocked by Corley's next words.

"I told Crosby the same things I'm going to tell you—and that was a week ago. He didn't listen, and now he's dead. You *listen!*"

Ted listened. The essence of Corley's talk was that in this war, platoon leaders, company commanders, and battalion commanders had no business leading their troops from the front, because doing so was almost certain death—and the troops needed their leaders alive. It sounded like good advice, although Ted realized it was probably something Corley himself seldom practiced.

Back in Japan, those infantry classmates who had finished airborne training were arriving at Camp Drake, and many of them were being assigned to either the 5th, 7th, or 8th Cavalry regiment of the 1st Cavalry Division.

Among those going to the 8th Cavalry were Kenny Miller, Roger Fife, Jack Hodes, Munro "Mo" Magruder, and Bill Wilbur. Hodes, Magruder, and Wilbur all had fathers who were generals. Mo had been born in China, raised in Switzerland and Washington, and had spent some time in the Navy before entering West Point. Bill Wilbur had also lived the transient life of an army brat, and his dad, West Point '12, had won the Medal of Honor in North Africa during World War II.

On the day they were leaving, Bill made a strange remark to '49er Joe Kingston, saying, "Well, Joe, which of us will be first to win the Medal of Honor?"

As long as they had known each other, Joe had never heard Bill talk that way. Was it possible Bill felt some sort of compulsion to measure up to his hero father?

"Forget that kind of talk!" Joe said. "That kind of thinking can get a fellow hurt mighty quick. Just do your job, Bill, and don't try to be a hero!"

Wilbur and Miller were both assigned to the newly formed 3rd Battalion of the 8th Cavalry, which had as its nucleus a group hastily put together at Fort Devens, Massachusetts. Commanding the battalion was Lt. Col. Harold K. Johnson, a survivor of the Bataan Death March and a future Army Chief of Staff.

The 1st Cavalry Division had already taken some heavy casualties. '49er Bill Marslender, arriving at the 7th Cavalry Regiment, felt the morale, rated on a scale of one to ten, was about minus five. He hoped it wasn't prophetic that the 7th Cavalry was the unit commanded by George Armstrong Custer at the Little Big Horn.

Back in Japan, Joe Kingston and Jack Madison learned they, along with Bill Kempen and Herb Marshburn, would be joining the 32nd Infantry Regiment of the 7th Division. Division headquarters at Camp Zama sent them along to Camp McNair, home of the 32nd Infantry, at the foot of Mount Fuji. Kingston and Madison reported in to Lt. Col. Don Faith, acting regimental commander, who asked them if they were prepared to die.

Joe and Jack, after looking at each other, murmured something like, "Only if necessary, sir." It seemed a strange sort of reception. The two of them then went looking for the 3rd Battalion, to which they'd been assigned. Among a row of empty squad tents, they found an officer sitting at a field desk with the sign "3rd Battalion."

"Where do we sign in?" they asked.

"Right here," was the reply. "You're only the second and third officers to report. We don't *have* any such unit yet; I guess it'll be put together as we get new people coming in."

In Korea, meanwhile, on the streets of Pusan and Taegu, a strange type of draft had been taking place. Men of military age had been snatched off the streets and told they were now part of the Republic of Korea (ROK) army, but that their service would be as part of the Korean Augmentation of the US Army (KATUSA). Without further ado, they were then shipped to Japan for a condensed form of basic combat training.

Joe and Jack, now members of the 32nd Infantry's I Company, were given twelve days to train a hundred of these involuntary recruits. To assist, they had US sergeants, who fortunately were both experienced and able. The Americans knew no Korean, of course, and only one of the Koreans, Kim Yu Jin, who had worked in an American laundry, had a smattering of English. The KATUSA soldiers were proud of all the expensive clothing and equipment they'd been given, and they took to the training with awkward enthusiasm. Bringing them even close to full combat readiness, however, was obviously a "mission impossible."

All this while, American replacements were arriving and being fitted into the company. To gain a measure of control, rank and file Americans and Koreans were paired off in a sort of buddy system, with the Koreans being told, "Wherever he goes, you go; whatever he does, you do too."

Periodically, trucks would pull up and dump off equipment in a helter-skelter fashion. Supply sergeants would sort through the jumble and try to determine what went where as best they could.

I left Diamond CP and headed for "Diamond Blue," the 3rd Battalion of the 21st Infantry, my temporary assignment. (1st, 2nd, and 3rd Battalions—with perhaps a patriotic touch—were, in order, Red, White, and Blue.) The battalion CP turned out to be a few tents and vehicles tucked away at the head of a draw. The battalion commander, Maj. John McConnell, was sitting on a footlocker outside the operations tent, stripped to the waist and enjoying the sunshine. "Major Mac," as everyone called him, had closely cropped silvery hair, a ruddy, rather handsome face, and a pleasant welcoming smile.

As a tanker, I didn't want to go to a rifle company, which seemed like a dangerous, unknown horror, but I was reluctant to say that, so I reminded Major Mac that my assignment to his battalion was only temporary.

"Okay," said Mac, "for now you can be our S-2." I didn't know how long I'd remain the battalion intelligence officer, or S-2, but a battalion staff job sounded almost prestigious for a second lieutenant.

As the afternoon wore on, I met the other staff members of the tiny headquarters, including 1st Lt. John Watkins, West Point '48, the assistant S-3. John was a tall, clean-cut officer, an army brat whose father had graduated from West Point in 1918.

Feeling insecure in this new environment, I welcomed John's presence. It wasn't that I yearned to talk old school tie or as the saying went, to "knock rings" with him, it was just that I had many questions, and it was far easier talking to someone with a common background.

John said he had been with the unit in Japan and had been leading a rifle platoon when they first came to Korea. Teaching me some basics, he said that I, as S-2, would be "Diamond Blue 2." Seconds in command, or executive officers, were called "5," commanders were "6." (This explained why they called Colonel Stephens "Big Six.") Our 3rd Battalion had four companies: rifle companies I, K, and L (Item, King, and Love) and a weapons company, M (Mike).

John told me of the first days of the war, the hastily established positions, the infiltrating enemy who appeared to your rear, the demoralizing retreats, the disastrous day of 11 July, at Chochiwon, when the 21st Infantry had been overrun and it had been every man for himself. Casualties had been high, and only a fraction of the original battalion had escaped. The battalion commander, Lt. Col. Carl Jensen, was among those killed that day, as was Lt. Leon Jacques, the S-2, the man I'd be replacing.

As darkness fell, we crowded into the small operations tent. Companies were required to report in every hour, or whenever something significant took place. Major Mac gave me the job of maintaining the battalion log, a routine task at best, but I was thankful finally to be making some sort of contribution. As S-2, I wrote down a summary of all messages, including the hourly reports, and relayed them to "Diamond 2" at Regiment.

In the morning, as Lt. Carl Bernard from Love Company prepared to return to his unit, I asked to go along. Maybe I felt guilty about being in comparative safety at the CP without having even seen the Naktong. Then too, I wanted to mark my S-2 situation map to show how much of the Naktong valley could be observed from various points along the line.

Carl said he would be proud to have me come along. It would be good for the men, he said, adding rather pointedly that it would be the very first visit to that location by a member of the battalion staff.

We started out by jeep, and after a while, I said we seemed to be going quite a distance. Carl agreed, saying he felt the battalion CP was much too far to the rear. Finally, on foot, we came to a cluster of huts at the base of a mountain, which Carl said was "Love Company Rear." Six or eight Americans were there, loading ration boxes onto the backs of a Korean carrying party. The Koreans, called "chiggi-bearers" by the Americans, wore A-frames which distributed the weight high up on their shoulders and allowed these short, wiry men to carry incredible loads.

The hike up the mountain was long and steep. By the time we neared the top, I was almost exhausted, and I marveled at the run-down looking Bernard, who wasn't even breathing hard. Along the way, Carl had pointed out the bug-out route, the predetermined path for an emergency retreat. "Bug-out," a term coined in Korea, seemed very much on everyone's mind.

At last we reached the crest. Looking down, I saw the Naktong, flowing serenely several hundred feet below us, and about a hundred yards to our front. Carl introduced me around as "the new Battalion Two, come to visit." The soldiers were a lean, scruffy bunch, evidently worn down by having fought, and lost, too many times the past month.

It was late afternoon by the time I had looked around and done some plotting on my map board, late enough that I decided to stay the night with Love Company. Across the river lay a sandy beach edged by a rice paddy and a two-lane dirt road. Beyond the road a mountain similar to ours rose abruptly; I wondered if there were enemy soldiers on it looking across at us.

L Company began calling for artillery fire, registering specific concentrations which they might be calling for during the night. Two nights before, they told me, enemy trucks had appeared on the road across the river. The convoy must have been lost, since the trucks had come driving along in full view with all headlights shining. Artillery and mortar fire had been brought down on the convoy, destroying enough trucks to block the road, and after that, the men said, it had been like picking off ducks in a shooting gallery. Through my binoculars, I could see some of the remains, hulls which were still smoldering.

Soon after dark it began to rain, and a short time later a curious message came from Battalion—at midnight the company would withdraw from the mountain. Midnight came, and in the darkness, I joined one of the squads which was starting single file down a steep, narrow path. The rain had slickened the trail, and suddenly I pitched head first, with helmet, weapon, and map board flying. Others were falling too, cursing softly since this was supposed to be a silent withdrawal. I fell again; my hands and feet were coated with mud. Feeling clumsy, I was glad the darkness made me anonymous.

The rain had changed to light mist as we gathered at the base of the mountain and waited. Early next morning, Love Company was ordered to march to a battalion assembly area well to the rear. After walking two or three hours, the company, with me tagging along, came to an open area where most of the 3rd Battalion, including a number of new replacements, was gathered.

We learned this was to be "organization day." People had been brought to where they could be sorted out, and where proper company, platoon, and squad assignments could be made.

Major Mac told me I had been replaced as S-2. An officer with intelligence experience had arrived and been given the S-2 position. I, in turn, would be going to Item Company, commanded by 1st Lt. Floyd "Gib" Gibson, a World War II veteran with a ready smile and a firm handshake. Gib introduced me to the other company officers: company executive officer, or exec, was 1st Lt. Ruff Lynch. Leading the 1st Platoon was my classmate Tom Hardaway. (What a pleasure to see a familiar face.) 2nd Platoon Leader was 2nd Lt. Jim Exley, who, like Gib, was a graduate of the Citadel. The 3rd Platoon would be mine, and Gib said I was lucky, that I'd be getting a fine platoon sergeant to work with, a man named Mont Robinette.

Things were happening too fast. Regardless of my armor background, I'd been made an infantry platoon leader, a job I'd always considered the dirtiest, most dangerous position an officer could hold, and a job I'd never wanted. Nevertheless, it was a chance to prove myself, and I felt an unfamiliar excitement.

With all the replacements who had just arrived, my platoon would be nearly at full strength, about forty men. Most were fresh off the boat. It was easy to tell the replacements; they were the ones who were reasonably clean.

"Hey, Lieutenant!" I was hailed by a sergeant in one of the other companies. He said he had been on the plane with me coming from Alaska. (Later I learned he had given me quite a build-up to his friends, presumably because of the box lunch episode.)

Sergeant Robinette, who looked wise but weather-beaten, led me to where our platoon was assembled, made up of mostly nervous new replacements, looking to me for leadership. I had more than a little self-doubt as Robinette introduced me.

"Men, this here is Lieutenant Maihafer, your new platoon leader."

Back at Fort Benning, meanwhile, Mike Wadsworth's wife Bette had given birth to a baby daughter in June, and by August, Mike had grown restless in his teaching job. His request for assignment to Korea was granted, and soon he and Bette left Benning to enjoy a forty-five-day preembarkation leave.

Wes Newman, Cec's wife, had received the film Cec had sent, with its travelogue-type pictures of San Francisco and Hawaii. Ernie and Gloria Denham watched the home movie with her, and since Ernie's original orders, like Cec's, had been for Hawaii, they wondered when—and if—the four of them would be in Hawaii together.

Cec by this time had joined F Company of the 5th Cavalry Regiment, and had gone into position some fifteen or twenty miles north of the 21st Infantry. George Tow was in the same regiment, as was George's boyhood friend, Beecher Brian, and six-foot-six Joe Toomey, the tallest man in our class.

On 14 August, Beech wrote home:

B Co. is in Bn. support. We are spread thin over 3 hills, 5 miles apart. We have been busier than you can imagine for a reserve

Company. In the last three days I have been on three patrols trying to clear out the Gooks from the rear. An unusual situation—
the river "front" is very quiet—but the rear is (or was) crawling
with Gooks. We took our first prisoner night before last. He just
walked in on us in a sort of daze. We didn't see him until he was
about five feet from our flank fox-hole. When the guard yelled "halt"
he jumped into a ditch and out of sight. I threw an illuminating
grenade behind him and he gave up very willingly.

Gib said we'd be returning to positions along the Naktong and
would start at once. He led off and we followed, nearly two hundred
men in single file.

We climbed a hill; descended into a valley; wound through a series
of rice paddies. It was hot—well over 100 degrees—and humid. Everyone was perspiring heavily as we started up another hill. I was wishing Gib would halt for a break, but he kept going steadily. We dropped
into a second valley but started climbing again almost at once. The
men were dragging, especially the new ones. Nearly three hours of
steady walking and climbing, and we were only now starting up the
final mountain, which looked monstrous. I wished we could let everyone rest for a few minutes, even though I realized we needed to be
on that mountain ahead of any North Koreans with similar ideas.

Each step became an agony. Up still higher we went, and now
men were dropping out, lying on their backs alongside the trail while
they tried to catch their breaths. A tall, blond-haired newcomer, who'd
been carrying a heavy mortar baseplate, was on all fours, retching and
moaning.

I too felt ready to give out, and dreaded the impression it might
make on the new platoon. When we reached the crest, Gib said the
three platoons, 1st, 2nd, and 3rd, would go in in that order from left
to right.

We followed a trail of sorts to the 3rd Platoon sector, where Robinette offered to put the squads into position. That was fine by me;
he was obviously better qualified than I to do it. I "established" my
platoon CP by collapsing just off the trail, on one knee, face flushed,
panting, looking most unimpressive to the men filing past. Each one—
or was it my imagination—seemed to stare critically as he shuffled
by. Well, one way or another, Item Company was now on position.

On Item Company's immediate right was an engineer unit, a detachment from the 24th Division's 3rd Combat Engineer Battalion,
manning a blockhouse on a knob about two miles north of us. In charge
was Monk Kurtz, who had graduated near the top of our West Point

class. By a remarkable coincidence, joining Monk's group was an artillery forward observer team headed by Earl Lochhead, who had been Monk's cadet roommate.

Earl and I had been on the boat together from Sasebo to Pusan and on the same train traveling to the replacement company at Miryang. From the replacement company, Earl had gone to A Battery of the 52nd Field. Arriving at the unit, he'd been impressed by the battery commander, but he felt most of the men seemed nervous and of very low morale. Perhaps they had a right to be; as part of Task Force Smith, they'd been the very first US artillerymen in Korea, and already their ranks had been decimated.

On the first morning after he'd joined A Battery, everyone, including the officers, had stared in wonderment as Earl began to shave. He felt like the innocent, shiny-faced shavetail from a Bill Mauldin cartoon. Soon he was on his way to that hill overlooking the Naktong, and to the pleasant surprise of finding his ex-roommate Monk Kurtz.

Farther to the north, on the right flank of the 24th Division, the understrength 1st Cavalry Division was defending its own portion of the Perimeter. A key terrain feature was Hill 303, overlooking the Naktong about five miles northeast of Waegwan. It marked the right flank of the Division, and for that matter, the right flank of Eighth Army. On their right was the 1st ROK Division, which came under attack in the early hours of 15 August. Before dawn, 1st Cav soldiers on Hill 303 saw about fifty enemy troops, accompanied by two tanks, moving boldly along the river road at the base of the hill. Another column was moving in their rear, hoping to encircle the Americans, and soon Cec Newman's F Company was under heavy fire.

After intense fighting, involving both F and G Companies, the enemy took Hill 303. A series of counterattacks failed to retake the hill, but two days later, following an air strike and heavy artillery fire, which inflicted an estimated five hundred enemy casualties, the North Koreans withdrew in disorder.

At some point during the fighting of 15 August, no one could say exactly when, Cecil Newman had been killed. Ironically, Cec, after surviving infantry combat in World War II, had lost his life in Korea in little more than a week.

My platoon on the Naktong had now worked out a fairly good routine. I'd had the men dig two-man foxholes on the forward slope of our hill. During the day, one hole per squad was manned; the rest of the men were allowed to spread out on the reverse slope and relax.

Night time was a different story, and following the advice of Gib and Robinette, I'd told the squad leaders, "When it gets dark, I want everyone in their holes on the forward slope. Two men to a hole; one of them to be awake at all times. Be extra alert, with *everyone* awake, right after dark and right before dawn. That's when we're most likely to get hit."

My own location was a shallow furrow I'd scraped for myself on the reverse slope, near the center of the platoon position and about ten yards down from the crest. Each night after dark, Robinette and I moved around together, checking with the squad leaders and making sure everyone was in position. We then returned to the Platoon CP, lay on our backs, looked at the stars, and talked most of the night.

The next day, the next, and the one after, evolved into a pattern of heat, boredom, and tension. For a time during each night I would fall asleep for two, three, even four hours. Just before morning, Robinette (I'd begun to call him Robby) would waken me. Together we would wait, hoping nothing unusual would happen. The first softening half-light would ease the tension a bit, but we wouldn't relax until the sunrise created full visibility.

Periodically a Korean carrying party would arrive with C-rations, ammunition, a few water cans. We would distribute the rations and ammo, but with the high humidity, and the temperature often reaching 110 degrees, the water was what we considered most important. Invariably we would run dry, and then we'd ask for volunteers to gather up canteens for a trip to the well in the valley behind us. When at the well, a man could take time to wash and shave, but even so, volunteers were few. Descending took about an hour and wasn't too bad; climbing back, however, took much longer and left a man enervated and worse off than when he had started.

The days merged together, and I lost track of time. One morning, just before dawn, the platoon guide shook me, saying, "Wake up, Lieutenant, it's almost light."

Suddenly, while I was still in that half-awake state, there was a loud burst of automatic-weapons fire at close range, just over the crest from me. Now fully awake and scared, I grabbed my weapon and waited for the next sound. There were no more shots, only a momentary stillness followed by a babble of voices.

A man came running over the crest, shouting, "Get a medic! Sergeant DiHerrera's been shot!"

I yelled for the platoon medic. He came with me as I scrambled over the ridgeline to DiHerrera's squad area. The sergeant, leader of the platoon's 3rd Squad, was lying on the ground and moaning; blood was coming from both his chest and shoulder. We carried him to the Platoon CP on the reverse slope, gently set him down as the medic put compresses over the wounds. DiHerrera's face was ashen; he seemed to be going into shock. We covered him with our jackets to keep him warm and tried to reassure him that he'd be okay. He said a few words somewhat incoherently, and asked someone to write home for him. Then he seemed to faint as we placed him on a litter. Volunteer carriers picked him up and started the long trek down the hill. We wondered if he'd make it.

"I found out what happened," Robinette said.

"What was it? Did one of his squad shoot him by mistake?"

"Yep. DiHerrera's been in the habit of checking his squad all during the night to make sure they're awake. Sometimes he creeps up and tries to grab their weapons away to teach them a lesson. Di was creeping up on all fours, coming from one of the holes farther down the hill. The Browning automatic rifle (BAR) man must have been dozing, and when he saw this figure getting close, he fired a burst almost without thinking."

"I can sure understand," I said. "Di made a mistake moving like that. Too bad it was so costly."

By this time the BAR man had come back to the CP, muttering over and over how sorry he was. He too looked on the verge of shock, and I talked to him a while, assuring him it wasn't his fault, that Di wouldn't blame him. Lying, I told him the wound didn't look too serious.

As the days passed, Robby and I talked of many things. For the moment at least, he had shed the natural reticence of an old soldier toward a shavetail second lieutenant. He spoke of the good times in Japan, when the 21st Infantry "Gimlets" had been stationed in Kumomoto. The atmosphere had been relaxed, and many men had Japanese girlfriends, called "musumas," or in the unlovely GI jargon, "mooses." Then, more slowly, he told of the first days in Korea. Time and again they had had to fall back. They would establish positions in the valleys, and the North Koreans would stream down the ridgelines and get behind them. Then, at Chochiwon, they had been overrun. Only a handful had escaped. Robby, by himself, had made his way south over the mountains, hiding much of the time to avoid enemy soldiers. Ragged, exhausted, and hungry, he had finally made it, but it was obvious the good ol' Kentucky boy, as he described himself, was much the worse for wear.

The platoon leaders, Tom, Jim, and I, weren't able to learn much from Gib about what was happening elsewhere, and the little he was able to tell us wasn't very encouraging. The enemy had crossed the Naktong and established bridgeheads on either side of us. Fighting was going on far to our rear on both flanks.

On 20 August, Ted Swett, now leading the 3rd Platoon of L Company, 24th Infantry Regiment, was rushed by truck to the vicinity of Haman, near the foot of Battle Mountain. His platoon had already had eight different platoon leaders; Ted made the ninth.

Their mission was to go to the aid of the regiment's C Company, which was being driven from the mountain. As Ted dismounted from the truck, he saw the smoke from close air support strikes at the top of the mountain and realized that the top of that mountain was indeed a long way off.

With the lessons of the Infantry School fresh in his mind, Ted sought out his company commander and asked, "When are you going to give us the attack order, sir?"

The company commander, giving Ted a blank look, just pointed to the top of the mountain, and said, "Move out, Lieutenant. *That's* your attack order!"

Trying to remember all that Colonel Corley had told him, Swett formed his platoon and started up the hill along a narrow path. Soon they were passing members of C Company, who were trickling down the hill in groups of two or three, dusty, sweaty, some of them bloody, and all of them discouraged.

The trickle of beaten troops continued, but then Ted, seeing someone in front of him, reasoned that C Company's remnants must have been sent back up the hill. He decided to investigate and finally caught up with the small group in front. It was Lieutenant Colonel Corley and his communications officer. So much for not leading from the front!

The climb grew steeper, the day grew hotter, and men began dropping out. At one point, Ted's radio operator, struggling with the heavy backpacked SCR-300, complained of a bad knee, so Ted unwisely offered to carry the radio himself. Fortunately, they met no North Koreans at this point, but when they finally came to a saddle, about 150 meters below the peak of Battle Mountain, Ted was exhausted.

Lieutenant Colonel Corley, who had set up his CP in the saddle, decided to use Ted's platoon as CP security. There were no enemy probes during the night, and things seemed eerily quiet. For a few hours at least, they were able to rest.

Next morning, Love Company was told to continue the attack.

Because of the narrowness of the terrain between the Battalion CP and the top of the mountain, the company would have to lead with but a single platoon, and Ted was given the job.

The ground was rocky, with only a few trees and bushes to offer concealment. As they proceeded toward the crest, the trees were left behind, and they began to receive small arms fire. Ted attacked the crest just as he'd been taught at Fort Benning—and it worked. Two squads led the way, their BARs chattering as they advanced. His third squad, plus a 60-mm mortar which had been set up in a draw, gave covering fire. An hour later, with the loss of only two wounded, the crest was secured and the enemy had been driven back.

At this point, Ted was feeling rather good about things. Moving around the position, he was struck by the spectacular view from the top of the mountain. It was high noon on a beautiful sunny day, and at least for a few minutes, there was no war, just tranquility.

Soon they were shocked back to reality by exploding mortar shells, signaling the beginning of a counterattack. Ted was crouched on the edge of a shallow hole which he'd made his CP, and the squad leaders were approaching to coordinate with him, when a mortar round landed near his left hip. The explosion killed his radio operator and two of the squad leaders.

Ted tried to move his legs, and couldn't. The mortar fire continued, and he realized he was quite alone—the troops that had been nearby were either dead or had disappeared. As he lay there, he saw some yellow fingers with dirty fingernails straining for a grip on the ledge, some twenty yards away. Apparently the enemy was about to occupy, unopposed, what had briefly been his platoon's position. He also realized he was weaponless; his carbine had disappeared in the explosion. Dragging himself out of the hole, he rolled down a rather steep slope, away from the still-struggling fingernails, and finally into a clump of bushes.

The platoon medic was hunkered down behind the same bushes, and Ted asked him to do what he could for his hip wound. As the medic took Ted's first-aid packet and began to open it, enemy soldiers, who by this time had occupied the top of the hill some fifty yards away, noticed the movement and began shooting. At that, the medic took off to the rear—with Ted's first-aid packet—just as another bullet hit Ted above the knee.

"This is a helluva way to die," Ted thought. By this time, he could see North Koreans walking around the top of the hill; one of them was kicking at the bodies which lay where the Platoon CP had been. Ted lay still, hoping the soldiers might think he was dead, and might not invesigate further. At this point he lost consciousness. When he came to, a fire fight was going on, diverting the attention of the North Koreans. He was hurting enough to realize he wasn't paralyzed, and that his right leg could move, so he decided to try making it back to the Battalion CP.

His thirst was overpowering, but reaching for his canteen, he found it had been shattered by the mortar round. Slowly, he began to crawl. As he neared the tree line, soldiers on the hill began shooting at him. A bullet zinged past his head, and he reached to adjust his helmet. In his weakened state, only then did he realize his helmet was gone.

As he paused to rest, he noticed a helmet lying on the ground a few feet away. He managed to get to it and put it on, even though it didn't fit very well.

Drifting in and out of consciousness, alternately crawling and resting, he dragged himself back toward the CP. Suddenly he was jolted to full alertness by the click of an M-1 rifle's safety being released, and by a voice whispering: "Here comes one now!"

Frantic, he rose up as well as he could and shouted, "Don't shoot, it's Lieutenant Swett!" As he was about to pass out one more time, he saw wary faces, from another platoon, looking down rather quizzically at his head, which was protected by an ill-fitting North Korean helmet.

Ted's next recollection, an hour or more later, was of being at Corley's CP, which was under small arms attack. Corley came over to see him, took his hand, and said he was sorry he hadn't had a chance to teach him more. Then Corley ran off to run the battle. (Almost single-handedly, the gallant Corley rallied his troops, and later that afternoon, retook Battle Mountain.)

To the best of my knowledge, the far shore of the Naktong, opposite Item Company's position, had long since been cleared of civilians. Early in the war, Korean police had forced the local population to evacuate, both for their own safety and because enemy soldiers had been disguising themselves as civilians for infiltration or observation purposes. Many North Korean soldiers, we had heard, even carried a white civilian overgarment as standard equipment.

Our company's weaponry at this point was both sparse and haphazard. We had one .30-cal heavy machine gun, two light machine guns, one 60-mm mortar with nine rounds, one 3.5" rocket launcher with three rounds, one 81-mm mortar tube with no baseplate or ammo, and not a single hand grenade. Gib had our light machine guns move several times a day and fire short bursts to make any enemy observers think we had seven or eight of them.

On most days, the other side of the river seemed lifeless. Occasionally, though, I could see white-clad figures through my binoculars, singly or in pairs, moving around in the village or the paddy fields. I wondered if they were merely returning civilians, or whether they were soldiers trying to study our positions.

One morning I saw two figures in the rice paddy, near a straw shelter we had used as a registration point for our mortar. The mortar crew attached to my platoon got ready and on my command fired three rounds in rapid succession. As the first round hit, the figures started running. The next round seemed to land almost on top of them, and the figures disappeared.

For the remaining days there was no movement opposite our position. Later I wondered, had those two really been enemy soldiers? Or had they been civilian farmers, maybe even a man and wife? If the latter, they of course had no business being there, but I was still troubled. Had I killed two innocents, or had I taken an action which kept the enemy from planning an attack? I'd never know. One thing is sure —we were *not* attacked as long as my platoon was on that hill.

A call came on the field phone. "Harry, this is Gib. Get your men ready to move out."

"What . . . why, what's happened?"

"Good news—we're being relieved! Come over to the CP; bring your platoon sergeant and guide, and I'll fill you in."

Along with Robby and Sergeant Dissinger, I walked to the CP. The two of them, with their unshaven faces and worn expressions, looked very much like Mauldin's "Willie and Joe."

Gib told us the 2nd Infantry Division, from Fort Lewis, Washington, had landed in Korea and a company from the 23rd Regiment would be relieving us. Tom Hardaway had gone back to guide their reconnaissance party forward. Up the hill they came, the company commander, platoon leaders, and key noncoms. In front was Tom, tall, strong, athletic, leading the way with tireless, long-legged strides. He looked fresh and unwinded, as contrasted with the newcomers, who were perspiring heavily and breathing hard.

Gib introduced himself and welcomed the new company commander, a captain. "Glad to see you, sir," said Gib and *meant* it.

"Well, we're glad to be here finally," the captain said, "although I sure wasn't ready for that climb. Next time don't send *Goat Legs* here; he was too much for us!"

Tom grinned, and I felt a surge of pride in him, the former cadet captain and hard-hitting varsity first baseman. He was every inch an officer.

The 2nd Division folks looked too good to be true—clean, well-equipped, professional. "Gee, Lieutenant," Dissinger said, "they've even got compasses!"

I led their third platoon people, the ones who would be relieving me, over to our position. Crouching, I moved onto the forward slope with my opposite number, a competent-looking Hispanic first lieutenant, to show him the terrain to our front. Immodestly, I felt pleased when he followed my example, walking upright or moving in a low crouch whenever I did. Gosh, this fellow looked on *me* as a veteran!

As we left our hill, wishing our 23rd Infantry replacements all sorts of good luck, there was an almost embarrassing contrast between these fresh, alert, almost eager newcomers, and our own dusty-looking I Company. Little did we know that many of those men would die three days later, when that same position was attacked and overrun.

That night we settled into a temporary rest area at a new "company rear," where we enjoyed the luxury of fires and hot food. Ruff Lynch, the company exec, had used the mess and supply people to prepare the area and to make us feel appreciated. As we got ready to turn in, Ruff offered Tom and me the use of his pup tent, complete with blankets and sleeping bags. We accepted gladly. Warm, full, and comfortable, Tom and I lay awake, talking and guessing about the future. Gib came by to see how we were doing, at which point I responded facetiously with "All right, sir," the phrase Tom and I had been using at bed check throughout our cadet years. Those days seemed far in the past.

4. Fighting Fires

24 AUGUST–5 SEPTEMBER

As August turned into September, the fighting along the Perimeter became, if possible, even more intense. When Gen. Walton Walker, the Eighth Army Commander, returned to his CP each night, he'd ask his chief of staff what reserves he had "found" during the day. Whoever they were, they would soon be headed to the latest trouble spot.

Next stop for Item Company was a congested, narrow valley, where rain, traffic, and the digging of emplacements had transformed the original green lushness into a wallow of oozing mud. Soon a truck convoy rolled to a stop, and dismounting from the trucks were dozens of Koreans, outfitted with new US Army fatigue clothing, helmets, rifles, and full field packs. These were the KATUSAs who would be joining us.

A few men from our battalion had gone back to Taegu and conducted basic training of sorts, which in truth amounted to not much more than learning how to load and fire a rifle. Now these South Koreans were ours—not truly soldiers, but at least warm bodies to help plug gaps in the porous defense line.

Item Company's KATUSAs, confused yet trusting, were split up and attached to Tom, Jim, and me. The group included two former college students, who had been named acting leaders—they were the only Koreans who could speak a few words of English. The taller of the two was named Chong. (Gib decided this sounded like John, and so John he became.) The shorter was called Kim, which seemed to be the Korean equivalent of Smith or Jones.

I soon realized John's and Kim's English was extremely limited. Not only was communication difficult, it was also dangerous, since each of them would smile reassuringly and nod agreement with whatever we said, pretending to comprehend even while failing to catch a single word.

"Well, Gib, what happens next?" I asked later that day. "Should we be doing anything in particular?"

"Just get your men cleaned up and ready," he said, "this is an assembly area."

"But what's our mission?" I persisted. "What are we supposed to be doing?"

"What the hell do you *usually* do in an assembly area?" he snapped as he walked away. Only then did I catch the significance of his having said "assembly" rather than "bivouac" area. We had learned the difference in school, but heretofore the distinction had never seemed very important. An assembly area, we'd been taught, was where a unit gathered before jumping off in an attack.

By now our Air Force classmates were entering the final phase of flight training, and they too were suffering losses. On 7 July, likable John Jenkins, saxophone player and model plane enthusiast, was killed in an air accident at Nellis AFB in Nevada. Eight days earlier, on 29 June, Wayne Moore, one of the few selected for jet fighter training, had been killed when his plane crashed near Williams AFB in Arizona. A month later, another jet crash at Williams claimed the life of Don Gabel, who before entering West Point had already completed flight training, been commissioned, and worn the wings of an Air Force pilot.

At Camp Drake, Lew Zickel had been given a job helping to process people for shipment to Korea. After a few days of this, he began feeling guilty about sending classmates to war while he stayed behind, so he asked to be released for combat. Within days, he was bound for Pusan aboard the *Kanda Maru,* a decrepit Japanese freighter.

That night, midway across the Strait of Tsushima, men on the ship heard a radio broadcast by Seoul City Sue, specifically mentioning the *Kanda Maru* and warning those aboard they were heading for disaster.

Lew was assigned to C Company of the 5th Cavalry Regiment, commanded by Tom Hoffman, USMA '48, and where '49ers Huck Long and Sam Coursen were already leading platoons. Jerry Paden, a member of the 61st Field Artillery, and another '49er, was the company's forward observer (FO). Lew joined the unit on a hill overlooking the Naktong, and his first thought was how tranquil the river looked.

Two nights later, however, as he led a patrol across the river to check for enemy activity, the Naktong's tranquility was no longer very reassuring. With a good deal of anxiety, Lew and his men forded the river in the darkness and reached their patrol objective, a nearby hill. They encountered no enemy, and the patrol returned without incident.

About the same time, Kenny Miller, along with classmates Gus Meyerson, Mac Odell, and Bill Wilbur, was joining the 8th Cavalry Regiment. They spent the night at Regimental HQ, then left to join their companies.

On his twenty-third birthday, 28 August, Kenny was given his first command, a platoon of King Company, and his main thought was a fear, which he kept to himself, that he might not be equal to what lay ahead. When he met M. Sgt. Ray Caplette, his platoon sergeant, Kenny said, "Sergeant, I have five years of schooling, but I'm as green as grass. I need all the help you can give me."

Caplette, a savvy veteran with a Silver Star from World War II, grinned and replied, "Lieutenant, you just leave it to me."

Shortly, Kenny and his platoon, in the darkness, were going into position along the Naktong, climbing a hill which was supposedly unoccupied. However, as they neared the top, they were challenged in Korean. When the challenge rang out, Kenny's mouth became so dry that his chewing gum stuck to his teeth. Fortunately the challenger turned out to be ROK, and they were able to assure him they were friendly. Kenny's nerves, already on edge, weren't helped any when he walked along his position and stepped on something spongy, the bloated body of a dead North Korean, buried under a few inches of dirt.

Item Company left its assembly area, with orders to take up a blocking position behind a ROK Division which appeared to be crumbling. We walked most of the day, a long, rambling approach march made doubly difficult by light rain and a chilling wind.

In late afternoon we started to climb, at first over foothills and then up a steep trail. The path became narrower, steeper, the rain grew heavier, and soon a dense fog had reduced our visibility to a few feet. As we continued to climb, our boots became layered with oozing mud and the trail became dangerously slick. At times we pulled ourselves upward by hanging on to weeds or bushes. In some of the worst places, men were designated to anchor themselves against trees and to pull the others up one at a time.

By the time we reached the crest, the fog and rain had closed in so thickly that the entire North Korean Army could have passed below us without being observed. Finally the rain stopped, the night passed, and we received orders to climb back down.

The threat in this sector had lessened, but another was developing elsewhere. After several more hours of walking, plus a few hours by truck, we arrived at an assembly area in a pleasant apple orchard outside Taegu, close to a river and also close to K-2, a critical airfield. K-2's security force included an antiaircraft platoon led by '49er Jack Hayne.

Taegu, a major city, contained not only our most important airfield, but also Eighth Army headquarters. Obviously the city would be a rich prize for the North Koreans, and they had been trying mightily to capture it. The corridor entering the city from the north had become known as the "Bowling Alley" and had been the scene of intense fighting.

For more than a week, the 27th Infantry Regiment, known as the "Wolfhounds," had beaten off fierce nightly attacks of North Korean infantry supported by tanks, self-propelled guns, and artillery.

"We're going to relieve a company of the Wolfhounds," Gib said. "You platoon leaders hop in the jeep, and we'll go check out the area." Gib took the right front seat of the jeep after having volunteered me as driver; Tom and Jim climbed in back. We followed directions into the center of Taegu, passed around a traffic circle, and headed north toward the Bowling Alley.

The narrow dirt road was congested, and we fell in behind a wheezing South Korean army truck crammed with boyish-looking infantrymen. Their helmets were covered with webbing into which they had woven leaves and branches, either for decoration or as an enthusiastic approach to camouflage.

The Koreans' truck stopped suddenly; I swung out to pass it but misjudged the clearance and brushed the truck's tailgate with my right front fender. No damage was done, but the jolt stirred a hubbub of chatter from the truck's occupants and gave a small thrill to Gib in the right front of the jeep. My passengers made unkind remarks about my driving, but I explained that I was actually misplaced as an infantryman — if I'd only had a tank, to which an armored officer was entitled, a little bump like that would have been inconsequential.

We made our recon, and on the return, Tom took over as jeep driver; my ungrateful passengers had voted me out of my position. Coming into Taegu, we decided to see if lowly foot soldiers could obtain lunch at an Army HQ.

An MP pointed out the Eighth Army Officers' Mess, and we entered without being challenged. Inside, we sat at a wooden table, ate off tin plates instead of mess kits, and were served by a Korean waitress in a long gown. Compared with life on the mountain, it

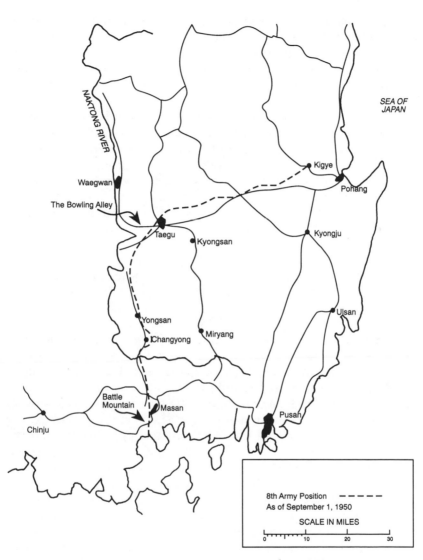

NAKTONG RIVER

SEA OF
JAPAN

Kigye

Waegwan

Pohang

The Bowling Alley

Taegu

Kyongsan

Kyongju

Yongsan

Ulsan

Changyong

Miryang

Battle
Mountain

Masan

Pusan

Chinju

8th Army Position — — — — —
As of September 1, 1950

SCALE IN MILES

0   10   20   30

The Pusan Perimeter, 1 September 1950

seemed quite elegant. After lunch, we headed back to the orchard, laughing, joking, and feeling pleased with ourselves for having crashed the sanctums of Eighth Army.

Our holiday mood changed abruptly. Back in the company area, men were rushing about with an air of urgency. Ruff Lynch, who had been in charge during Gib's absence, said our orders had been changed. "We're still in the role of fire brigade," Ruff said, "but now the fire's to the east, over in the ROK area."

We mounted up in "deuce-and-a-halfs," the familiar 2½-ton GI trucks, this time from an Eighth Army Transportation Company. I rode alongside the driver in the cab of the lead truck, and the bumpy ride, over rutted secondary roads, took nearly three hours. The driver told me he'd been shuttling units constantly to plug holes in the line.

"I wonder how long we can keep it up," he said. I was wondering too.

Then—end of the line—another assembly area, near a place called Kigye. I said good-bye to the driver, hating to see the trucks pull out, since they represented a link with the safe rear area, if indeed there was such a haven.

As Item was being shuttled to Kigye, almost the entire 1st Cavalry Division was engaged in heavy fighting. Within a two-day period, three '49er platoon leaders were killed: boyish, blond-haired Fred Eaton of the 7th Cavalry Regiment, plus Mac Odell and Mo Magruder of the 8th Cavalry.

Fenton McGlachlin "Mac" Odell had been with his unit only three days when he was told to take a crucial hill north of Taegu. He told his men how the Americans fought the British during the American Revolution by using "walking fire."

"If they hit the man in front of you," he said, "just keep walking and firing. We've got to take that hill." Mac was in front, walking and firing, when the enemy got him with a grenade, but his men walked on to take the hill.

I remembered Munro "Mo" Magruder for many things, such as the time in history class when we were discussing the issue of states' rights, and Mo brought the house down by saying, "Well, since I was born in China and spent much of my boyhood in Switzerland, I'm not sure which side I should be on!"

Mo and his platoon had been defending a hill north of Taegu when he was killed by automatic-weapons fire. Although we had once considered Mac Odell and Mo Magruder to be confirmed bachelors, they had each fallen in love with girls they'd met at Fort Benning, and they'd each been married in June, shortly before embarking for Korea.

Our whole battalion had been transported to the Kigye area and dispersed along the base of a mountain at the edge of a wide valley.

To our rear was a South Korean artillery battery, equipped with outmoded 75-mm pack howitzers.

Item went into position between King and Love companies. For the moment all was quiet, so our 3rd Platoon relaxed and cleaned up. Suddenly the artillery pieces behind us began to shoot over our heads at targets beyond the mountain. A few minutes later, there was a crashing roar a few yards away. There was another explosion, then another: counterbattery fire, enemy gunners trying to knock out the South Korean 75s. And here we were in the middle. Our South Korean allies were ruining the neighborhood.

Some of the enemy shells were landing among the American infantry, and soon the whistle of incoming rounds was followed by cries from the wounded and calls for medics.

Our platoon shifted position, moving higher and hugging the mountain, trying for a spot the high trajectory incoming rounds couldn't reach. The artillery duel continued throughout the night. To make it worse, occasionally our friendly Koreans would miscalculate, their shells would fail to clear the mountain, and would hit instead on the slope above us. We could hear the rush of outgoing shells, the whine of incoming.

"If someone will give me a whistle, I'll stand up and direct traffic!" That was Sergeant Sullivan, trying to add some humor to the occasion. It helped, but only a little.

By morning the firing had stopped, and once again it was time for a reconnaissance. Gib told us, "We'll be attacking in a day or two, so we're going to a Korean Observation Post (OP) to get a look at the terrain up ahead." At the OP, two members of the ROK Capital Division, a captain and an interpreter, pointed out the mountain that was to be our objective. We studied it through our binoculars but could see no sign of movement.

A shot snapped by overhead. We looked at each other, puzzled because it seemed to come from the very hill we were on. I raised my head, began to study the objective hill again.

Zing—another shot. Tom Hardaway was standing next to me, and this time the bullet seemed to pass right between us. We ducked down, and the Korean captain spoke rapidly to his interpreter.

The interpreter leaned over saying, "The captain, he say please to keep head down. Captain he tell men not to show selves. If anybody place head up too much, he tell men to shoot that person. But captain, he not want them shoot at you!"

It seemed a harsh way of enforcing camouflage discipline, but it surely made an impression. We descended the hill and returned to our jeep, thankful to leave while still intact. Tom, my replacement as officer-driver, took the wheel and we started back. As we came to an open valley, a shell landed in a field about twenty-five yards to our right. Seconds later, another shell hit in the road a few yards ahead of us. Evidently we were in a stretch visible to some enemy observer, and he was adjusting fire, with us as a target. Another shell landed— this time just to our rear.

"Should we stop this thing and jump in the ditch?" Tom shouted.

"No, keep going!"

Tom jammed his foot to the floor, and we careened down the road, rounded a bend, and passed behind a sheltering hill.

Two days later, our attack was canceled, but again trucks came to move us to a threatened area. This time it was to Pohang on Korea's east coast. During the past two weeks, Pohang and the hills north of it had changed hands many times. Recently the NKs, who'd been heavily reinforced, had broken through, and the ROKs, trying to retake lost ground, had suffered heavy losses. Now it would be our turn to attack.

By early September, the North Koreans had infiltrated so many men behind the 7th Cavalry Regiment that it was decided to withdraw the whole unit to new positions in the rear. That was easier said than done, since the enemy held certain key hills *behind* the 7th Cavalry, and in effect, before they could fall back, they would have to drive the North Koreans from their proposed route of withdrawal, especially the key terrain feature, Hill 464.

George Company of the 7th Cavalry was given the job of taking 464. As it happened, '49ers led each of George's platoons: Dick Tobin the 1st, Curly Lindeman the 2nd, Larry Ogden the 3rd, Hal Anderegg the 4th. In darkness, amid a pouring rain which made the valleys a sea of mud, they waited for word to begin the attack. Finally, at 3:00 A.M., they were told to jump off.

The company, which was down to eighty men, moved out cautiously, well aware that enemy soldiers were all around them. By midmorning, Tobin's platoon reached a position short of the crest. Captain West, the company commander, halted the column while he and Tobin went forward to take a look. Moments later they came upon three enemy soldiers preparing to eat breakfast. In the ensuing melee, all three North Koreans were killed.

At this point West told Tobin to lay down a base of fire while Larry Ogden's platoon circled and assaulted the hill from the left. Larry and his men got within fifty yards of the crest before being stopped by heavy fire from the North Koreans. Every avenue to the top was blocked. Throughout the day, with both Larry and Curly Lindeman heavily engaged, the company held its ground but could make no progress. Finally it was decided to wait until nightfall, then to drop down the hill, detour to the east, and try taking 464 from a new direction. They had to abandon seven dead on the hill, but their five wounded they brought with them, and it made for slow going.

In the middle of the withdrawing column, Anderegg and his men, followed by Tobin's platoon, reached a trail intersection at the bottom of the hill, turned right instead of left, and got lost. Before long, Hal sensed he was out of contact with the remainder of the company, but decided to continue along as he was going, since the path seemed to lead toward the top. From time to time, they stopped to rest. They'd been exhausted when they started, and now, carrying three of the wounded with them, as well as a machine gun and a mortar, they had trouble putting one foot in front of the other.

At one point, Anderegg realized five of his men were missing. When someone went back to look for them, he found they had fallen asleep during a rest break. An hour before daybreak, they reached a small, flat area, where they stopped and rested.

As it began to grow light, they continued upward. To the east, they could see Hill 464, and as they reached the crest of their own hill, they found a series of empty North Korean foxholes. Two men were put into each of four of these holes. Corp. Lou Tebodo (who later attended West Point, graduating in 1955) and PFC Harper, with the light machine gun, noticed another hole, about five yards away; it was covered with pine boughs, and as they looked, something inside moved.

Tebodo yelled at Sergeant Link, "I think there's somebody in this hole."

"Hey," Link shouted, "GIs in this hole?" The only answer was a cough. Sergeant Link left Tebodo to cover the hole and moved up to Sergeant Reed's hole.

"I think there are gooks over there."

Anderegg, arriving on the scene, said, "Well, clean them off." Tebodo, with his rifle, and Harper, holding the light machine gun, stood guarding the hole as Reed walked up and pulled off the brush. There sat four North Koreans, rifles between their legs. Reed gestured for them to come out, but no one moved.

Reed grabbed a man wearing officer insignia and pulled him out of the hole. The man twisted loose and ran, and Harper shot him down with the machine gun. Others of the platoon shot the other three men in the hole and fired into still another hole that was covered with brush. When they removed the brush, they found two more bodies.

Suddenly they spotted other North Koreans, some twenty-five to seventy-five yards away. Firing continued, and before it was over, seven more enemy were killed and three taken prisoner. From papers found on the bodies, it was learned that this had been a Regimental CP. The man who had twisted away and run to his death had been the regimental commander.

Later that morning, Anderegg and Tobin were reunited with the remainder of G Company. By 8:00 A.M. G rejoined the battalion, after being out of touch for some twenty hours and surrounded by North Koreans all that while.

Just north of Pohang, we unloaded near a snug, horseshoe-shaped draw, in the middle of which was the customary rice paddy. Our I Company platoons curved around the hillsides under some sheltering trees. We rested, cleaned our weapons, wrote letters home, and wondered what would come next.

The following day, Gib returned from a company commanders' meeting and told us our battalion would attack at dawn.

"This is a big one," he said. "We'll have more people supporting us than you can believe, artillery, mortars, air, and offshore we've even got the battleship Missouri!"

"Everybody's being so good to us it makes me worry," Jim remarked.

Gib agreed. "Yeah, there's often someone who'll help, but in the end it's the poor miserable infantryman who has to do the dirty work."

"Fortunately I'm assigned to the Regimental Tank Company, so I don't worry about things like that," I said. It had become a running joke, not terribly funny, but an exchange with which we were comfortable.

"Forget about the tanks, Maihafer. Ten years from now we'll be infantrymen slogging across Mongolia, and you'll still be muttering about a mistake being made, that you're actually a tanker."

"But sir. . . ."

"Don't call me sir!" That was another of Gib's standards, inevitably followed by, "One lieutenant doesn't call another lieutenant 'sir'. Rank among lieutenants is like virtue among whores!"

An hour before dawn, we were on our feet. In the dark, we ate an abbreviated breakfast and started double-file along the road to our attack position. Around first light, we turned to our left, moved off the road and up a hill, pausing just short of the crest.

The top of the ridge was the Line of Departure, which we would cross on signal. To the rear, our artillery began to rumble. Shells whooshed overhead, on their way to soften up, we hoped, whatever lay ahead. Then the artillery interrupted its firing as the Air Force took over. Fighter planes passed overhead and dove toward suspected enemy positions, firing rockets and machine guns.

Item was on the battalion's left. To our right, on the same hill, was Love Company. Across the road on another hill, King Company was assembled. When Item moved out, our 3rd Platoon would be on the company's left, with Jim and Tom to our right, thus putting our platoon on the battalion flank, with nothing friendly to my left.

In theory, you made an approach march from assembly area to attack position, deployed, and then moved promptly across the Line of Departure. But here we were, holding up and waiting. It was a mistake to be so long in an exposed location, and soon we began to pay for it. Enemy artillery and mortar shells began landing, with Love and King getting the worst of it. As we watched in horror, a three-round concentration landed squarely on a cluster of bunched-up King Company soldiers.

The minutes ticked off, and finally my radio operator said word had come for us to jump off.

"On your feet, let's go!" I yelled. As we reached the crest, an awesome, surrealistic panorama was laid out before us. Hills, valleys, villages — all stood out vividly in the morning sun. Columns of smoke and burning houses showed where the air strikes had hit. A P-51 zoomed low across our front, close enough for us to see the pilot's face. As he pulled up, he fired a salvo of rockets into a village that was already burning.

We picked our way single-file down the forward slope. Two scouts were in the lead; I was directly behind them. We came off the hill, started across a dry paddy field, and as we came into the open, all hell broke loose. A string of shells landed, bursting all around us. I dropped to one knee, wanting to hug the ground, but when caught in the open, it was best to run through the concentration, even though every instinct screamed for you to stay down. But what if I started running and no one followed? I was scared, my mind was racing, and those thoughts flashed through my consciousness faster than it takes to tell about it.

Trying to sound calm, I stood up and told 3rd Platoon, "On your feet, let's go." One by one, the others followed as I began walking forward. Once they were moving, I started jogging, and the platoon stayed with me. More shells landed, but by this time many of them were falling behind us.

We ran quite a ways, then spread out and climbed our first objective, a small hill that offered some cover. Robby moved among the squad leaders, getting a count of casualties. "We had three wounded, Lieutenant. Two were able to walk and I sent 'em to the rear. The other was Archie, the automatic rifleman in Sully's squad; he got it pretty bad. One man stayed to take care of him until the medics take over."

We dug in and caught our breath. Ahead was a valley which appeared even wider than the one we'd just crossed. The second objective lay just beyond that valley, and when we moved out, we'd again be in the open.

Sullivan's assistant BAR man came running up—white faced and shaken. I saw him talk to Sully and then head back to the rear. Sullivan came over to report.

"Sir, Archie's dead. The man stayed with him until he died. The medic never showed up."

"Where's that man going?"

"I sent him back for Archie's BAR. Wouldn't you think he'd have known to bring it without my telling him!"

"You mean you sent him back—to cross that valley *again?*"

"Of course! Our squad needs that automatic rifle; you can't just go leaving it behind!"

I shook my head in amazement. Despite the shock of hearing about Archie, Sully had reacted so quickly, so *correctly*, by making the man return for the valuable automatic rifle. Personally, I hadn't even thought of it. These noncoms were good instructors.

Firing in our area was sporadic, but off to the right it seemed to be intensifying; I could hear the popping sounds of US rifle fire and the chatter of our machine guns. Mixed in was the low-pitched buzzing of enemy automatic weapons, the Soviet-made "burp guns."

Farther to the east, and nearer the coast, the regiment's 1st Battalion was also attacking. FO Earl Lochhead was with Charlie Company, whose CO was Jack Doody, USMA '48. As they approached the Line of Departure, shells from Navy 16" guns, so large they could almost be seen with the naked eye and sounding like freight cars, were passing overhead. Several rounds landed prematurely near the company's line of march, and Earl, trying to be funny, picked up a 6" shell fragment, showed it to the infantry, and told them not to worry, these were "friendly" shells.

The company went into position on three fingers which ran north-south. The 4.2" mortar observer was with one platoon, and Earl's FO party was with another. There was a break in the line, with about fifty to a hundred yards between platoons. During the afternoon, Earl saw his first enemy, as a Maxim machine gun with a square metal shield began firing from about seventy-five yards away. The gun was on the crest of a ridge, making it a difficult target for artillery, and the battalion's Fire Direction Center (FDC) told Earl they didn't want to waste too much ammunition on it. Later, Earl brought fire on what appeared to be a tank, backed into a house and further camouflaged with vines, but he couldn't tell if they actually knocked it out.

I Company started out again, three platoons abreast, across the open paddy fields. Once again enemy mortar shells began falling. Our own artillery was landing on the next objective, and the North Koreans occupying it decided to take off before we got there. As we climbed the next ridge, Objective Two, I was still on the left, Jim in the middle, and Tom on the right. The ground dropped off sharply to our front. In the distance was yet another ridge — Objective Three. This side of it, out in the open, we saw a crowd of enemy soldiers heading northward. Our artillery FO quickly called in a fire mission.

To our right, on Hill 99, King Company was meeting stiff resistance, from enemy artillery, mortars, and automatic weapons. There was a constant crash of exploding shells, mixed with the rippling buzz of the burp guns.

It appeared Item would be holding this position for awhile, waiting to see if King Company was able to come abreast, so we began to dig in. The sun continued to beat down; my canteen was nearly empty, and my mouth felt like cotton.

A few hundred yards away, to our left front, another hill looked down on us. I hoped no "bad guys" were on it, for if they were, they would be staring down our throats.

A radio message from Gib said to keep our heads down; an air strike had been scheduled against the trench network on Hill 99. King was taking heavy casualties; every time they tried to reach the top, they were being met by a shower of hand grenades from well dug-in enemy. Two of King's supporting tanks had also been lost — one in a NK minefield and the other because of a thrown track.

Moving cautiously, trying to stay under cover, I headed toward

Gib, wanting to tell him the dominating hill to our left front should be occupied. Between us was an open area; I ran across it and dove to the ground on the other side. As I started up Gib's hill, the P-51s appeared for the air strike, moving perpendicular to our line of advance. The first plane made its pass almost directly overhead, loosing its rockets against the enemy's ridge. Up ahead I saw Ruff Lynch, who grinned and waved. As the next plane dived, the pilot must have mistaken our hill for the enemy's. His first rocket made a rushing sound like a freight train, followed by an explosion just ahead. Then, suddenly, another roaring sound was right on top of me. It was a moment of stark terror, as the concussion, felt rather than heard, slammed me down like a punch from a giant fist. Clods of earth and stones rattled against my helmet, and I lay still, shaking, not wanting to look up, afraid of what I might see. Could it have hit Ruff?

"You all right, Harry?" It was Ruff; the rocket must have landed between us.

As I rose up, my ears were ringing and I felt groggy. I also felt lucky. At the Company CP, our artillery FO was screaming into his radio to "lift the G.D. air strike!"

Gib said our battalion was being held up; by this time King Company was down to thirty-five men. We discussed the hill to our left front, and Gib agreed it should be occupied.

"Do you want to try it, Harry?"

"Not really, but I guess my guys are the logical ones to go up it."

"Yeah, but be careful." Back at the platoon, we placed some mortar fire on the other hill to soften it up. Then, warily, we spread out, covered the intervening few hundred yards, and began climbing, fearing that any moment might bring a spasm of fire from hidden positions.

We reached the top, found a few holes and a lengthy trench network which had recently been abandoned, but that was all. Squad positions were assigned and we settled in, still feeling apprehensive.

The sun beat down, and I became even thirstier. Crazily, some lines from *Gunga Din* kept running through my head:

> But if it comes to slaughter
> You will do your work on water,
> And you'll lick the bloomin' boots of 'im that's got it.

The words kept droning, over and over, like a tune that couldn't be shaken.

The FO arrived to stay with our platoon, since we were holding the key piece of ground in the area and were the only people securing the battalion's left flank. Throughout the night, the two of us called for sporadic fire missions to discourage any counterattack. It was a long night.

Earlier, over in the C Company area, Earl Lochhead had lost communication with his FDC. The land lines had been severed, perhaps by exploding shells, and the battery for his radio had gone dead. He tried two more batteries—both proved defective—and Earl cussed the practice of using equipment salvaged from Pacific islands after the end of World War II.

His only recourse was to repair the land line, and not wanting to ask his men to do something he wouldn't do, he set out down the hill to find and splice the break. A sniper began shooting; unfortunately he could see Earl and Earl couldn't see him, so it was back up the hill to try another battery.

Soon after dark, the question was asked if anyone wanted grenades. Earl raised his hand and, though he'd only wanted a couple, was given a whole box. None of the infantry seemed to want any, but when the company came under attack, everyone wanted one, and Earl was only too happy to share.

At one point, Earl thought there was a North Korean in their position, so he went to a sergeant and said, "I think our position has been infiltrated."

"Sir, why don't you go capture him?" the sergeant said. Earl drew his .45 and approached what turned out to be a bush moving in the wind.

The enemy began attacking the side of the hill, and Earl called for artillery fire from his supporting 105s. The enemy kept coming, and Earl brought the fire even closer, at one point using himself as the aiming point. Fragments fell on his own position, but the attack was broken up. Next morning they saw many dead bodies outside their perimeter.

It was with a sense of relief that we saw the first streaks of dawn appear, rising out of the Sea of Japan. With this first light came word that we would be withdrawing. To the west of us, the enemy had broken through the ROK Capital Division, which had all but collapsed, and we were badly needed in the vicinity of Kyongju.

One by one the platoons withdrew. My 3rd Platoon, plus our attached Koreans, covered the company's withdrawal and pulled back last—across fields which were now silent.

Sergeant Robinette, who was with me as we fell back, said he had arranged to have a new medic assigned to our platoon.

"That other guy, Lieutenant, he didn't stick with us when that concentration hit. If he had, he might have saved Archie."

"I know, but it's a hard thing to prove. Anyhow, Robby, I'm glad you managed to have someone else assigned. How did you do it?"

"I told that last guy that if he ever came near my platoon again I'd kill him."

On 4 September, the 2nd Battalion of the 5th Cavalry attacked and captured Hill 303, northeast of Waegwan, the very hill on which Cec Newman had been killed three weeks earlier. That night the NKs counterattacked in force, and by midnight G Company of the 5th Cavalry was surrounded.

One of George Company's platoon leaders was '49er Jim Scholtz, a huge, powerful athlete who as a cadet had set a world's record in the hammer throw. Jim had joined the company on the Naktong two weeks earlier. Perhaps happiest to see him was his classmate, and fellow track star, A. G. Brown. Brown had been leading patrols across the Naktong almost nightly, and Jim, on his second day with the company, had volunteered to take the next patrol himself so as to give A. G. a bit of relief.

The situation for G Company grew worse as the NKs tightened the noose around 303, and a decision was made to withdraw. First, however, they wanted to expend as much of their ammo as possible to prevent it falling into enemy hands. Jim took a rocket launcher and decided to try hitting an enemy group behind a slight knoll about two hundred yards away. To clear the knoll, he needed elevation, so Jim stood fully erect and put his eye to the sighting device on the launcher's side. As he did so, he was hit by a bullet which entered his left shoulder, passed across his body, and exited through his right shoulder.

As the company withdrew from 303 in the darkness, fighting all the way, Jim managed with help to get down the hill and into a litter jeep alongside another wounded man. The jeep, trying to make its escape, came under still more fire, and the man alongside Jim was hit for a second time.

Back at the battalion aid station, '49er artilleryman Frank Sarsfield, himself a casualty, saw Jim, who was by then unconscious. Frank wondered if Jim was going to make it.

To the south, in the 25th Division sector, it took nearly five hours to bring Ted Swett down from Battle Mountain. His four Korean litter bearers did the best they could, but every jolt intensified the pain, and at one point, as a short round from friendly artillery landed nearby, the bearers dove for cover and dropped the litter in a rice paddy.

At the foot of the mountain, Ted was strapped to the hood of a jeep which joined a convoy carrying wounded to a Mobile Army Surgical Hospital (MASH) unit near Masan. As they arrived, a softball game was in progress, and to Ted it seemed the ball almost stopped in midair. Bats and gloves were thrown aside as corpsmen and nurses raced to help the wounded. Ted thought the nurses were the most beautiful creatures he had ever seen. Soon a young doctor performing triage came by.

"Lieutenant," he said, "when you come out of surgery, you may not have that leg."

"That's okay, doc. I'm alive." Luckily, they were able to save the leg; Ted's canteen, fragments of which would remain permanently in his hip, had absorbed part of the blast, probably saving the leg, and perhaps even saving his life.

Further evacuation brought Ted to Tokyo Army General Hospital, where his roommate turned out to be Winston Churchill's son Randolph, a correspondent for the *London Daily Telegraph*, who'd been wounded while covering action in Korea. (According to *Time*, when Randolph arrived in the Far East, he had caused an uproar by being thrown out of the Tokyo Press Club after demanding he be allowed to sign chits for drinks before he had plunked down his membership deposit.)

With a Churchill for a roommate, Ted met a host of celebrity visitors, including Joe Alsop, Jimmy Cannon, and the British ambassador. The latter, to his credit, and contrary to hospital regulations, provided the room with an ample supply of excellent Scotch whiskey. Each afternoon, Churchill would announce, "Leftenant, it is the Hour of the Aperitif! Have a neat one!"

Later, Ted was also visited by Barbara Buffington, Ralph's widow, who came up from Yokohama to see him. During cadet days, Ralph and Barbara had often double-dated with Ted and Cay, Ted's future wife. Barbara talked the doctor into giving Ted a wheelchair and pushed Ted, out of bed for the first time, to a hospital auditorium to hear a memorable performance by Al Jolson.

Also arriving at Tokyo General was Jim Scholtz, happily assigned to the same ward as Ted. Soon Jim, regaining his strength, became ambulatory. Because of the bullet which had entered one shoulder and gone out the other, Jim wore a brace which made it impossible to wear any kind of shirt, and the tiny Japanese nurses' aides stared in awe whenever the muscular blond giant roamed the hallways.

Some sixteen years later, Ted Swett, having been medevacued

from Vietnam, was talking to Col. Marty Pfotenhauer, hospital commander at Camp Drake. One evening, reminiscing about the Korean War, they discovered they had both been near Masan about the same time, and Ted asked if Marty remembered Battle Mountain.

"Of course," Marty said. Then he wondered out loud whatever happened to a young West Point lieutenant who had received a direct hit on the hip from a mortar round, because he had told the lieutenant he would probably lose the leg. Ted, who still owned both his legs, was happy to identify himself.

Bill Marslender had been with his platoon of Able Company, 7th Cavalry, for only three days when they went on line northeast of Waegwan. His first attack order was far from Infantry School standards, as his company CO merely pointed to a hill on his map and told Bill to occupy it. Bill, who had no map of his own, led his platoon to what he hoped was the right location.

Next morning, the company commander, who had never left his CP, told Marslender to attack Hill 518, the looming hill mass known as Suam-San. He and his men started out, up a ridge which kept getting sharper and steeper, still wondering if they were in the right place. At this point, Bill barely knew the men in his own platoon, let alone others in the company. Consequently, when he met another unit, he and the other lieutenant first introduced themselves, then mutually agreed Bill would take the right edge of the ridge, the other would take the left.

They kept climbing, and any doubt about being in the right place was soon dispelled, as they began receiving automatic weapons fire together with a thundering mortar barrage. One of the first mortar rounds made a direct hit on the weapons squad. The shelling continued and casualties mounted. Unable to move, they crowded against a cliff face, which provided some measure of protection.

It was now about 5:00 P.M., and Bill's original thirty-eight men had been reduced by more than half. About a hundred yards to the rear, he saw what appeared to be an area offering some sense of security, and he radioed for permission to pull back. The company commander, still at the CP, assumed Bill meant "withdraw all the way," and said he'd ask Battalion.

At this point, the other platoon leader, who'd been slightly wounded, crept over to Bill's position. His exact words, implying a need for leadership from his fellow lieutenant, were, "Sir, what are we going to do?"

Bill pointed out the proposed position to him and suggested he

William H. Marslender. Courtesy US Military Academy Archives.

start withdrawing there, one squad at a time. Bill would offer cover and then start his own men back. They would bring their wounded, but of necessity would have to abandon the dead. The pullback was nearly completed when the radio operator received a message saying their request to withdraw was denied.

"Don't acknowledge it," said Bill, "and turn off the damned radio!" By this time only six men with Bill were still alive, and two of them were badly wounded. Carrying the wounded in slings made from ponchos and rifles, they managed to make it back to the new location. The only one there was Bill's platoon sergeant; the others had scattered.

As it began getting dark, the firing let up. Marslender told his four men to dig in. The platoon sergeant, ignoring his own wounds, went out in the darkness, calling out and whistling, and eventually returned with twelve additional men. It wasn't much of a force, but at least sixteen were better than four.

Soon after daylight, they spotted a North Korean patrol coming down the mountain to look for them. The Americans fired and the patrol withdrew, but now the American position was known. Thirty minutes later, mortar fire began landing, causing still more casualties.

Finally someone at a higher level acknowledged that the operation had failed, and about 10:00 A.M. Bill was ordered to withdraw. It was supposed to have been a battalion assault, but the attack, along a narrow ridge line, had resolved itself into a column of platoons, and finally a column of squads. Later attacks on Hill 518 also failed, and a captured prisoner said there had been twelve hundred NKs on that hill.

Indirectly, Bill heard the company commander wanted to court-martial him for withdrawing without orders, but had abandoned the idea when told directly by Bill's platoon sergeant that if that were to happen, he, the sergeant, would have to blow the whistle about the company commander never having left the CP!

Simultaneously, a few miles away, the 8th Cavalry Regiment was involved in almost continuous fighting. Bill Wilbur had been with I Company of the 8th Cav only a few days, but he had already distinguished himself by volunteering for several hazardous assignments. Perhaps he was trying to emulate his hero-father, the World War II Medal of Honor winner.

Wilbur had led a number of reconnaissance patrols deep into enemy territory, securing important information as to enemy gun emplacements and troop dispositions. Then, on 3 September, Bill's company was given the mission of stopping the enemy's advance by cutting the road north of Tabudong, even though the enemy already held the village and terrain to the company's rear. Bill's DSC citation for the action read in part:

> Realizing the necessity of clearing the enemy from the village, Lieutenant Wilbur volunteered to lead a thirty man patrol into it. Although continually harassed by enemy small arms fire, he succeeded in clearing a sector. Then, despite the heavy small arms and machine gun fire, he aggressively led the patrol to the far side of the town, where they successfully recovered and evacuated a seriously wounded man. While clearing out the remainder of the village, Lieutenant Wilbur skillfully directed his patrol in repelling an enemy attack, killing six. When the enemy, approximately seventy-five in number, launched a second attack and nearly overwhelmed his troops, Lieutenant Wilbur called for fire upon his own position and broke up the hostile force, allowing his patrol to withdraw to his Company's position.

As this was happening to Bill Wilbur, '49er Jack McDonald, a member of the 99th Field Artillery Battalion, was nearby as an FO with another of the 8th Cavalry's frontline rifle companies. The situation became critical, and in the words of his Bronze Star for Valor citation (two months later he'd win a second one) Jack, "realizing that artillery fire was needed to stop the advancing hostile hordes, moved to an extremely exposed position where he could effectively observe and direct supporting fire. Despite the heavy volume of enemy automatic weapons and small arms fire in his area, Lieutenant McDonald courageously remained at his post until the following day . . . and played a major part in preventing the hostile forces from overrunning the area."

For Item Company, it was another bumpy ride, this time to a bivouac area near historic Kyongju, the country's ancient capital. Kyongju, with the world's oldest astronomical observatory and its many temples and monuments, was held in special esteem by all Koreans. However, I suspected this wasn't the first time men at war had disturbed its tranquility.

Our battalion was spread out in an attractive, park-like grove. Flat, shady, peaceful—a place to relax, to eat hot food, to write a letter home. An hour after our arrival, however, my platoon was given the mission of protecting a newly arrived tank unit.

We trudged out of the bivouac area, which by now looked more appealing than ever, and joined the tanks at a roadblock north of town. The tankers had been in Korea only a few days, and compared with our grimy, bearded bunch, they looked marvelously clean and rested.

We formed a perimeter, with our machine gun and rocket launcher covering the road, and I told the squad leaders only a minimum number needed to be awake; the others could get some badly needed rest. After comparing this place with Pohang, it was hard to become too concerned. However, the "virgin" tankers saw it otherwise. On the horizon, far in the distance, a mountain held by the ROKs was receiving fire, and one of the tankers told Robby and me, rather breathlessly, that through his binoculars, he had actually seen puffs of exploding artillery.

"Pretty damn close, huh?" he said. Robby just looked at him. Later that night it began to pour. Driving sheets of rain, whipped by the wind, soaked us thoroughly. The tank platoon leader invited me to share the lean-to they had constructed by attaching a tent flap to the side of his command tank. He and I stayed awake and talked, sharing experiences and comparing backgrounds. Surprisingly, we both had been sergeants during World War II, and both had attended aerial gunnery school. He was further surprised to learn that I, like himself, had been commissioned as a lieutenant of cavalry.

"Y'know," he said, "I think that having been a sergeant gives us an advantage. We understand what it's like to be an enlisted man—how the men think, who in their eyes makes a good officer and all that. Y'know who never understands that sort of thing—it's those goddamned West Pointers!"

I showed him my Academy ring, and our newfound friendship seemed to cool. Fortunately it made little difference, since next morning another platoon came to relieve us.

5. The Perimeter Holds

6–14 SEPTEMBER

For those fighting along the Pusan Perimeter, the second week of September was a kind of turning point. The North Koreans kept pressing their attacks, often successfully, but were never able to make a complete breakthrough. Battles continued to rage, from Pohang in the east to Waegwan and Taegu in the west, and Masan in the south. Gradually the momentum was shifting, and UN forces along the Perimeter were becoming more and more like a compressed spring, ready to explode once the pressure was released. It was costly to bring this about, and a significant part of that cost was borne by junior officers.

It was early afternoon, and once again it was time for Item to move, out of Kyongju's park-like grove and toward a range of hills in the distance. Major Mac was on hand to see us off, and as I passed him, he waved and called, "Good luck, Harry." Somehow it sounded ominous.

My platoon was in the lead as I Company set off cross-country, and I asked Gib, who was walking with me, if we were replacing a friendly unit, and if not, whether the hills ahead were supposed to be empty.

"Well, there aren't any friendlies out there," he said. But whether there were enemies, he couldn't say. In midafternoon, as we came to a fork in the trail, Gib pointed out two peaks joined by a ridge line.

"Harry, take your people and head for that right-hand peak. When you get there, extend your line to the left. I'll be with the rest of the company. We'll take the left-hand peak and then extend to the right. Let's hope we can link up."

Our platoon split off and began moving faster, hoping to reach our objective before dark. Suddenly we came to a dead end—a ravine with a stream at the bottom. Eventually, after an hour's delay, we found a ford and waded across in water that came up to our knees.

We pressed on in the fading light, but it was dark when we reached the foot of our objective. The peak, outlined against the evening sky, loomed high and forbidding. We tried to call Gib, but our radio frequency was jammed with Korean voices, perhaps friendly Koreans, perhaps not. As we huddled at the base of the mountain, fearing what might be on top, the darkness made each man anonymous. For an instant, I wished I could forget my responsibility and fade away into the night. What right had I to lead men up that slope when I myself had no idea what to expect? Shaking off the doubts, I found the noncoms and whispered instructions. We spread out and moved upward—cautiously. An eternity later we made it to the crest. Fortunately, the ridge was unoccupied.

The situation in the 1st Cavalry Division that week was nothing if not fluid. Much of the time, it was impossible to say who was surrounding whom. Frequently a unit would seize a hill, then find the enemy was already occupying terrain to their rear.

To Kenny Miller, with his platoon of King Company, 7th Cavalry Regiment, it seemed they climbed hills and dug holes all day, then tried to stay awake all night. On 6 September, his weary group, accompanied by a platoon of engineers, was ordered to climb Hill 466. It had rained hard during the night, making the trail muddy and difficult, and soon a dense fog closed in, reducing visibility to about fifteen feet. As the fog lifted, they began receiving small arms fire, and King Company hugged the ground. A string of machine-gun bullets plowed a furrow near Kenny's shoulder.

I Company of the 7th Cavalry, across the road on an adjacent hill, was being overwhelmed, and Kenny, watching helplessly, saw North Koreans streaming down the I Company ridge. Listening on his radio, Kenny overheard a plaintive cry.

"Sir, Lieutenant Wilbur is dead . . . *all* our officers are dead!"

Kenny was jolted. It was a cruel way to learn the fate of a friend and classmate. Bill Wilbur, unlike his dad, would never win the Medal of Honor, but his courage was fully attested to in a letter to General Wilbur written by Bill's battalion commander, future Army Chief of Staff Harold K. Johnson: "Your son was utterly fearless, in fact he seemed to have a total contempt for danger in any form. . . . He was supreme in combat, confident of his own ability. He faced grave danger without fear and suffered his mortal wounds without comment."

Two days earlier, Bill Marslender, in Able Company of that same 7th Cavalry Regiment, had started up Hill 518 with thirty-seven men. Of that number, only six remained, and perhaps since his group now resembled a squad more than a platoon, he was the one chosen to establish an outpost in a valley to the battalion's front. It wasn't clear how far up the valley he was to go, nor when he was to return. They borrowed an SCR-300 backpack radio so they could talk to Battalion, then set off after dark in a heavy rain. After advancing a mile or more up the valley, they covered themselves with their ponchos, spread out in a perimeter, and waited.

During the night, heavy firing, like fireworks, broke out to their rear as the battalion came under attack. Next morning, their radio calls went unanswered, and Bill wondered if the battalion had been overrun. Marslender and his radio operator climbed a knoll to improve their chances of communicating, but there was still no response. They climbed still higher, to a nearby ridge, and Bill, standing behind the operator and holding the radio handset, suddenly saw four North Koreans coming down the ridge. There was no time to say anything; he just returned the handset to the operator and began fumbling under his poncho for his carbine.

A North Korean with a red star on his cap, possibly an officer, fired at them with his burp gun and the four enemy then began to run away. Bill took aim—he had a clear shot—but his carbine wouldn't fire!

The rest of Bill's men, who had remained in the valley, heard the firing and came hurrying up the ridge to join him, just as the operator, with blood on his shirt and pant leg, said he'd been hit. After they'd removed first his shirt, then his trousers, but still couldn't find anything, the man said: "Sir, I guess I'm not hit. I was just scared."

The blood, it turned out, was Bill's. Bullets had hit both his hand and his carbine. The impact had jammed the butt of the carbine against the operator, which explained both the blood and the carbine not firing.

Moments later, looking across the valley to an opposite ridge, they saw a frightening sight—a body of troops, deployed in combat formation and coming their way. Bill realized there was no place to go, so he told his men to spread out and hide.

As the troops drew closer, someone was shouting instructions. Incredibly, Bill recognized the voice. It belonged to Larry Ogden, who'd been calling out to fellow '49er Curly Lindeman.

"Larry! Larry Ogden! Is that you?" Bill yelled.

"Yeah! Is that you Bill?" It was a joyful reunion. Larry explained that the battalion had been driven back, and Larry's company had been sent out as a rescuing force. Soon Bill, whose wound was more serious than had first appeared, was on his way to a hospital at Pusan, where doctors had to cut off his West Point ring so as to work on his swollen hand.

North of Kyongju, Gib assembled the platoon leaders and said: "The battalion is jumping off in an attack, with K and L leading, us in reserve. Better stick around so we can get together fast if we have to plan a quick move."

The three of us, Tom, Jim, and I, eased to an open spot on the next rise. It was a beautiful day, with warm sunshine, blue sky, fluffy clouds. We lay on our backs, talked idly, wondered whether we'd be called on to join the assault. We had borrowed one of I Company's two SCR-300 radios; Gib had the other. With our own walkie-talkies, the SCR-536s, we could talk to each other and to Gib, but with the 300 we could hear Battalion and the other companies. With more than a casual interest, we tuned to the battalion net.

King and Love Companies were reporting heavy opposition. As their messages came in, we could hear heavy firing in the background. The situation sounded bloody, and I felt the hollowness gather in my stomach.

More messages came in; more staccato sounds of machine guns in the background; more reports of casualties. I looked at Tom and Jim. No one wanted to say the obvious—that we were glad to weren't the ones making the attack.

An unexpected message came for Gib from the battalion adjutant. "We have a couple new officers here who've been assigned to Item. Shall we send them forward?"

"No," Gib replied, "why don't you just hold them back at Battalion Rear until I need them."

"Until he needs them?" I laughed. "That's a hell of a thing to say!" Tom and Jim agreed; Gib had sounded as though he expected to lose some platoon leaders. Didn't he know all three of us were invulnerable?

Our turn came the next day. Item, accompanied by tanks, and with my platoon leading, would assault a series of hills to the north. Shortly after daybreak, five General Sherman M-4s clanked into position. Their bumper markings showed them as belonging to the 70th Tank Battalion, the school unit from Fort Knox. Three months earlier I had been training on some of these same vehicles.

We spread out and followed as the tanks moved forward into an open valley. There they halted and began firing their cannons at a hill to our front. By this time Gib had joined me.

"I'm confused," I said. "Which one of those hills is my objective?"

"It's *that* one," he said, pointing to the left front.

"Then why are the tanks shooting at that one to the right of it?"

"You're right; it's *that* one, not the one I said."

After all my tactics classes, at West Point, at Riley, at Knox, "Take that hill; no, *that* one!" seemed rather brief for an attack order. However, I got the idea.

I located the platoon leader's tank, climbed onto the rear deck, and banged on the turret with the butt of my carbine. The hatch opened—slowly—and a wary lieutenant, looking like a turtle reluctant to emerge from his shell, raised his head.

Briefly we discussed how far the tanks would advance and when they would lift fire. During the conversation, I flashed the crossed sabers under my lapel to show that I too was a tanker. (Like most infantry officers, I didn't wear my officer insignia openly.) Ironically, it turned out that *he* was an infantryman, and he joined me in disparaging the assignment system. However, he made no suggestion about trading places.

After the tanks had finished shooting, we headed for our hill, at the right side of a ridge line. Once on top, we moved to the forward slope and dug in, four squads abreast, with the attached recoilless rifle section bending back on the right. For protection to the rear, I had each squad put its two-man automatic rifle team on the reverse slope.

The 2nd Platoon passed through and went in to our left; beyond them, the 1st Platoon and the Company CP were on the far left. All around us were recently abandoned trenches.

A figure appeared to our right front, moving rapidly away from us. Some of the riflemen started shooting at him.

"Hold your fire!" Robby called before I had a chance to react. The man dove into a gully and disappeared from sight. I was relieved. Maybe he was a soldier, but then again maybe not.

"Do you think he was a civilian, Robby?"

"I dunno, Lieutenant. But y'know, I don't really care. Once, after Chochiwon, I was all by myself, caught in the open, and a bunch of North Koreans were shooting at me while I zigzagged and ran and ran. They were laughing and having fun, and I felt like that guy must have just now."

I could surely understand Robby's order to cease fire. Robby, who described himself as an "ol' Kentucky boy," had only the day before been promoted to master sergeant. It was well deserved; he was a fine soldier and a fine man. His reaction to the promotion was, "Wait'l mah pappy hears about this—he won't believe it! Probably he'll even get mad; it took him about thirty years to make master!"

Somehow it made me realize for the first time that Robby was a young man, probably still in his thirties. I'd been looking at his seamy, weatherbeaten face, with his walrus mustache and tired eyes, and thinking of him as ageless.

We settled in for the night. I found a shallow gully on the reverse slope, which let me stretch out more or less protected. Rain began to fall, and I put on my poncho. Though I tried to sleep, I soon found myself sliding downhill as rain gathered in my gully.

I groaned, roused myself, and moving cautiously in the darkness and rain, checked the squad positions. Water had gathered in the bottom of most foxholes, and the discomfort level was high. I wanted to try sleeping, but after squirming a while in my wet clothes, I realized it wasn't much use.

Well to our rear, almost to Kyongju, there was a spasm of firing. Streams of tracer bullets curved into the night sky. Instead of the usual white or red color, some of them looked greenish. Were the green ones being fired by the enemy? And what was the enemy doing that far behind us? Had there been a major breakthrough, or was it merely a patrol which had been discovered? There was a whole fireworks display by now; more machine-gun tracers, flares, colored pyrotechnic signals, then the flashes of tank cannons. We discussed what was happening, finally deciding it might be an enemy probe trying to get at the tanks.

As the first gray streaks of dawn appeared, the rain had stopped but a fog still hovered in the valleys, obscuring our vision. All at once there was firing to my immediate left, in the 1st Platoon area. The firing, including the ugly hum of burp guns, became heavier, and a few shots began coming our way.

An enemy patrol had traveled up the draw behind our position. An automatic rifleman later said he had seen them moving along— some fifteen or twenty men—but in the dimness of early morning he had assumed it was a carrying party bringing rations and ammo to us. Maybe the patrol in turn had seen us, and the BAR teams I'd placed guarding the rear had caused them to detour. In any case, the patrol had circled and blundered into Tom's area.

Meanwhile our rations and ammo *were* coming forward, not with a carrying party but on the back of tanks. The tanks arrived at the base of Tom's hill and began firing their machine guns and cannons. As I watched, there was a large explosion where the Company CP had been. A spatter of machine-gun bullets followed, and I hoped the CP group had already moved.

When the enemy patrol came upon the rear of the CP, the company communications sergeant had been first to see them. He called out, fired his carbine, the enemy fired back, and then all was confusion. The CP group ran, crawled, tumbled tail-over-teakettle onto the forward slope to get out of the way. About that time the tanks arrived and began shooting. Next, Tom had some of his men cover him while he led a group to drive off the enemy. The North Koreans started falling back. Tom, leading a charge, heaved three or four hand grenades, killing or wounding several of the enemy. Tom then called for more grenades; someone handed him a couple. He stood to get leverage for one last throw; a North Korean fired a parting burst from long range, and one bullet found its mark.

Time passed. The firing subsided, then stopped altogether. My own men still hadn't come under attack and I was frustrated, not knowing the situation and unable to establish radio contact. Finally a messenger arrived, saying Gib wanted me at the Company CP. I asked where my regular runner was.

"I don't know, sir, but I think he got hit. They just told me to go find you and Lieutenant Exley."

Making my way along the ridge, I noticed that Jim's 2nd Platoon people, like mine, were only now starting to stir around and to poke up their heads. Jim's platoon sergeant came up to me and said, "I'm sorry about your friend, Lieutenant Hardaway."

"What about him?"

"He's dead. I thought you knew; I'm sorry."

Disbelieving—or at least refusing to believe—I kept going until I came upon Gib. He was sitting on the ground, looking tired.

"Is it true about Tom?"

"I'm afraid so, buddy. I can't believe it either. He was one of my favorites. We all knew you'd take it hard, Harry, that you two guys were close."

Gib began to recite, in a hushed, almost childlike tone, "Maybe it was that poncho . . . it made him awkward . . . and he had to stand to throw . . . and he was such a big target." His voice trailed off; he began again. "They were all around us . . . everybody was confused . . . then Tom got things organized . . . drove them off . . . they were down in there . . . just over that ridge."

I shook my head, still rejecting what had happened. Gib went on as though he needed to get it all said.

"He was lying there, Harry, and you know, all I could think was that his face was dirty, his mouth was open, and rain was dripping from his helmet and running down his face . . . and it'd go in his mouth . . . so I closed his jaws and wiped his face clean . . . his mouth being open . . . that means he died instantly, from that one bullet in his heart. I wrapped his personal things in this scarf so we can send them home to his widow."

Gib had trouble going on. I said, "Gib, let me keep Tom's West Point ring." I took the ring, put it on my right hand, and made a promise to myself to wear it in Tom's memory and someday to deliver it to Tom's wife, Terry.

Tom, my closest friend, was dead. As for me, I was tired, wet, and filthy. My feet hurt; I was hungry and weak. In a daze I started back to my platoon. Tom's platoon sergeant, Gypsy Martin, stopped me to say that Tom was the "best damn officer" he had ever known. Farther along the ridge, 1st Sgt. Roy Cano came to me and said simply, "I'm sorry about Lieutenant Hardaway; he was a fine officer."

In that moment I came unraveled. My eyes brimmed over, and tears poured down my cheeks. Roy put his arm around my shoulder. I kept sobbing, almost whimpering. Roy said, "Lieutenant, you've got to pull yourself together. You don't want the men to see you like this, do you?"

He was right. I tried to shake it off, and back at the platoon, with my red eyes, I kept to myself. Someone told me about my missing runner, who'd been lucky. A machine-gun bullet had hit him in the side, curved around the rib cage, and emerged without puncturing anything.

Next day we withdrew, back again to the orchards of Taegu, and to the same area we'd occupied earlier. It would be a chance to clean up, to lick our wounds, and to recharge our emotional batteries. As for me, I kept thinking about Tom.

That week the 1st Cavalry Division was fighting for its very life. The North Koreans, stalled elsewhere, still had hopes of striking a final blow, making a major breakthrough, and opening a corridor to Pusan. If they pulled it off, victory in the south might still be theirs. For the 5th Cavalry Regiment, action was almost nonstop.

In the Taegu area, east of Waegwan, Hills 174 and 188 were critical terrain features. Over a four-day period, Hill 174 changed hands seven times. On 12 September, as he led his platoon up 174, Roger Kuhlman was killed by mortar fire. That same day, on Hill 188, Courtenay Davis, Kenny Miller's best friend, was killed by machine-gun bullets. Then, on 13 September, the enemy recaptured both 174 and 188.

Next day, I Company of the 5th Cavalry, with Beecher Brian (1st Platoon) and Joe Toomey (2nd Platoon), learned it was now their turn to assault 174. The plan called for Beecher to swing to the west through some rice paddies and to climb 174 from the left. The 3rd Platoon would be in the center; Joe and his men would be on the right.

Before they even started, mortar fire began landing, and once they were in the open, the fire intensified. Beech had his platoon form more or less in a line, and told them to move through the paddy as quickly as possible, heading for the base of 174. The rice was waist high, and even though they were hurrying, the going was slow. Men began falling. One round landed about ten yards to Beech's left front; the concussion folded him in half as though he had run into a tripwire. A few feet away, a piece of shrapnel had torn a hole about the size of a silver dollar in the stomach of the platoon medic, a youngster they called Smitty.

Smitty was crying with pain, saying, "I don't want to die!" Beecher sent for litter bearers and tried to reassure him. Smitty, screaming with pain, told Brian he felt sick to his stomach and stuck a finger down his throat. As soon as he did so, his stomach heaved, and the pressure forced about a foot of intestines out of the hole in his stomach. Beecher put a compress over the wound to keep out the flies, strung a bandage from Smitty to the nearest rice paddy dike as a marker, then ran to rejoin his platoon at the base of 174. (Later, Brian learned the litter bearers had missed finding Smitty, whose body was recovered several days later. The man sent to guide the bearers had stayed in the rear and never come forward. Beecher was furious, just as I was when my BAR man, Archie, died through neglect in that similar incident near Pohang.)

The firing intensified as Beech and his men moved up 174. Over on the right, Joe Toomey's 2nd Platoon was almost to the top, and Joe urged the commander to send the rest of the company to join him there for a final assault. However, the 3rd Platoon was decimated, as was Beech's 1st Platoon, and the CO reluctantly ordered Joe to pull back. Toomey, not wanting to give up ground they'd paid for in lives, argued about it, but finally had to withdraw and join the others in forming a tight perimeter. The ground was rocky, and there was no way to dig in, so they tried to get cover in little folds in the rocky surface and built small rock walls out of loose shale, which covered the ground.

By this time the company had lost half its men. The enemy continued to counterattack, and throughout the night, I Company desperately held on, calling for supporting artillery and mortar fire,

Adrian Beecher Brian. Courtesy US Military Academy Archives.

heaving grenades, sometimes shooting, but often hesitating to fire, since no one wanted to give away his position. Frequently the North Koreans, creeping around in the darkness, were so close that they and the Americans could hear each other breathing.

Next morning at 11, Battalion allowed the company to withdraw. The following day, however, despite their weakened condition, they were ordered back up the same hill. It was a nightmare—dead bodies, both American and Korean, littered the hillside. For five more days, the men of I, now nearly punch-drunk from constant shelling, stayed where they were. When they finally pulled off, of the forty Americans and fifteen Koreans who had started out in Beech's platoon, only twelve Americans and five Koreans remained.

During our first two years at West Point, we had lived three to a room. During the final two years, however, as an upperclass benefit, we'd lived with only a single roommate. An exception was made for Bill Marslender, Roger Kuhlman, and Fletcher McMurry, who got along so well as roommates during plebe year that they asked not to be broken up. Their requests were honored, and they were probably the only three members of our class to room together for all four years.

In many ways, they were as close as brothers. The day after graduation, in fact, Fletcher McMurry had married Bill's sister Linda in the West Point chapel. Now Bill, back in the hospital in Pusan, was stunned as he learned of Roger's death. It brought back a flood of memories, of their both choosing the infantry branch, of being together at Riley, and at Benning—both for the basic course and for jump school—and of driving together from Roger's home in Wisconsin to Seattle and Fort Lawton.

Unlike Bill and Roger, their roommate Fletcher had, upon graduation, gone into the Air Force, and at the time of Roger's death, Fletcher had just received his pilot's wings at Vance Air Base in Oklahoma. He and Linda were a popular couple, and during flight training "Mac and Linda's Grill" was the scene of many happy get-togethers, one of the highlights being Fletch's recounting of the exploits of his great uncle, the illustrious Confederate, John Pelham.

Next stop for the McMurrys was the advanced flight school at Tinker Air Base. Fletcher and Linda, saddened by Roger's death, vowed not to forget him, and when their infant son was born, they named him William Roger in Kuhlman's memory.

Kenny Miller and his platoon of K Company, 8th Cavalry Regiment, had been moving and fighting constantly for over a week. By

8 September, as their company attacked Hill 573, everyone was exhausted, both physically and mentally. At one point, when one of their sergeants was killed, Miller heard the company exec lamenting, "why couldn't it have been me . . . I'm so fuckin' tired."

Late in the day they pulled back to an assembly area, where they ate for the first time in over twenty-four hours. Two days later they moved to a large hill mass opposite the walled city of Kasan. The hill mass had five knobs on it, and Americans owned three of them. Arriving on the third knob, they found a quantity of abandoned US equipment, grim evidence of a unit that had been overrun.

The fourth knob was captured on 10 September, but by this time Kenny's platoon, which contained thirty-two men when he took command on 28 August, was down to about fifteen. Other platoons were in similar condition, so when I and K companies assaulted the fifth knob on 11 September, the attacking force was more like two platoons than two companies.

Fortunately the able Sergeant Caplette was still on hand, and off they started. For the first part of the climb, the contours of the ground offered some protection. When they arrived at the military crest, Kenny looked back to the fourth knob, where his company commander (well to the rear as always, Kenny thought) was motioning for him to keep going.

"Let's go!" Miller yelled. After a few steps, he looked back and saw he was the only one moving. He yelled again, adding a few choice words for emphasis, and the platoon got to its feet. Almost immediately they were greeted by mortar bursts and automatic-weapons fire, plus grenades which came rolling down the hill into their formation. Seconds later a bullet plowed into Kenny's stomach, spinning him around. As he dropped to the ground, he felt he'd been hit by a sledgehammer.

A soldier came running over. "Where you hit, Lieutenant?"

"In the belly," Kenny gasped. The pain had begun, and his right leg was growing numb. The soldier put a first-aid packet over the wound, and Kenny told him to get on up the hill. As the man started to move, a bullet hit him in the head. He fell beside Kenny, holding his face and gurgling, "Mama," as he died.

The platoon went on to take the hill, and for a few moments all was quiet. Kenny felt warm in the groin area, and he knew he must be bleeding internally; his fingers were getting numb; he decided the numbness would spread and that very shortly he would die. For some reason, it was more a feeling of resignation than of panic.

A medic came and patched a large exit wound in Kenny's right hip. "Am I going to die?" Kenny asked.

"Nah, Lieutenant, you're going home to sleep between sheets." After that, the pain became more bearable, even though a thunderous mortar barrage began landing, with each round producing more screams from the wounded.

Without orders, the men began to leave the hill, and Miller could hear Sergeant Caplette yelling, "I'll shoot the first son of a bitch that leaves here without a wounded man with him!"

The medic grabbed two soldiers who came running by. "Get the lieutenant out of here!" Kenny put an arm around each man, and they literally dragged him back down the hill.

When they reached the company commander's location, the CO asked, "Miller, is it bad?" Kenny decided that was the dumbest question he'd ever heard.

Sergeant Caplette, carrying a wounded man under fire (and winning his second Silver Star) was the last man off the hill. At the end of the day, only seven remained of the thirty-two who had started out two weeks earlier.

Since Kenny's wound was in the stomach, they couldn't give him anything for his thirst or his pain. All they could do was to place him on a litter and assign four KATUSAs as bearers. The trek down from the hill mass took four hours. At least twice, the Koreans stumbled and dropped the litter.

Finally Kenny was loaded into an ambulance, which had to remain where it was until the artillery shelling let up. It wasn't until the following morning that Kenny arrived at a MASH unit, where his bloody litter, placed on sawhorses, became an operating table, and where a skillful surgeon repaired the internal damage and cleaned the hole in his hip. He was then put on a train, taken to an airfield, and flown to Tokyo General Hospital, where he joined Jim Scholtz, Ted Swett, and others.

One evening, heavily sedated and semidelirious, he realized it was raining, and he asked a nurse captain if he could bring his men in out of the rain.

"You bring them on in," was her unhesitating reply. She stayed by his bedside and held his hand until he drifted back to sleep.

In our bivouac at the Taegu orchard, Gib and I decided it would be better if I were the one to write the first letter to Terry Hardaway. It was a hard letter to write, but I tried my best to make it meaning-

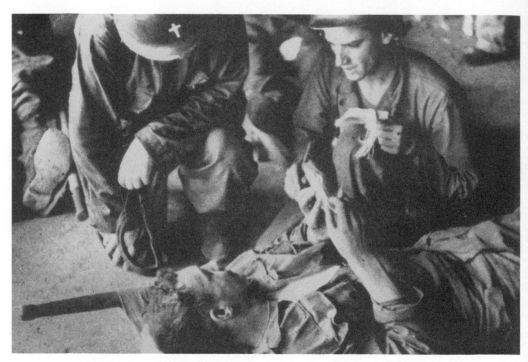

Kenny Miller on litter, tended by a medic and chaplain and showing them
something on his map. Battalion Aid Station, 3rd Battalion, 8th Cavalry Regi-
ment, September 1950. US Army photo.

ful, telling how we all felt about Tom, describing the circumstances
of his death, and ending by saying: "I have some small knowledge of
how great your loss really is, and I too share that feeling of loss with
you, as do the men who served in Tom's platoon, including Tom's platoon sergeant, a hardened veteran, who said he had actually grown to
love Tom, and that he was the 'best damned officer he'd ever seen.'"

After that, I wandered over to the Battalion HQ, where Father
Dunne was setting up shop, arranging an altar cloth on the hood of
his jeep. "I'm going to say Mass after awhile," he said. "But first, Harry,
I want you to do something for me."

"What's that, Father?"

"Go over to my pup tent, crawl in, and rest a while. Frankly, you
look like hell! Look under the folded blanket, where you'll find a bottle, and take a couple of good stiff belts. Then, take one of the paper-
backs in there, read a while, and try to relax."

"Okay, Padre, I'll try. Thanks." It seemed to help, both the relaxing and the knowledge that Father Dunne was someone who cared. At Mass, I used one of his missals and read the familiar Introit words. Events of the past month had given them new impact:

> I will go unto the altar of God,
> To God who giveth joy to my youth.
> Judge me, O Lord, and distinguish my cause from the nation
>   not holy. . . .
> For thou, O God, art my strength; why hast thou cast me off?
> And why do I go sorrowful whilst the enemy afflicteth me?

6. Striking Back

15–20 SEPTEMBER

As early as July, Douglas MacArthur had decided upon an amphibious landing well behind the North Korean lines. Such an encirclement, reminiscent of his brilliant island-hopping campaigns of World War II, could be the master stroke to end the war. For the first two months of the war, however, General Headquarters (GHQ) planners were unable to gather an invasion force, since North Korean successes required all available units to be sent to General Walker's desperate Eighth Army.

On 23 July, at a high-level conference in his Tokyo headquarters, MacArthur defended his choice of Inchon as the invasion site. His skeptical audience included both Army Chief of Staff J. Lawton Collins and Chief of Naval Operations Forrest P. Sherman. Despite the inherent difficulties of the plan, especially Inchon's treacherous tidal situation, MacArthur prevailed, and approval was granted for a mid-September landing.

The invasion force would be made up of the 1st Marine Division and the 7th US Infantry Division, which together would comprise the newly formed X Corps under Gen. Ned Almond.

After 23 August, nearly all the army personnel arriving in Japan, including many '49ers, were funneled into the 7th Division, which earlier had been stripped of 140 of its officers and 1,500 of its enlisted men. Consequently, the units now being assembled were more or less starting from scratch, with most officers and men meeting each other for the first time. Further adding to the confusion was the need to integrate more than 8,000 KATUSAs into the division's ranks.

Among the late arrivals assigned to the 7th Division was artilleryman Don Gower, whose orders had been delayed because of a baby due in August. Soon after arriving in Japan, Don went shopping, and mentioned to a sales girl that he was joining the 7th Division in Hokkaido.

"Not Hokkaido," she said, "you're going to land at Inchon." Don assumed she didn't know what she was talking about. Next day he reported to the 7th Division in Yokohama harbor, and learned his unit, the 48th Field Artillery Battalion, had already embarked, which meant he couldn't join them until after he'd gone ashore in Korea. In other words, he was part of an amphibious operation as an unattached individual, without even having had a chance to draw ammunition, and it was a naked feeling. During the trip to Inchon, he was able to talk a soldier out of a clip of ammo for his carbine.

By this time, word was out that the 32nd Infantry would support the 1st Marines in the Inchon operation. Bill Kempen and Herb Marshburn were in the 1st Battalion of that regiment; Lew Baumann and Curt Anders were in the 2nd; Joe Kingston, Jack Madison, Sam Barber, and Jack Thomas were in the 3rd.

Kingston and Madison, with I Company, put to sea on an old Liberty ship, the *Private Sadale Munomori,* named for a Nisei hero of World War II. It was truly a makeshift outfit—new recruits fresh from the States, a hundred KATUSAs (including at least two known communists), plus a last-minute supplement of soldiers released from the Eighth Army stockade. Through a happy coincidence, their company commander turned out to be Capt. Jim Spettel, an older brother of '49er classmate Chuck Spettel.

On 11 September, Jack Madison wrote a letter home from aboard ship, saying: "I certainly do wish we had an opportunity for more training. I feel sure we will get some more when we arrive. It would be nothing but foolish to commit us in this state of combat efficiency."

Also coming aboard was ex–Air Force man Lew Baumann, who was assigned as a spare officer to George Company, where Curt Anders had the 1st Platoon. Conditions aboard the ships were crowded and uncomfortable, but the true misery lay just ahead. On the second day at sea, their convoy ran into Typhoon Kezia. Hour after hour, violent, stormy seas tossed the ships about, with a foreseeable impact on already nervous stomachs. Soldiers told each other they'd gladly trade the sea for the shore, even for a shore defended by hostile North Koreans!

Early on 15 September, the initial assault was accomplished by Marines who seized Wolmi-do at the mouth of Inchon harbor. Later in the day, landing ships, tank (LSTs) brought the 1st and 5th Marines ashore at Inchon itself, and by the afternoon of 16 September, a solid beachhead had been secured.

Lew Baumann. Courtesy Col. Lewis R. Baumann (Ret.).

That afternoon the '49ers of the 32nd Infantry went ashore, taking up positions on the Marines' right flank, and with a mission of sealing off the road leading into Seoul from the south. As Curt Anders left the transport *Ainsworth* and headed for Inchon, he realized the fighting had already moved inland. Nevertheless, an amphibious landing was an amphibious landing, and enough to cause a bit of apprehension. However, when the clamshell doors of his LST opened, the first two people he saw, rather than enemy troops, were Gen. Ned Almond, his corps commander, and Marguerite Higgins, the attractive correspondent from the *New York Herald Tribune*.

George Company moved east toward Seoul, with Lew Baumann (who was still an "extra" officer) and the first sergeant bringing up the rear. Soon men began discarding equipment and dropping out of ranks.

The first sergeant, a tough World War II veteran, let some of them pile equipment on the litter jeeps in the rear of the column, but steadfastly refused to let anyone ride, saying if they fell out they'd just be left behind. Baumann was shocked by the troops' wretched physical condition, and before the day was over, he ended up carrying, in addition to his own rifle, two other weapons, and an apron with 60-mm mortar ammunition.

The 1st Marines were north of the Inchon-Seoul highway, and Curt Anders's platoon, miles away, was supposed to be the 7th Division's link with them. Looking up, Curt saw Marine F4U Corsairs, coming in low and firing their machine guns. Curt leapt to his feet, ran into the open, and began waving a Day-Glo panel to show the pilots they were strafing friendly troops. A North Korean machine gunner opened up, and a bullet, after clipping the top of Curt's combat boot, entered his leg.

That night Lew Baumann led a squad-sized contact patrol to let the Marines know George Company's location. As they neared the Marine lines, they heard firing, which meant reaching the Marines without being fired on themselves would not be easy.

"Army patrol, requesting permission to enter your lines!" Lew called out. A Marine sergeant responded, and the patrol was allowed to enter, first Lew by himself, then the others. The Marine CO was more than friendly, and when he learned the patrol members hadn't eaten that day, he even provided some hot C-rations and coffee.

All was going well, and after coordinating their exit with their friendly hosts, sometime after midnight they filed out through the Marine outposts. Minutes later, however, it appeared someone hadn't gotten the word. The newfound friendship was sorely tested as Marines began shooting wildly in their direction! Lew and his patrol found a sheltering ditch and made a hasty withdrawal.

The night's work was not yet over. On the way back to their own company, they heard Korean voices, accompanied by the sound of digging, making them realize they were caught between the North Korean enemy and the US Marines. They made an abrupt turn and somehow managed to avoid both. Then, when they reached George Company, they entered the company perimeter without being challenged. Nearly all the green, out-of-shape recruits were fast asleep. It was not a comforting discovery.

Jack Madison, leading I Company's Weapons Platoon, received his baptism of fire a few nights later as his company neared a town where they were supposed to link up with the Marines. KATUSAs with his platoon were used primarily as ammo bearers, an important job, since Jack had been told not to expect any ammo resupply, particularly for the 57-mm recoilless rifle. However, when white phosphorus mortar rounds began falling up and down the column, the KATUSAs promptly threw their ammo carrying bags in the rice paddies and took off. Jack was probably as much concerned about retrieving his precious ammo as he was about the incoming mortars.

As they continued down the road, the head of the column was almost wiped out when their village rendezvous point turned out to contain North Koreans rather than Marines. At that point they pulled back to some high ground and spent the night being shelled by friendly artillery. Next morning the situation straightened out and the Korean ammo bearers returned, presumably looking for breakfast.

The following day, Joe Kingston and his platoon, mounted on tanks, went rolling south, heading for the key town of Suwon. Inside the town, an enemy T-34 tank, hidden behind a building, opened fire on the leading American tank and knocked it out, killing the tank company commander. Eventually the situation was stabilized, and the 32nd Infantry, after being replaced by the 17th Infantry, went on to a new mission.

Don Gower came ashore on 17 September, and after hitching a ride with an obliging chaplain, finally joined up with the 48th Field. '49er Clay Moran was also in the 48th Field, which was commanded by Lt. Col. U. G. Gibbons, a former English instructor of ours at West Point. Don was assigned to C Battery, and next day was further assigned as an FO with G Company of the 32nd Infantry, just missing Curt Anders, who had been evacuated to the Marine hospital at Inchon after gaining the dubious distinction of becoming the first '49er Inchon casualty. (Fortunately the wound wasn't serious. A few days later, Anders went AWOL from the hospital and rejoined his company.) Meanwhile, Lew Baumann had taken over Curt's platoon.

The Marines had been held up, and the 32nd Infantry was ordered to attack Seoul from the south, crossing the Han River opposite South Mountain, which extended from the river northwest into the heart of Seoul. For the crossing, they'd use Marine amtracs, the amphibious tractors known as "water buffaloes." George Company would be in the lead, with FO Don Gower accompanying Lew Baumann and the 1st Platoon. Newcomer Gower realized with some satisfaction that he'd be the first army artillery officer to enter Seoul.

After an artillery preparation, and helped by an early morning

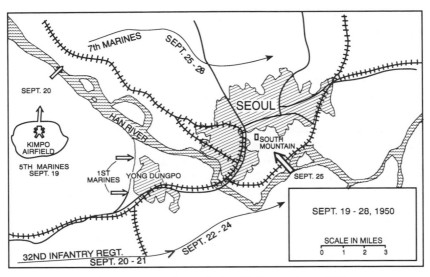

The Capture of Seoul, 19–28 September 1950

fog which limited visibility, the amtracs plunged into the water and began firing their machine guns. Inside one of the lead tracks, it sounded to Lew Baumann as though someone was banging the top of the vehicle with a club. As Baumann's amtrac neared the far side, the track commander realized the bank was too steep for the track to climb.

"Lieutenant, we're going to drop you here!" he yelled. When the ramp dropped, Baumann grabbed the cosmoline-covered cable attached to it, lost his grip, and went sliding into the Han River. The soldiers in the track went rushing forward and up the bank, most of them managing to stomp on Lew in the process.

Baumann scrambled up the bank, reassembled his platoon, and proceeded on his mission, which was to secure a walled compound containing troop barracks. The squads deployed in a wedge formation and crossed a wide area without seeing anyone or meeting any opposition. Then, a few yards short of the compound gate, Lew noticed a bush which seemed to move erratically. He signaled a halt, stared at the bush, and once more saw it move.

Lew pointed to the bush and told a BAR man to cut it down. The BAR barked out a long burst, the bush shook with the impact, and an enemy sniper slumped to the ground. With that, all hell broke loose. North Korean troops on nearby high ground opened up with everything they had. The platoon rushed through the gate and into the compound, where the buildings and the surrounding wall provided a good bit of cover.

Next job was to clear the buildings, American-built barracks which had once housed US occupation troops. The squads spread out, and after a search, it appeared the place was unoccupied. When the platoon reassembled, however, Lew's 1st Squad was missing. After waiting fifteen minutes, with no sign of the missing squad, Baumann took one of the other squads and went looking.

He found his men, almost immobilized, at a building not far from the gate. "What's going on?" he asked the squad leader.

"They could see us from that ridge up there, Lieutenant. We've got some wounded up on the second floor, and I told everyone to keep still so we don't draw any more fire."

"But you can't just leave those wounded men lying there! It's been at least fifteen minutes, and a man could bleed to death in that amount of time!"

Baumann entered the building, and at the top of the stairs, found a soldier, who had not been hit himself, but who cautioned Lew not to go any farther. "They can see you if you do, Lieutenant, and you'll get hit. There's a couple of men lying there and we told them not to move or they'd draw fire!"

Lew told the man to go to a window, stay concealed, but to fire at the overlooking ridge. This brought return fire, but as Lew went to the wounded men, he stayed clear of the windows, and the enemy rounds were ineffective.

The first man had been wounded in the arm and shoulder, and with Lew's help, he made it down the stairs. The next man, however, had been hit in the legs, so Lew had to drag him to safety. It took a while, but eventually Baumann was able to report the compound was cleared. (For his actions during the day, including this saving of two wounded men under fire, Lew received the first of two Silver Stars.)

Baumann's 1st Platoon rejoined George Company, which was scaling the slopes of South Mountain. By midafternoon they were on top, near the center of Seoul. When Don Gower arrived at the crest, the infantry had knocked out all opposition except for a few enemy holed up in old Japanese antiaircraft bunkers. After the company commander's jeep made it up the little road to the top, he and Don took the jeep's five-gallon can of gasoline, poured it into the back of the main bunker, and set it on fire. The North Koreans promptly came out and surrendered.

From his vantage point on South Mountain, Gower could see

Marine positions to the west, and NK soldiers in Russian-type helmets, pulling wheeled machine guns and mortars, heading east right below him. Excitedly, he called for his very first fire mission, but it was no go. The FDC said the sector to his front belonged to the Marines, and they couldn't be sure where they were. Much as he tried, Don couldn't convince anyone he had a great target.

That night the NKs began shelling South Mountain with 120-mm mortars, followed by an attack designed to cover the main force's withdrawal. Casualties in George Company, which held the highest knob, were light. On their right, however, Fox Company was overrun. The battalion commander, Lt. Col. Charles Mount, who had been one of our tactical officers at West Point, launched an all-out counterattack. Shortly after daybreak the position was restored. As it became light, Don saw masses of NK bodies in front of, and in, the Fox Company position. Overall, the night's action had cost the NKs nearly 400 dead and over 170 prisoners.

Later that day, Joe Kingston was part of a force trying to clean out the rest of Seoul. As his platoon advanced up a steep hill, they came upon a North Korean trench network. Joe sent scouts out to either side, then led the way into the trench itself. The trench made a right-angle turn, and suddenly Joe came face to face with two armed North Koreans. Joe pulled the trigger of his carbine — and nothing happened. Before the Koreans had time to react, and almost by instinct, Joe began screaming at the top of his lungs.

"Drop those guns! Drop 'em! Do it right now!" To the Koreans, the broad-shouldered, 6'2" Kingston must have looked and sounded frightening indeed. Unhesitatingly, they dropped their burp guns and surrendered. Joe then teamed up with one of his men and cleaned out the rest of the hill, which was honeycombed with entrenchments, capturing nine more NKs before they had a chance to fire on his platoon.

Back at the Taegu orchard, we received a few replacements and were happy to have them, although many were rear area types whose background made them ill-suited for combat. A case in point was Ed Walsh, a personable first lieutenant of infantry, who had spent his army career running either a PX or an Officers' Club. Despite Ed's seniority, Gib made him my assistant platoon leader, supposedly so he could learn from my "expcrience." I laughed at Gib as he said it, reminding him I'd been an infantryman for a mere month. (Over in the 1st Cavalry Division, Beecher Brian had a similar reaction when, after two weeks on the job, he was transferred to a newly formed company, and told it was to take advantage of his "seasoning.")

On 16 September, as my classmates far to the north were landing at Inchon, a meeting was called for all officers and key noncoms
of the 21st Infantry. We assembled in an open field on a bright sunlit
morning, and the formation, with more than a hundred officers and
twice that many noncoms, somehow let us view the regiment in a
new perspective. Gathering this way for the first time, looking at those
who had shared a common experience these past weeks, most of whom
we were seeing for the first time, gave us a sense of confidence, of
comradeship, even of power. It was a far cry from our usual feelings
of stretched-out, understrength isolation. Maybe that was the idea.

While we were waiting, there was almost a carnival atmosphere,
a chance to visit with friends in other companies, some of whom we
hadn't even known were in the same outfit. In the C Company area,
I saw Jack Doody, my friend from the class of '48, along with Earl
Lochhead, his FO. A year and a half earlier, in my hometown of Syracuse, I'd been in a wedding party with Jack and two of his USMA '48
classmates, Marty Nelson and Charlie McGee. Marty was the groom,
Jack the best man, and Charlie and I the ushers. Now Jack changed
my carnival mood by telling me that both Marty and Charlie had been
killed in early August.

Colonel Stephens, looking tough, stood on top of a truck and
began to speak. He had big news—Americans had pulled an end run,
an amphibious landing at Inchon, far up on Korea's west coast. Stephens told what he knew of the landing, then said our own part in
the counteroffensive was about to begin.

"We're breaking out of the Naktong Perimeter, and the 21st is
going to spearhead it. I want you to be aggressive, bold, and to move
fast! If anyone delays you, move around them. We have the numbers
now to overflow 'em, so don't worry about leaving any enemy bypassed;
there'll be lots of people behind you to mop up."

Big Six was a leader. I for one felt charged up and inspired. His
was the emotional talk of a coach at halftime: hard hitting, go-get-'em
words that aroused. Maybe the turning point had come. Maybe a big
offensive would send the North Koreans reeling and we could all go
home. But considering what had gone before, maybe it wouldn't be
that simple.

Near Seoul, Don Gower's unit, C Battery of the 48th Field, was
part of a task force that included a tank platoon and a truck-mounted
company of the 17th Infantry, one of whose rifle platoons was led by
'49er Bob Fallon. With the tankers leading the way, the force made
about six miles before running into North Koreans on hills on both

sides of the road, overlooking a concrete bridge. The tank platoon leader, riding with the hatch open, was killed immediately, which took a lot of fight out of his green platoon. Between the second and third tanks were three jeeps, carrying the task force commander, the liaison officer (LNO) from the 48th Field, and Don, the company's FO.

Hiding behind his jeep, the LNO told the battery to go into position and sent them a fire mission. The task force commander ran back across the bridge, was shot through the foot, and rolled under a jeep. Since the LNO was tying up all available guns, Don couldn't do much on his own, so he went forward to talk to the LNO. On his way back, still under fire, he rescued the task force commander, and then moved the jeeps so the tanks could get started again, an action that won him the Silver Star. (Bob Fallon said all he got from the day's work was a chewing out because his men jumped from their trucks on both sides of the road, making them difficult to control!)

In the south, the Eighth Army was getting ready to cross the Naktong and move north for a link-up with Almond's X Corps. Before doing so, however, it was necessary to deal with the many areas around the Perimeter, particularly in the Taegu sector, where the enemy still held a great deal of commanding terrain. Several key hills, fortified with 82-mm and 120-mm mortars, had been converted into mini-fortresses with extensive trench networks. The job of reducing these fortifications was made doubly difficult by a shortage of artillery ammunition; supply priority, because of the Inchon invasion, had for several weeks been given to X Corps.

The 5th and 7th Cavalry Regiments were given the task of reducing fortifications in the Taegu-Waegwan sector. Bloody fighting followed, and '49er lieutenants were in the thick of it.

On 17 September, the 5th Cav's 1st Battalion attacked a commanding hill on one of the key approaches to Taegu. George Tow (the friend who'd kidded me about my birthday, with "how old would you have been next year, Harry?") led his A Company platoon as part of the attacking force. Soon after they jumped off, Able Company began receiving heavy small arms fire from the objective and the attack bogged down. George saw that he could help if he could get his machine gun and some riflemen on a lower side hill. He worked his way on reconnaissance to the flanking hill three hundred yards to the right front of his platoon and signaled his gun team and riflemen forward. Going back part way to meet them and to lead and direct them personally into position, he was hit by a sniper's bullet and instantly killed.

George William Tow. Courtesy US Military Academy Archives.

Beecher Brian, George's boyhood friend, wrote home a few days later:

> I have some bad news for you, Mother and Dad. George Tow was killed in an attack last week. It was during a series of attacks in which some hills changed hands many times. His Bn. attacked a hill 600 yards to the left flank of the hill our Company I was holding. We were watching the attack by George's company just as if we were in a grandstand, and were putting fire on the Gook flank. It was a beautiful, well-executed attack with relatively few casualties. We had all zeroed in our rifles at 600 yards with tracers and I know we did a world of good for them. I never, never dreamed I was watching dear old George Tow get killed. It has made me absolutely sick. I pray that this mess will end soon. I'm sorry to write you about things which will cause you worry but I do think you should know about George.

A Battery of the 61st Field Artillery was part of the same attack, and Jerry Paden, as an FO, brought fire on a series of objectives, helping the infantry to advance. Then, as a final assault began, and despite the heavy incoming fire, Jerry volunteered to accompany one of the lead platoons so as to provide maximum fire support. As he was adjusting fire, a series of mortar rounds landed near the FO party. Jerry, seriously wounded, was given first aid and evacuated.

Late that afternoon, Lew Zickel, in C Company of the same battalion, went up the steep slope of Hill 300, and before dark, the company had seized the crest, a razorback ridge. That night the NKs launched a series of fierce counterattacks, but the company, with every weapon firing, managed to hold. After one such attack, Lew and another man went back to battalion to replenish the company's supply of grenades and .30-cal bandoleers. The trip back, with a heavy load and up a steep slope in the darkness, was sheer torture, but they made it, and just in time. Another counterattack was under way.

A North Korean threw a concussion grenade toward the foxhole Lew was sharing with his platoon sergeant. Lew saw the grenade coming and threw his arms wide. A fragment passed under his arm and slightly wounded the sergeant. Lew felt an enormous impact and was momentarily stunned by the blast, but surprisingly, no permanent damage was done. Next morning, however, his chest ached, his head ached, and he found in his shirt pocket a mechanical pencil that had been bent double by the blast.

Jerry Paden, at a field hospital in Taegu, was visited by his classmate Jack Hodes, a platoon leader in the 8th Cavalry. They talked a while, and after Jack left, Jerry learned he was being further evacuated to a hospital in Japan.

Jerry's wounds were critical, and surgeons performed emergency surgery soon after his arrival in Japan. Complications set in, and despite the best efforts of the medical staff, Jerry died that night.

Gib sent for Bud Hay (who had taken over Tom Hardaway's platoon), Jim, and me. Company commanders and platoon leaders would be going forward to recon the proposed Naktong crossing sites. We climbed into Gib's jeep and moved out as part of a 21st Infantry convoy. Along the way, we forded the Kumho River by means of an underwater bridge the engineers had put together with sandbags. Finally we came to the road running along the Naktong and headed north. There were more than a dozen vehicles in our convoy, and we drove along in the open, clearly visible to any observer on the far shore. I felt dangerously exposed.

The convoy broke up, and we moved to an apple orchard that would be our assembly area. The plan called for the troops to come forward later that afternoon. Meanwhile, we would make our plans for the crossing.

The day after George Tow was killed, another attack in the same area was launched by the 2nd Battalion of the 7th Cavalry, and a leading role was assigned to the 7th's G Company, where '49ers Larry Ogden, Hal Anderegg, and Dick Tobin were all platoon leaders. Another classmate, Curly Lindeman, had also been in G but had been evacuated with serious wounds a few days earlier. Their CO was Capt. Fred De Palina, a recent arrival whom they didn't yet know too well, but who was obviously a good man. As they started out, Larry Ogden's platoon was supported by a machine-gun squad led by a good-natured ex-Navy man they called Swabbie. They reached the base of Hill 253, and began receiving heavy mortar fire.

The order was given to move out, and Larry called to Hal Anderegg, "Where's Swabbie?"

"He's dead!" Anderegg called back.

Trying to shake it off, Larry and the others started climbing. The shelling intensified. A round exploded next to Larry, knocking him down but strangely leaving him unmarked while killing a man on each side of him. As they approached the crest of the hill, the previously hidden NK riflemen and machine gunners opened up. Larry felt a sort of slap, and looking down, he saw a hole where a bullet, without touching him, had gone through his pant leg. George Company hugged the ground, and anyone bold enough to raise his head was inviting a quick burst of fire.

Suddenly, something seemed to snap. Perhaps it was being pinned down and taking casualties without striking back. Or perhaps it was the frustration of the past several days coming to a head. In any event, George Company, yelling, firing, screaming like madmen, stormed upward in an all-out assault.

They swept over the top, and the remaining NKs bolted. The Americans kept running, and on they went, still screaming insanely, down the far slope and into a village containing the enemy's mortar positions. Everything and everyone was swept aside. Two North Korean majors were among those killed as the mortar positions were overrun.

The advance continued, and George Company found itself in a rice paddy in an open valley. Off to the right, a road came down from between two hills, followed the contour of the hills, and then skirted the edge of the paddy.

Suddenly they saw an enemy company coming down from the hills. The enemy troops, quite unaware of the Americans, were marching along the road in formation, and someone in front was carrying an unusual green flag.

Captain De Palina passed the word, "Everyone stay down, keep quiet, and hold your fire."

Moments later, however, someone panicked and started shooting. The NK's quickly left the road and went into the hills. Now they could look down on the Americans, who, out in the open, made easy targets for the Koreans' plunging fire. George Company's position was completely untenable. Soon there were screams as one man after another was hit, and it was obvious they had to get out of there as best they could.

Among the wounded was Fred De Palina, who said he'd give some cover as the others tried making it back. Larry Ogden made it to a ditch alongside the road, began moving along on his hands and knees, and crawled over the body of a dead North Korean. Suddenly he heard a shot ring out behind him. It turned out the Korean hadn't been dead after all. He had risen up and taken aim at Larry, but an American coming along behind had seen him and fired first.

Many more died before the remnants of G Company returned to friendly lines. Among the dead was Captain De Palina, who had personally killed six of the enemy before he himself was killed, and who was posthumously awarded the Distinguished Service Cross. In the fighting, the effective strength of the three rifle companies of the

2nd Battalion had been reduced by nearly 75 percent. However, they had done their part, and thanks to them and others like them, the stage was set for crossing the Naktong and breaking out of the Perimeter.

During the afternoon, the four of us from Item's recon party were guided by an engineer to our proposed crossing point. Lying on our stomachs, hidden in the shade of trees just off the beach, we studied the opposite shore through glasses, paying particular attention to "Objective Hill," a towering cone with steep, scarred slopes. About all we knew was that our battalion would first take that hill, and then work northward, parallel to the river.

Soon after that, B-29s passed overhead and bombed Waegwan, five miles north of us, in support of an attack by the 5th Regimental Combat Team (RCT). Even at this distance, the noise and concussion from the exploding bombs was almost overpowering. Could any NKs be left alive in that town after such a pounding? And if they were, could they still be effective? I guessed we'd find out.

The plan kept changing. At first, we'd been told about a river crossing at dawn by the 1st and 3rd battalions. A new order, however, called for an attack at midnight.

By 10:00 P.M., the troops had still not arrived. There had been problems at the Kumho underwater bridge, and the infantry, forced to leave the trucks, were having to walk the last eight or ten miles. I didn't relish the thought of telling them, as soon as they arrived, that we'd have to jump off in an attack almost immediately.

That long march, plus the operation that lay ahead, made me concerned about Robinette, my platoon sergeant. He was burned out, physically and mentally, and had been keeping up only by sheer force of will. Robby had never complained, of course, and I knew he'd keep going until he dropped.

Another message from battalion—traffic at the Kumho bridge was still backed up. The assault boats wouldn't be here in time, so it would be a daylight crossing after all.

The troops began to arrive. I assigned areas to the 3rd Platoon squads, and after much stumbling, bumping, and cursing, they managed to take up positions. Having twenty-five South Koreans mixed in with the forty GIs in the platoon added considerably to the fun.

Tired as they were, they first had to dig foxholes, and fortunately the ground in the orchard was soft. Next I met with the noncoms to tell them the plan. We would organize ourselves into "boat teams" of ten men each. Twelve men would cross in each boat, our ten plus two engineers who'd do the steering and also paddle back on the return trip. There would be six paddlers and four men kneeling in the middle. We decided to let the Koreans kneel and get a free ride, since we doubted our ability to tell them much of what was going on anyhow.

A bit later, to no one's surprise, the plan changed again. Now it stood that the 1st Battalion would cross by itself, after which our 3rd Battalion would cross with two companies abreast: our own Item on the left, King Company on the right, Love in reserve.

We continued to dig in, and after much thought, I made a painful decision. As usual, Robby had bunked down near me. With his matted hair, walrus moustache, stubble of beard, and all-encompassing poncho, he looked more than ever like a suitable companion for Mauldin's Willie and Joe.

"How you feeling?" I asked.

"Mah feet hurt a little bit."

"Well, I've decided to leave you back tomorrow. You've been needing a rest for a hell of a long time. You stay back with the kitchen truck and come up when those people do."

"I can keep up okay, Lieutenant," he told me, his voice not changing at all from the usual monotone. "I'd just as soon go along."

The only thing was to convince him it was for the good of the platoon, and that his own welfare didn't enter into it. "Yes, I know, but that last march we made, you had a hard time keeping up. We're going to be doing a lot of climbing tomorrow, I expect, and I'll probably have to push the guys pretty fast."

"Yessir," he said, and shuffled away. I wondered if I'd be able to run the platoon without him.

Nearby, in the 1st Battalion area, Earl Lochhead learned he and his FO party would be just behind the first wave. His driver and jeep, with the powerful radio, would have to stay behind initially. Therefore his commo man would have a heavy backpack radio, and another man would be prepared to lay wire once they got across. Earl and his FO party, as a favor to the infantry weapons platoon, offered to carry a few 60-mm mortar rounds.

Soon after dawn, the artillery and air began to work on the mountains across the river. First the artillery 105s and 155s fired their high explosives and white phosphorus. Then a flight of P-51s came in, launching rockets and strafing with their guns. Then more artillery concentrations were fired, followed by yet another fighter attack.

There had been no sign of enemy on the far shore; Earl and the others wondered if they'd be able to cross unopposed. Soon their question was answered. As the first wave landed, enemy artillery, mortar, and machine-gun fire opened up. One boat was literally blown out of the water. A swarm of bullets created patterns of water spouts; other shots ripped into the flimsy boats. (Earl noticed several boats going around in circles after men stopped paddling and crouched down to take cover. They learned to their sorrow that plywood would *not* stop a bullet.)

The beach on the far side was less than two feet wide, with a yard-high embankment. Earl jumped out of the front of his boat; his radio operator jumped out the back and, along with the radio, went under, thus putting the radio out of commission for the rest of the day.

Lochhead and his party crouched behind the berm for protection. During a lull in the firing, they noticed a 60-mm mortar lying nearby; apparently the crew had been hit. They ran to the gun, set it up, and fired off the rounds they had been carrying.

Just then four Marine F4U Corsairs appeared, releasing their napalm while they were still over the river. Earl saw the tanks floating lazily overhead, and then dropping about seventy-five yards in front of his position. This suppressed the fire that was holding them down, and Earl and his party started moving again, running along a dry stream bed.

We often chuckled at the way Koreans could eat C-rations, almost as though they wanted to finish every can before someone took them away. Now, as Earl rounded a bend in the stream bed, he saw a Korean sitting on the ground and eating a can of fruit cocktail. Earl and the other artillerymen, too scared to think about eating, could only marvel.

Looking back across the river, Lochhead and the men with him could see artillery fire landing on the troops who were still waiting to cross. Most of that fire was being directed toward the orchard where Item Company and the rest of the 3rd Battalion were assembled. Round after round plunged into our assembly area.

We had just learned the plan had changed still again. In the latest version, our battalion would lead off with just Item Company, which would cross with two platoons abreast.

During a pause in the shelling, I decided my hole wasn't quite deep enough after all. After a flurry of rapid shoveling, which slowly slacked off, Gib came over. We started talking, and I persuaded him to scoop out a few shovelsful for me while he was there. He laughed, squatted down, and had enlarged my hole a bit when suddenly—zing-*crack*, zing-*crack*, zing-*crack!*

"Dig your own damned hole!" he yelled as he went running to

cover. Another five or six rounds came in. They were spaced five or ten seconds apart and sounded as though they came from a high-velocity weapon.

Soon the yells began.

"Medic—over here!"

"Aid man. Hey! Aid man!"

"Litter bearers. Where're the damn litter bearers? Hey, somebody get a litter over here!"

Some litter cases came by, followed by a man with his trousers cut off at the thigh and a bandage on his leg. He was limping along, supported by one of his buddies. Another man came by, sobbing over and over, "I don't wanna die. I don't wanna die." His squad leader, with an arm around his waist, was walking him to the aid station and trying to comfort him.

A few more quiet minutes passed. I sat up and started to shovel more dirt out of my hole. By now I was *convinced* it wasn't deep enough. Without warning it started again—the sickening whines and the sharp crashes after each. I piled into my hole and cuddled into as small a space as I could—knees under my chin, hands locked under my thighs, trying to hide my whole body under my steel helmet.

Nearby a soldier from my platoon was hit in the scalp by a fragment from an exploding mortar. He had been in a two-man foxhole, and although the wound wasn't critical, blood spurted over both men. The wounded man kept calm and said, "I guess I'd better go to the aid station."

His partner, however, one of the original 24th Division men in Korea, became hysterical, broke down completely, and had to be evacuated. The casualties mounted, and among those killed was Earl Lochhead's jeep driver.

There was a call for the I Company platoon leaders. We gathered around Gib, who said the plan had changed yet again. For some reason, perhaps a shortage of boats, battalion had decided to lead off with just *one* platoon.

"So when you get over there, Harry . . ."

"Oh no," I groaned, trying to make it sound funny. They all grinned, and someone said something about "Lucky Pierre."

Just then the enemy guns started firing again, and we scuttled back to our holes. The briefing continued, but on an individual basis. Platoon leaders took turns wedging into Gib's hole to get the picture and to study his map. My platoon was to cross over, work northward to Objective Hill, and secure it if possible. Other units would follow until the whole battalion was across and tied into a tight defensive bridgehead. We would jump off at one o'clock, which gave me about an hour.

We heard the 1st Battalion had had a rough time of it. The enemy was well dug in on Hill 174 opposite the crossing site, and the battalion had suffered heavy casualties, both during the crossing itself and during the subsequent assault on 174. At noon, however, as I was being briefed by Gib, the firing had died down, so perhaps their bridgehead was secured.

Following Gib's briefing, I returned to my platoon, which had been fairly fortunate. Only three men had been evacuated. There were one wounded Korean, one wounded American, plus the man who had cracked up.

I briefed the squad leaders as best I could, and told them to pass the word. To replace Robby as platoon sergeant, I named Sgt. Larry Sullivan, a tall, good-looking Irishman with a large portion of common sense. He was in good shape physically, the men respected him, and I figured he'd be able to command the platoon if something happened to me.

I began to saddle up. First I buckled my pistol belt, holding a canteen, folded-up poncho, and first-aid packet, over my field jacket. Then I slipped an extra bandoleer of ammo over one shoulder, my binoculars over the other, folded my map to the proper place and put it inside my helmet liner, picked up my carbine, and that was that. Ignoring a sinking feeling in my stomach, I called out, "Okay, 3rd Platoon, on your feet, let's go!"

Slowly the men rose from their holes and began to file out of the orchard. We came to the beach, a naked stretch of sand which suddenly looked as though it were ten miles wide. Before I'd taken a dozen steps, there was a sudden crash. Some enemy observer must have spotted us, and I wondered if he was now saying, "Right 50, repeat range, and we've got the bastards!"

Holding our breaths, we walked on—much more rapidly. At the water's edge, helped by engineer crewmen, we pushed the first two assault boats into the water, climbed awkwardly aboard, grabbed paddles, and shoved off. It wasn't any Poughkeepsie regatta, and we moved by clumsy lurches, but eventually our nose hit the muddy bank of the far shore. We pulled ourselves out and headed for a cornfield about two hundred yards inland. The men spread out, using the cornstalks for cover, while we waited for the whole platoon to reassemble.

As the last of my men cleared the boats, I could see the 1st Platoon starting across the beach on the other side. Just then a solitary mortar round landed near them, hitting at the same place as the one that had been fired at us.

I waved to my runner, who was carrying, in honor of our special role, the longer-range SCR-300 radio instead of our usual short-range and undependable walkie-talkie. He came up, and I radioed back to Gib, who was traveling with the 1st Platoon, that we'd reassembled and were moving on.

We had about two miles to go before reaching the base of our objective, and a pair of short but steep hills to climb en route. I'd selected a rather meandering route, but one that would keep us fairly well hidden from any enemy up ahead.

As we advanced, we saw welcome evidence of the air and artillery preparation — shell craters, ground scorched by napalm, tail fins of exploded mortar shells. We also passed a number of zigzag trenches and a series of one-man foxholes, all of which had apparently been abandoned without having been used.

We reached the top of the first hill and started working forward, keeping several yards down from the crest to avoid skylining ourselves. It appeared the best way to reach the second hill was by a trail winding through some rice paddies, even though we'd be moving on a course perpendicular to our general line of advance.

Back on the opposite side of the Naktong, the battalion staff, watching us through binoculars, must have thought we were lost. This prompted a call to Gib, and a further call to me.

"Harry, this is Gib. Harry, this is Gib. Over."

"Gib, this is Harry. Over."

"This is Gib. Mac seems to think you're heading the wrong way. Can you see the objective okay? Over."

"This is Harry. Yes, I can see the damned thing, and I think I'm heading the best way. Over."

"Roger, boy. You know what you're doing. Keep 'em moving. Out."

As we reached the top of the second hill, an artillery preparation was slamming into the face of Objective Hill. The platoon was moving at a crawl, so I signaled a halt, and everyone dropped in place for a short but welcome break.

While the men were resting, I took the chance to study the objective again. The wide "scars" were actually deep ravines, and we'd have to avoid them. Slowly we wound down to the valley floor, skirted a small village, and then regrouped in a dry stream bed, about 150 yards from the base of our objective. We crossed another paddy and started up the hill. It was steep, seemingly straight up, and the going was slow. I kept putting one foot in front of the other, breathing loudly after every step. About halfway up, we arrived at the first of the ravines, and as planned, the leading squad went to the left, spread out in line, and waited for the next squad to come abreast just across the ravine. Before long we were climbing again, wondering if anyone was on top waiting for us.

We kept going; still no fire. We climbed some more, and finally we had reached the top. It was quite a view. Upriver we could see well beyond Waegwan. The platoon hastily formed a rough perimeter. I took a quick look around as the men slumped to the ground, weapons bristling outward, ready to fire on any possible counterattack. The only sign the enemy had ever been there was a pair of small foxholes, probably a former observation post. I radioed back to Gib, who by then was at the base of the hill with the 1st Platoon, that the objective was secured.

Roughly, the ridge system in that area formed an "H," legs parallel to the river, with two peaks at the intersections of the legs and crossbar. We were on the right peak, having come up what would have been the lower right leg of the "H." The plan called for the 1st Platoon to pass through us, then to move along the center ridge and secure the other high point.

A change in orders came over the radio. We were to continue the advance ourselves. I told the squad leaders and pointed to the other peak. We all groaned in unison. Slowly the men of the 3rd Platoon got to their feet. We began inching forward along the connecting ridgeline.

The sun was beating down in earnest by this time. As we started up a steep slope leading to the final objective, feet were beginning to drag, and no one looked very alert.

I called out in a loud voice, "Okay, you guys, don't forget there may be a whole mess of North Koreans looking down our throats from up there." That seemed to do the trick. We all became a little more cautious as we climbed, and our eyes searched warily for hidden weapons.

My leading squad had made it to the top. Moving at a snail's pace, breathing hard, I kept climbing and finally managed to join them. Once there, the squads spread out in a new perimeter.

Things were looking up. By this time the rest of Item Company was climbing Objective Hill. From our vantage point, we could see, back on the Naktong, tiny assault boats ferrying other companies across.

The hope now was that King and Love Companies could get in position and secure our flanks before anything happened. While Item defended the crossbar of that "H," Love Company was supposed to take the upper right ridge, bending back to the river. King, on our left, would have the lower left portion, tying in to the 1st Battalion.

It took time, and also much hollering and guiding on our part. I went around checking the squad positions, and some of the men asked about chow. As far as I could see, there wouldn't be much chance of anyone getting rations to us until morning. A 57 recoilless rifle crew came on up, and we assigned them a sector of fire. Later a 75 recoilless from Mike Company arrived, and I fitted them into our positions too. That brought my own personal "army" to over a hundred men, with lots of firepower, and it felt good.

Everyone kept looking to the front, searching valleys, villages, other mountains. Far off we could see people moving, but we decided they were probably civilian refugees.

The sun had set by the time the first men from King Company filtered into position on the left of my platoon. Eventually, however, all three rifle companies managed to get in place. By then it was dark, and getting cold again.

Gib got a radio message from the battalion commander, who along with his staff was still on the far shore: "Well, Gib, we've got our bridgehead. If nothing hits us tonight, and we hold, we've got it made. If something does hit us tonight, and we still hold, we've still got it made."

Nothing hit us that night.

7. Heading North

20 SEPTEMBER–4 OCTOBER

MacArthur's "hammer and anvil" plan was beginning to unfold. With the X Corps, now in Seoul, acting as the anvil, the Eighth Army would come hammering north, destroying or capturing whatever lay in its path. It was hoped the news of Inchon would break the spirit of NKs in the south and cause them to collapse. Unfortunately it was not that easy. At first, the NKs, many of whom were unaware of the Inchon landing, continued to fight tenaciously.

However, Walton Walker's Eighth Army, including the lieutenants of USMA '49, sensed the tide had turned.

Morning—20 September—and for the moment it was calm. Looking back and down, we could see the Naktong winding an untroubled course. The river reflected the morning sun as more units, including our own division's 19th Infantry, continued to cross. To the north in Waegwan, engineers were trying to repair the major highway bridge so tanks and trucks could reinforce the bridgehead. To our left front, a peaceful green valley, gracefully terraced, opened invitingly; the only discord came from the right front, where a dark, bulky hill mass loomed. An intelligence report had it that a North Korean counterattack would use that particular mountain as a springboard.

In the late morning I heard on the radio that an air strike had been called against a particular hill, but the pilots couldn't identify it. If no one could mark the target for them, they would have to turn around and go home. I entered the conversation, said the hill was one I could see clearly, and we could mark it with white phosphorus mortar rounds. The offer was accepted, we marked the target, and the 3rd Platoon had its own airshow. The pilots wagged their wings in appre-

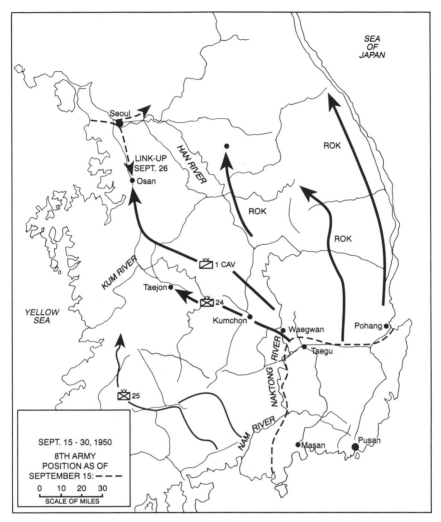

Breakout, Pursuit, and Link-up, 15–30 September 1950

ciation, zoomed in low over our heads, and made their passes, firing their guns and rockets at the suspect hill.

In midafternoon we intercepted another message, this time from a company on our flank. They had fired on a group of enemy soldiers who had retreated around the brow of a hill into another valley—the one in front of me. A Korean had reported that the enemy soldiers had hidden out in a cave.

A cave—there appeared to be one far to my front—a dark rectangle at the base of a steep slope. I pointed it out to the leader of the 75-mm recoilless rifle crew. The gun was brought into position, sighted carefully, and fired. There was an ear-splitting roar, the characteristic sheet of flame to the weapon's rear, and an instant later a puff of smoke in the distance, about fifty yards short of the cave. The crew resighted and fired again. This time the shell hit on the hillside, a few yards to the left of the cave's mouth. I called an adjustment, and a third round was fired. This one was almost exactly on target and hit only a few yards from the opening.

I looked through my binoculars and waited for the smoke to clear so as to make another adjustment. Suddenly I saw frenzied activity. People came running from the cave, waving their arms and holding up strips of white. Soon there seemed to be a crowd, a hundred or more, apparently all civilians. They moved slightly in our direction, then stopped. Three figures detached themselves from the group and kept coming.

The three were a long time getting to us, but eventually we saw they were older, white-bearded men carrying flags of truce—bamboo poles with white articles of clothing tied to the ends. They labored up our hill and told their story to an interpreter.

When the fighting had come this way, the people of their village had taken refuge in a large cave known to all who lived in this area. Earlier in the day, enemy soldiers had come and tried to join them in the cave. But the people, especially the women, had shrieked that the Communist soldiers must go, that they would only bring trouble for all. Some of the villagers had wanted to come tell the Americans what was happening, but the Communists had threatened to kill them. Finally the soldiers had left, but only after cautioning them not to go to the Americans, who would be sure to kill any who came forth.

The leader had come to ask safe passage for his people. He and his two courageous companions were offering themselves as test cases—possible victims—in case the Communist warnings were true. I assured the leader they could pass through without harm, and the three patriarchs returned and led their people forward. Slowly the column, a ragged procession of old men, women, and children, wound its way up our mountain. I shuddered to think what would have happened had one of our shells actually entered the cave.

It was twilight by the time the column faded from sight, heading if not to happiness at least to temporary safety. They said the North Koreans had all left the area moving north. Evidently they were right; at least there was no enemy activity that night.

Although the 19th and 21st Infantry Regiments were both in the 24th Division, there had been little chance for intermingling. At one point I'd heard that John "Rigger" Ragucci was in the 19th Infantry, as was Leslie Kirkpatrick, my pal from precadet days at Lafayette. However, when I saw the 19th Infantry crossing the Naktong on 20 September, I didn't realize one of their platoons was being led by my classmate Roger Kelly.

Happy-go-lucky Roger, with his ready smile and cheerful Irish face, was one of the most popular men in our class. He'd been a member of the Cadet Glee Club and the Catholic Chapel Choir, a director of the traditionally irreverent Hundredth Night Show, and an all-around great guy. For the past few weeks, he had also been a hard-working combat infantryman.

During the latest operation, however, Roger had been suffering from severe headaches and fever. His condition grew worse, and shortly after they crossed the Naktong, his company commander urged him to report to the aid station. Roger refused, saying he didn't want to leave his men. He struggled through for another day, at the end of which he was near collapse. Finally the suggestion became an order, and Roger begrudgingly consented. At the aid station, he saw his battalion commander, and just before he was evacuated, said, "Colonel, don't think I'm deadbeating." The colonel assured him he didn't. Back in Pusan, Roger learned he had acute encephalitis.

It was still calm on the morning of 21 September, and our spirits were high as we came down from the hill, for this time we were not retreating or shifting laterally to plug a gap in the line; we were moving *forward*, and it gave a new bounce to each step. Had the turning point actually come? Were we really moving toward a decision, and with a hope of winding this thing up?

We descended to the valley and began moving northward in a column of two's, spaced on either side of the two-lane dirt highway. The road, paralleling the Naktong, was lined with tall, thin poplars and wild-blooming cosmos. The sun was shining and the world was bright.

We halted opposite Waegwan and rested. Looking across the river, we could see engineers working on the damaged spans of the all-important bridge. Once that bridge was repaired, US tanks could come across and join the column.

Standing alongside the road was our battalion commander, wearing not only a broad grin, but also new silver leaves. Major Mac was now Lieutenant Colonel Mac. Gib and I were very sincere in our congratulations. Mac was a good man—able, compassionate, good-natured, and equally important, a team builder.

We started up again, pausing frequently because of slowdowns at the head of the column. Whenever we halted, I had two men from each squad move into the fields to guard against a surprise attack from the flank. As the day wore on, I began to get gripes; these halts were for a break—to rest—yet my flank guards were getting worn-out from trudging into the fields each time we stopped. I urged the squad leaders to rotate the men who were used for this, but said we'd continue to put out security.

"But none of the other platoons are doing it, Lieutenant."

"That's *their* business. I'm responsible for the safety of this platoon, and if that makes me a mean SOB, well, that's too bad." I tried imagining what I'd do if suddenly the enemy came swarming from an unexpected direction. I'd have been embarrassed if anyone knew I was quoting to myself Napoleon's maxim to the effect that if you were marching a column of troops, you should always have in mind what you'd do if the enemy unexpectedly appeared to your front, rear, or one of your flanks. And if you *didn't* know that, you had no business being in command.

Alongside the road we began to see assorted items of enemy equipment, some destroyed, some simply abandoned. It surely looked as though we had the NKs on the run.

We turned off the road in the late afternoon and made camp on a hillside dotted with burial sites. The graves were circular mounds, three or four feet high. It seemed an admirable custom—burying one's honored dead on a hillside, in a tranquil setting close to the sky.

The enemy was still putting up fierce resistance in the Taegu area. The 7th and 8th Cavalry regiments combined in an encircling move, but the NKs, well dug in on key hills, were not giving up.

North of Tabudong, as A Company of the 8th Cavalry attacked Hill 624, three '49ers were involved: platoon leaders Lou Messinger and Roger Fife, and artilleryman "Snuffy" Smith, the company FO.

Unfortunately neither Beecher Brian nor I had seen Roger, our fellow member of Cadet Company E-1, since before we landed; we would have enjoyed his comradeship and hearing more about Oklahoma and his beloved horses. A line about him in our yearbook put it nicely: "Here's to you, Rog—may there be an abundant supply of hoss-flesh and friends, for you do right by both."

On 22 September, the weary Able Company, which the week before had been cut off and had gone three days without food, was

Men of the 3rd Battalion, 8th Cavalry Regiment, 1st Cavalry Division, and tanks of the 70th Tank Battalion, 1st Cavalry Division, move out on an assault of a Communist-held hill in Korea. US Army photo #8A/FEC-51-3010.

making its second attempt to take Hill 624. During the course of the attack, as he neared the summit of 624, Roger Fife, who was in front of his platoon, turned to shout orders to his men. As he did so, he was hit by enemy rifle fire and killed instantly.

In writing to Roger's parents, Lou Messinger said in part: "Here in Korea, Roger and I became very close and his death was a terrible blow to all of us. His men admired, respected and loved him. We have lost a fine friend and a great and fearless leader."

The day Roger was killed, Item Company continued north along the Waegwan-Kumchon highway, passing a number of burned-out hulls of Soviet-made T-34s. Each time we did so, we gave thanks for our fighter planes and their deadly rockets.

Up ahead, some shots were fired toward the road, and John Uffner of King Company, USMA '50, saw enemy soldiers in a valley off to his left. It appeared some of them were changing from uniforms into civilian clothes. Uffner's report was relayed to battalion, and Colonel Mac told Gib to send a platoon into the valley to clean it out.

Gib called me to him. "Harry, some soldiers in that valley have been shooting at our column. We want you to go up there and make 'em stop!"

"How many are there?"

"We don't know. Maybe fifty—but some of them may be changing into civilian clothes, so possibly they're just trying to get away."

"Right. But I still don't think I should go straight in at them. Maybe I'll take the platoon up into the hills and try to circle around behind."

"Good idea. And use your radio if you get into trouble. We have lots of people following behind who can go in after you."

"Okay, I'm on my way." As our platoon left the main column, I told the squad leaders we'd head into the hills, follow the ridge away from the main road, and try coming in behind whoever was in that valley. Back on the road, the 1st Platoon was coming into view. Gypsy Martin saw me, waved, and called, "Go get 'em, Lieutenant!"

We found a trail that twisted vaguely through the hills. We climbed, became tired, rested awhile, then climbed some more. After nearly an hour, I decided it was time to descend. A path led downward through a dark, gloomy canyon and past a group of huts where an old woman was washing clothes.

I sent Kim to ask if she had seen any enemy soldiers. He reported, "Old woman she say all Communist soldiers they gone long time."

Maybe she was right. Or perhaps she was lying, just another bystander not wanting to get involved. As we neared the valley floor, I asked Ed Walsh, the former PX officer who was acting as my assistant platoon leader, to take a squad and station them at the mouth of the valley as a killing party. If we flushed any enemy, Ed could be waiting to capture them or take them under fire. Walsh seemed to wince at the term "killing party," but he took the squad and left, evidently happy to have an assignment.

We emerged from the wooded hillside. Unfortunately our circling hadn't been very deep; we might still be heading into something frontally. As the platoon moved onto a narrow footpath, I was up front behind the two lead scouts. Suddenly there was a snapping sound and a high-pitched whine. Behind me someone yelled.

"Hey, are they shooting at us?" I shouted. Just then I felt a sharp sting. A quick needle of pain jabbed my left thigh. It took a moment to register. Why—I'd been hit! I sat down, eased myself off the path, and took cover behind a low rice paddy berm.

Sullivan came running up in a low crouch and slid into place alongside me. "Are you hit, sir?"

"Yeah, I think so." A circle of red appeared on my leg. I unbuckled my cartridge belt and pulled it free, then undid my trousers and pulled them down a few inches. Blood bubbled from a jagged hole about the size of a half-dollar inside my left thigh.

I thought, "Why, it's a pretty big bullet that caused that, and there's only one hole, so it must still be in me." Then I saw another oozing of red, several inches to the left. Impatiently I brushed away the blood and found another hole, a small neat circle, and realized the smaller hole was where the bullet had gone in. The bullet, after tumbling, had made the larger exit wound which I'd seen first.

As I was becoming aware of all this, Sully was unwrapping my first-aid packet. He put a compress over the wound, tied it in place, then yelled for the medic to come forward.

Sully and I talked about what to do next. Although the platoon had tried to take cover, we were still more or less in the open, and shots were still keeping us pinned down. The fire was coming from a low hill about a hundred yards away. I tried to think, while Sully and Dissinger, the leader of the 3rd Squad, crept ahead to reconnoiter.

Long minutes passed. The platoon medic came forward, and since I needed to think clearly, I shook my head when he offered to give me an injection of morphine.

Sully returned and said there was a small village up ahead. If we could get someone in there, we might use the protected position to provide covering fire while a squad or two went up the hill to clean out whatever was there.

As I was debating how to do all this, Dissinger took matters into his own hands. He grabbed a BAR, ran across the open space, firing as he went, and made it safely to the edge of the village. From there he kept the enemy pinned down while the remainder of his squad moved forward to join him. As the men squeezed past me and saw my wound, some offered a word of encouragement, others just clucked sympathetically. The Koreans, unable to communicate in English, were almost comical as they made strange gestures to convey their regrets.

I took the radio and tried to raise a response, thinking we might get someone to come up behind the enemy from the far side of the valley. No luck. Apparently I Company, with the only radios which would net with mine, had moved on. I called again, "Any station, any station, please come in. Over."

Silence. No doubt the rest of Item was long gone. Obviously they'd had no choice in the matter, but nevertheless I somehow felt abandoned.

The platoon runner came crawling up. "Sorry you got hit, sir."

"Thanks a lot. I'll be okay. Look, I need you to go back toward the highway. If you find Lieutenant Walsh, ask him to come forward to take over the platoon."

About twenty yards behind me, the medic was working on Kang, a Korean ammo bearer who had been hit in the foot and who, judging by his moans, was in considerable pain.

I lit a cigarette and, strangely enough, remembered something I'd read as a boy. At the Battle of Oriskany, in the Revolutionary War, fought not far from my home in upstate New York, American General Herkimer, after being wounded in the leg, had been propped up and had continued directing the fight, all the while puffing on a long clay pipe. I had no pipe, but in lieu thereof, I smoked my cigarette.

A messenger came with a note Sully had scrawled on a page torn from a notebook: "Send second squad forward. Hold the A-6. Can get up hill from here if you cover us. Will fire grenade to lift fire. Okay?"

I sent the second squad forward, less the A-6 light machine gun, then rolled over on my stomach to watch as Sully and the assault squads worked their way across the valley and onto the enemy's flank.

I passed the word, and we began firing to keep the enemy pinned down. It didn't take long. A few minutes later I saw a grenade explode and gave the signal to lift the covering fire.

We'd made it! Men were sweeping along the crest of the hill. Apparently they were unopposed; whoever was up there had either been neutralized or had run away.

The valley was clear, and before long Ed Walsh arrived with news that our encircling move had worked. Several North Koreans, a mixed bag of soldiers and civilians, had surrendered when they saw we had gotten behind them. An enemy headquarters had been located near the mouth of the valley, and this was the group left behind when the main force had fled.

While searching the headquarters, someone had found a primitive litter, a straw mat attached to two carrying poles. I told Ed he now had the platoon, wished him luck, and gave him my binoculars, compass, and map. Then the medic punctured me with one of his morphine syrettes and I was placed, with surprising gentleness, on the litter. Four volunteers lifted me into place, and we started back. Faces kept peering down, murmuring wishes of good luck, sympathy, and encouragement.

Sully, walking alongside, said: "I told you I'd take care of you, Lieutenant. You've got a million-dollar wound, just like three lieutenants I had in the last war. Before you know it, you'll be getting fussed over by all those pretty nurses!"

Then we were back at the highway, where a litter jeep was waiting, and where I was lifted onto one of the back-deck stretchers. There was a clasping of hands, a last-minute wave, and we were under way. I was on my own again, an individual rather than a member of a unit, and there was an abrupt, panicky feeling of loss.

Just before the breakout, '49er Jack Bender, a veteran after three weeks in a rifle company, had been assigned to the 1st Cavalry Division's Reconnaissance Company. The company had lost several officers in the recent fighting, and its CO, from the West Point Class of '47, remembered Jack and had arranged the transfer.

While the term "veteran" might be used here facetiously, those three weeks had indeed been memorable. Jack had joined Fox Company of the 7th Cavalry Regiment on the Naktong, and with about seven GIs and eight KATUSAs, had been responsible for nearly a mile of river frontage. On his second day with the company, he had taken a patrol across the river and run up against an enemy machine gun. He and his men had engaged the gun and knocked it out, but as they were doing so, they had seen NKs circling to cut them off. Fortunately they'd been able to get back safely, but it was an all-too-sudden introduction to combat.

Then, a few days later, Jack and his men had been isolated by a North Korean breakthrough. For three days, their only food had come from a case of catsup they had found, together with some wild onions. They had wiped off the onions as best they could, doused them with catsup, and in their hungry state, had found the combination to be superb.

Now Jack was on his first independent patrol mission with his new recon platoon, a unit with two light tanks, four scout jeeps with machine guns, and an infantry squad mounted in a personnel carrier. As they crossed a narrow valley with finger-like ridges leading down to the road, they came under machine-gun and mortar fire. Jack left his vehicles, with the platoon sergeant in charge, to give covering fire. Then he and the infantry squad went into the hills. In the action, which won Jack the Silver Star, they knocked out the automatic weapons and mortars and routed the enemy foot troops, thus allowing the mission to proceed.

There were two litters on the back of the jeep. I lay facing to the rear, occupying the one on the left. Alongside me, rather than another patient, was a North Korean woman who had been picked up at the headquarters we'd overrun and who was being sent to the rear for interrogation.

We jolted along, past an advancing column which included KATUSAs. The woman, evidently a devoted Communist, or at least a loud one, began to jeer at them. A Korean riding alongside the driver said she was insulting the South Koreans for fighting alongside the Americans.

"Be quiet!" I growled.

She ignored me, pretending not to understand, and continued her harangue. I raised up and lifted my arm, as though I were going to swat her with the back of my hand. She glared at me, but at least she quieted down.

We came to a battalion aid station alongside the road, where a doctor bandaged my wound and ordered me onto an ambulance for further evacuation. While I lay on the ground waiting, several men came by to ask how things were going "up front."

The ambulance had four litters, an upper and lower on each side, plus a bench in the middle. Riding the bench was a young soldier from I Company who had developed an eye infection and was being sent back for treatment. He seemed embarrassed about being along as a noncasualty and kept trying to cover me with a blanket or to be otherwise helpful and sympathetic.

I was on a lower litter, and above me was a critically wounded North Korean. He was bleeding badly, and some of his blood was dripping down. Across the aisle, a slightly wounded American tried to make small talk. Above him, the fourth casualty, also an American, was ominously quiet.

I felt a change in the roadway and was told we were crossing over the Naktong at Waegwan. For us at least, the bridge had been patched back into service just in time. The ambulance stopped, the doors opened, and we were unloaded at a former schoolhouse serving as the 21st Infantry Collecting Point.

Litter bearers found a vacant spot of floor and set me down. I closed my eyes, tried to rest, and for a while all was fine. Suddenly

I started to shake. At first it was a minor trembling, but then it quickened into severe, visible shaking and twitching. Violent spasms sent my legs jerking and kicking until the blanket was thrown loose. I grabbed the sides of the litter and hung on, feeling embarrassed and hoping no one had noticed.

A medical corpsman came over, put a hand on my shoulder: "You all right, Lieutenant?"

"Yes, I think so . . . I'm sorry . . ." I said. He gave me another shot of morphine, and I calmed down. Later in the evening, half asleep, I looked up and saw Father Dunne.

"Hi, Father. How long have you been there?"

"It's okay, Harry. You needn't try to talk. Just lie there and relax while I say a few prayers." He put a purple stole around his neck and began to murmur in Latin. He then took a few drops of oil from a small vial, spread some on his thumb, and made the Sign of the Cross on my forehead. Only then did I realize I was receiving Extreme Unction. Back in grammar school, the good nuns had taught us this was a sacrament which gave "comfort to the sick and grace to the dying." I trusted I was in the former category.

Next morning, along with three others, I was loaded into an ambulance that jolted us for hours over mountain roads, into a valley, across a river, then back over hills until we came in late afternoon to a railroad station in the center of Taegu. The station was congested, gloomy, full of foreign sounds and smells. Our litters were deposited unceremoniously on a sooty platform alongside the tracks. Korean civilians waiting for trains regarded us with curiousity.

Suddenly I saw Kang, the Korean from my platoon, lying a few yards away. At my request, some soldiers standing nearby moved my litter next to his. Kang, like most Koreans, usually displayed little emotion. Now, however, I could hear him moaning in pain.

As the soldiers set my litter alongside him, Kang looked at me, tried to smile, and said, "Lieutaenan' Ha-ree—okay?"

"Okay," I said. Kang turned to the Korean lying on the other side of him, evidently explaining who I was. He winced again; obviously he was suffering quite a bit. Slowly he extended a hand to me. I reached out from under my blanket, took his hand in mine, and squeezed reassurance.

"Okay, Kang . . . okay." Eventually a train clanged into the station and snorted into place a few feet from us. Hands picked up my litter and started to move me.

"Wait," I said, "I want that Korean to come with me."

"Can't do it, Lieutenant. The Koreans are going on a different train to their own hospital. This train is just for the Americans."

Kang, confused, looked at me pathetically.

"Goodbye, Kang," I said. "Okay, okay." He looked young and frightened. I never saw him again.

We arrived in Pusan about midnight. Outside the train, lit by the glare of headlights, we were loaded into waiting ambulances and driven through winding streets which, in the darkness, took on an air of mystery.

The ambulance stopped and the doors were opened. Flashlights probed the interior, obscuring the faces behind them. Soon I was lifted and carried into a shabby, sprawling building, evidently another converted schoolhouse. The bearers put me down in a narrow corridor, alongside the wall.

Quickly the grim triage got underway, with emergency cases being rushed to surgery. A medic came by and looked at my tag, a card on a string attached to my shirt like a mailing label. He grunted and moved on.

People were standing in the corridor alongside the litters, and when I turned my head, my face was only inches away from their boots. An hour or so later, a motherly Red Cross lady recorded my next-of-kin information and told me I was at the 8054th MASH. I gave her Jeanne's address in New Jersey, but said my records might still show my mother as emergency addressee.

I said, "Make sure any telegram goes just to my wife, since my mother is in poor health and shouldn't be upset." (Months later I learned that notification had happened just the way I'd tried to prevent; the telegram went only to my mother; no word went to Jeanne.)

It was near midnight before a doctor looked at my leg. He asked if I felt okay, then told the orderlies to put me to bed. They carried me into a large hall, formerly the school's auditorium, where beds were set up row upon row, then unlaced my boots, peeled off my fatigues and underwear, and helped me into some blue hospital pajamas. It was a pleasure to shed the fatigues, which had acquired an unlovely crusting of mud and dried blood. Before long I was asleep.

During September's final week, most of the Eighth Army continued to push north. An exception was the 7th Cavalry's shattered 2nd Battalion, which had lost two-thirds of its fighting strength. Larry Ogden, Dick Tobin, Bill Hoffman, and other '49ers of that unit were temporarily given the imposing designation of Eighth Army reserve, and held back until they could be reconstituted as an effective force.

On 26 September, at Osan, other units of the 7th Cavalry, driving north, met elements of the 7th Division's 31st Infantry coming south from Seoul. The linkup of Walton Walker's Eighth Army and Ned Almond's X Corps had been achieved, and by 29 September, Seoul was secure to the point that South Korean president Syngman Rhee, accompanied by Douglas MacArthur, flew into Kimpo airfield, and at the bombed-out National Assembly Hall, declared that Seoul was once more the seat of South Korean government.

Roger Kelly and I were probably in the same Pusan hospital, but neither of us was aware of the other's presence. That was unfortunate, because it might have helped Roger to know a friend was nearby. Roger's encephalitis was a particularly virulent form. His fever grew worse, he sank into a coma, and on 28 September, the good-natured, music-loving Roger breathed his last.

About that same time, stateside hospitals also had their share of '49ers. Ted Swett had been transferred from Tokyo General to Washington's Walter Reed, where he had a prolonged stay as his wounds refused to heal.

Ted's wife Cay had taken a small apartment nearby, and in the evenings, when Ted was free to leave the hospital, he and Cay often got together with Doug Bush, Ted's cadet roommate, and Doug's wife Carolyn. Flying the F-80 Shooting Star, Doug had graduated first in his class at Williams AFB, and it was also at Williams that a son, William D. Bush III, was born to Carolyn and Doug. Doug was now stationed at Andrews AFB, flying the faster, more advanced F-86 Sabrejet. The foursome spent many happy hours together, even though Doug, eager to test his newly acquired fighter pilot skills in Korea, grew more and more restless.

Dave Bolte, West Point '49, whose major general father was the Army Acting Chief of Staff for Operations, G-3, was also at Walter Reed. Dave, a member of the 8th Cavalry Regiment, had been in Korea for only ten days when a bullet smashed into his shoulder as he peered at enemy lines through his binoculars. Many of his memories were frustrating ones, of inadequate equipment and untrained soldiers, of not having the proper tool to remove a ruptured machine-gun barrel, of seeing a green soldier clumsily dropping a primed grenade into his own foxhole and blowing himself to pieces, or having to take over, under fire, an abandoned machine gun when one of the crew members was wounded and the others used the familiar excuse of taking him to the rear.

Ted Swett was one of Dave's frequent visitors, and one such visit was "memorialized" by a front-page picture in the *Washington Star*,

William Douglas Bush, Jr. Courtesy US Military Academy Archives.

captioned "West Point Classmates Reunited," showing Ted with Dave's mother at Dave's bedside.

Meanwhile, Kenny Miller left Japan by ship, landed in San Francisco, and next day rode from Letterman Army Hospital to March AFB in an impressive white Cadillac ambulance. From March he was flown to Maxwell AFB in Alabama, spent a night there, and then went on to Fort Bragg, arriving at last in his home state of North Carolina. At Bragg, more surgery was performed to close the open wound in his right hip. Kenny had gone from 155 pounds to 110, and looked like a scarecrow.

After my first week at the Pusan MASH, the nurse said I could get up and walk around awhile, even take a shower. An orderly offered to get some clothes for me, and I had a hard time telling him my sizes. In less than two months, I had lost nearly thirty pounds, but at least I still outweighed Kenny Miller!

Now that I was ambulatory, I could go to meals in the hospital mess and, for daily sick call, go to a doctor rather than having one of them come by my bed. On my first trip to sick call, I noted unhappily, but not unexpectedly, that it involved standing in line. But there were *two* lines, and one was considerably shorter than the other. With what I considered commendable shrewdness, I moved to the shorter line, which led into an office on the left of the corridor. I wondered idly what the letters "NP" over the door signified.

My turn came and I entered. A friendly first lieutenant, wearing doctor's caduceus insignia, offered me a chair.

"How are we feeling today?"

"Pretty good, doc."

"Is there anything you'd like to talk about?"

"No, not particularly."

"Well, are we having any particular problems?"

That "we" sounded a bit artificial, but he seemed a nice guy, and I didn't let it bother me.

"Well, to tell the truth, doc, I *would* like to get my bandage changed."

"Oh, we have a bandage, do we?" For some reason, he seemed dubious, so I began unbuckling my belt to show him. Suddenly he realized I was a "regular" patient, just as I remembered that NP stood for neuropsychiatric. We both started laughing. I apologized for getting in the wrong line, but he said to think nothing of it, that it was a nice change to see a "healthy" gunshot wound.

A few days later, I read in the *Stars and Stripes* of a series of UN victories, including triumphs by the 24th Taro Leaf Division. To make it even better, General Walker was saying that the North Korean Army, for all practical purposes, had ceased to exist.

I had visions of I Company returning to Japan without me and decided I'd best get back to my unit. The impersonal hospital atmosphere had made me aware that the men of I Company had become my family, and frankly I missed them.

"I'll release you in a week or so," the doctor said. "But it sure is strange to see someone in a hurry to return to the infantry."

"Don't worry, doc. Maybe I wouldn't be acting this way if I didn't think the war was almost over."

Beecher Brian's letters home about that time were reflecting not only the weariness and agony of the past few weeks, but also the cautious optimism most of us were feeling.

He wrote his sister Libby: "My own dear Lib, Remember the 'Bon Voyage' letter you sent me? Well, I just got it the other day. I am glad it didn't get to me until it did because I really did need it when it came. Things have been very rough up here for the last few days and your letter was most welcome. . . . It gives me comfort to know that my loved ones at home are praying for me."

On 21 September, he wrote home: "The gooks are finally on the run, but the last week has been awful. . . . I hope the war is almost over. I hope it does some good for posterity. . . . Well, we are about to load up on trucks and moving North."

In another letter, on 29 September, he wrote: "The main trouble now is that the NKs have all changed into civilian clothes, dropped or hidden their weapons and are joining the refugees. We spot them by looking for a group of 10 or 12 young men with crew cuts and dressed in spanking clean civvies. Yesterday our company took 200 prisoners. . . . We are all speculating when the war will end. I am afraid it will not be as soon as most people around here think, especially if Red China comes in. That would be the last straw."

In the latter part of September, the troopship *General A. E. Anderson* arrived in Japan carrying members of the airborne 187th Regimental Combat Team. Five '49er artillerymen—Boyde Allen, Dene Balmer, Jim Coghlan, Ward Goessling, and Dave Freeman—had attended jump school and been assigned to the artillery battalion of the 187th. The '49er "Redlegs" were in high spirits as they met up with their unit in Ashiya. However, their mood changed abruptly after they ran into '49er Jack Wogan, a C-119 pilot with Troop Carrier Command, who told about the many classmates who'd been killed or wounded along the Pusan Perimeter.

The first leg of my return journey was by train. We reached the end of the line around midnight, spent the night in a one-room stone building, and next morning transferred to trucks, sitting in back and bouncing into the air as each new rut was encountered. We rolled north, from Waegwan toward Kumchon, past the valley where I'd been wounded, and on toward Taejon. All along our route we saw the debris of war: burned out trucks and tanks, discarded ammo boxes, C-ration cans, empty shell casings. On the shoulders of the road, plodding south in a constant stream, were the pitiful refugees — an old man with a wispy beard, wearing a white robe and a black horsehair hat, bending under a heavily loaded A-frame; a sad-faced woman with a bundle balanced on her head, with one child strapped to her back and another holding her hand. Sometimes a child, perhaps a newly created orphan, would be walking alone. Farther on, as we neared the scenes of more recent fighting, we began to see bodies of dead enemy soldiers sprawled grotesquely in the paddy fields.

We spent the night in Taejon, the city where General Dean had been captured early in the war. In the street was a knocked-out T-34 tank, appropriately lettered, in true American tourist fashion, as having been destroyed under the direct guidance of General Dean.

Next day our truck dropped us in Seoul, where I hitched a ride with a driver from the 24th Division. He drove me to a valley a few miles north, where the 3rd Battalion of the 21st Infantry, including I Company, had been camped for nearly a week.

The truck stopped; I threw out my duffel bag and climbed down. A shout went up, and I found myself being greeted and pounded by friends who hadn't expected to see me again.

Gib had acquired something new since I saw him last, the railroad tracks of a captain. They looked good, and I congratulated him heartily.

"But you've been promoted too, Harry. Let's go see Colonel Mac and make it official."

We walked to Battalion CP, where once again there were happy greetings. Then Mac and Gib, acting jointly, pinned on the silver bars making me a first lieutenant. It was a good moment.

Later that day I went to the medics, who put a clean bandage on my leg. The wound was healing nicely and starting to scab over.

Nevertheless, when Gib saw the bandage, he said, "That makes me mad. They had no business sending you back so soon; you should still be in the hospital!"

"But I wanted to get back in case you guys were shipped out to Japan. What's the matter, don't you think that's likely?"

"'Fraid not. They're sending trucks for us tomorrow and we'll be going on line again. Looks like this thing isn't over yet."

8. Pursuit into North Korea

5 OCTOBER–3 NOVEMBER

For all practical purposes, the North Koreans had been defeated in the south, and MacArthur called on them to surrender. The victorious Americans, including every '49er lieutenant, felt certain the war was over, and we just hoped the other side accepted that fact and acted accordingly.

Of course, if the enemy *didn't* surrender, the question became whether or not to pursue him into North Korea. Unfortunately the desire for complete victory was tempered by a very real concern. Might not a border crossing into North Korea cause either the Soviets or the Chinese to intervene?

At Lake Success, the UN General Assembly, despite considerable misgivings, and after lengthy debate, gave approval for the UN forces to cross the 38th Parallel. By that time, as it turned out, the question had become academic, since ROK divisions on the east coast, without fanfare, had taken the initiative and advanced several miles across the border.

Meanwhile, MacArthur had made the decision to withdraw the 1st Marines and the US 7th Division of Almond's X Corps from the Seoul area, and to prepare them for an amphibious landing at Wonsan, well up the east coast. The Eighth Army's IX Corps, with the 1st Cavalry and the 24th Division leading the way, would pass through Seoul, cross the Imjin River, and advance to the 38th Parallel. It would then make preparations to cross the border into North Korea once permission was given.

Jack Madison was back in Pusan, waiting to board ship, when he wrote home:

The news is slowly coming back, naming our classmates who have been killed or wounded. Here they are: I don't need to tell you how some of them hit home. I lost some of my best friends. It's hard to believe that they are actually dead. . . .

Roger Kuhlman, 1st Cav, one of the finest men I ever knew. Munro Magruder, my roommate at Riley, a wonderful friend. Married ten days before we left. Bill Wilbur, a very good friend. Ran into him in Chicago, and we flew on to Seattle together. He must have had a premonition; he took out a $30,000 insurance policy before he left. Fenton Odell, a fine chap. His father is a classmate of yours, dad. Married two weeks before he left. Courtenay Davis. I knew him slightly, but he was a good friend of Joe's. Tom Hardaway. A fine chap of great promise. Wounded were Dave Bolte, Ted Swett, Jim Scholtz, George Tow [actually, George was KIA], and Curly Lindeman. No word from Bill Marslender. I hope that no news is good news. I know what a blow Roger's death must have been to him.

It's hard to make yourself believe that the lives of these young men are worth the whole damn stinking country of Korea!

Well, rumors are flying as to what the future holds. The more conventional is back to occupation duty in Japan. The more radical is "we land at Bremerhaven." Your guess is as good as mine. I hope they won't need the help of the 7th to finish this off. However, they might. So, until you hear us mentioned again, don't worry. We're a long ways from the action at this point.

Based on that last paragraph, it must have seemed to Jack, as it did to others of us, that the war was about over.

A day or two later, the 7th Division loaded aboard assault shipping and headed for Wonsan. At that point, probably none of them had ever heard of the Chosin Reservoir.

Back at Item Company, I visited the 3rd Platoon, where the noncoms brought me up to date. The day I was wounded, and while I was on my way back to the aid station, the platoon had continued north and rejoined our battalion, just in time to take part in an after-dark march around Kumchon, an all-night wandering which blended fear, confusion, and a numbing weariness.

Next day, so they told me, Robby had berated Sully for having "let" the lieutenant get hit. Sullivan, on the other hand, said he felt proud for having arranged my two-week vacation in a clean hospital bed.

"I'm glad *you're* still okay," I said to Dissinger. "You sure did act foolish that day, running across that rice paddy with all those bullets flying around."

"Aw, Lieutenant," he said sheepishly, "I heard you got hit and I guess I just got pissed off."

Word had come out, meanwhile, that I had been named company executive officer, so the 3rd Platoon would no longer be mine. My new job, I suspected, rather than a true promotion, was Gib's way of keeping me a bit more out of harm's way.

As Eighth Army moved north from Seoul, I Company of the 5th Cavalry Regiment, with platoon leaders Joe Toomey and Beecher Brian, was first in line. At one point, Beech was in front as the column entered Munsan-ni. Civilians lined the road, smiling, raising their arms, and shouting, "Manzai." A twelve-year-old boy was pushed forward to extend greetings in broken English, and Beech lifted him onto the hood of his jeep. The Koreans cheered some more, perhaps thinking the lieutenant was a kind and gentle liberator, whereas Brian's main thought was that the civilians wouldn't let the child ride with him if the road ahead was mined!

A mile beyond town, Beech took a fork in the road and headed east. It was a heady moment for a second lieutenant—to be the first American soldier leading the division and the Eighth Army into enemy-held territory. About a half-mile farther along, however, Beecher received a frantic signal to stop; he was leading Eighth Army down the wrong road! It might have been easier if someone else had taken over the lead. Instead, the decision was made to turn the regiment inside out on that narrow dirt road, and a red-faced Brian had to turn around and double the column as he made his way onto the other road. That night the Eighth Army password was "Wrong Road."

Next day, as the column reached the Imjin River, it was Joe Toomey's turn to be in the lead. Joe came to the river's edge, where the bank on the near side sloped gently into the water. On the far side, however, the bank rose steeply, about a hundred feet to a ridgeline that extended along the north shore. As ordered, Joe and his platoon stepped into the water and began wading across, unaware that the river bottom was covered with slimy mud and, in places, with quicksand. Joe and one of his men made it to the far shore and started uphill. Meanwhile, most of his men were still struggling in the mud, the quicksand, and the swift Imjin tidal current.

Joe looked back, yelled for his men to hurry, and took off his helmet to wipe his forehead. Just then an enemy grenade came arching through the air, hitting Toomey on the forehead. The grenade bounced off, it going one way and Joe the other. Fortunately it failed to explode, but it left a large gash in Joe's head, which began to bleed profusely. With blood flowing into his eyes and blinding him, Toomey called for someone to relieve him, and Beecher Brian was ordered to cross the river to take over.

As Beech started across, the tide began coming in, and the water, which initially had been only two feet deep, soon became waist high and was still rising. Beech's feet became caught in the quicksand, and he felt himself sinking, just as some North Koreans maneuvered into position and began shooting. Bullets spattered into the water, as Brian, holding his carbine above his head with his left hand, reached down with his right hand, pulled his right ankle free, and knelt on his right knee. Then he reversed the procedure and pulled his left leg into a kneeling position. He now had enough surface on the bottom to keep from sinking further, and his head was just above water. Nearby, Pfc. Victor Fox, a small man, stepped into deep water, which went over his head. He began thrashing about, just as the man in front of him was hit, with his body floating out of sight. Fox managed to struggle to shore, as did Brian, who finished the crossing on his knees.

Brian's 3rd Platoon, as soon as they were across, spread out in a skirmish line and assaulted the nearby ridge, firing all the way. That night, as they dug in and counted noses, they realized that three of their men, two Americans and a KATUSA, had drowned during the river crossing.

As the 1st Cavalry Division advanced north, it was supported by the 14th Combat Engineer Battalion, the unit in which Ralph Buffington, '49's first fatality, had served. Bill Moore was a platoon leader in the 14th Battalion, as was Terry Powers, a blue-eyed, Georgia-born '49er.

At a selected point on the Imjin, Terry was given the mission of constructing a "flying ferry," an engineer raft device, powered by outboard motors and kept on course by a line attached to a rope spanning the river. Terry managed to get a rope across and then built his raft, using rubber pontoons and prefabricated aluminum bridge parts for the decking. Theoretically the raft should have been able to handle a tank, but because of the swiftness of the Imjin current, Terry wanted to make a trial crossing before trying to do it with a load.

An impatient tank commander waiting to cross, however, said there was no time to waste. Everything looked okay to him, and he insisted on driving aboard. Off they went, and halfway across the Imjin, which may have been two hundred yards wide at that point, the outboard motors quit. The thin rope and bridle, unable to hold against the swift-flowing current, promptly snapped, and the raft, carrying

Terry and the tankers, began drifting downstream out of control. As they made their way toward the Yellow Sea, enemy soldiers on the far shore began shooting at them.

The raft sailed on, and finally started to slow as they reached the Imjin estuary. Just then the tide shifted, and with a rush the tiny craft started back upstream! Back they went, mile after mile, once more passing North Koreans who fired a few shots in their direction. They reached their initial starting point and kept going. Finally the raft careened into shore, where they managed to beach it and where Terry (who Bill Moore ever after called "Steamboat Powers"), shaken but unhurt, began the construction process all over again.

By the evening of 8 October, the 1st Cavalry Division had reached the 38th Parallel and secured the border town of Kaesong. Jack Bender, with his recon platoon, was told to get ready. When and if the signal was given to cross the border, his platoon would have the "honor" of leading the way.

Our company had been moving north against light opposition for two or three days when Colonel Mac gave me a new task.

"We'll be moving out in truck convoy at dawn," I was told, "and we want you to take a jeep and bring up the rear of the column. Watch for any broken-down vehicles, radio in their position, stay with them until they get going or until the maintenance people get with them. Take charge of things in case any NKs decide to hit the rear of the convoy.

"Sorry we don't have any map to give you; maybe we're outrunning the map supply people. Don't worry, though, we'll be on the same road all day, and there'll be road guides posted at all the critical points."

It was almost relaxing, being a passenger while the driver did all the work, staying in convoy, maintaining his interval, and trying to avoid the dust clouds kicked up by the lead vehicles. I even had time to read a copy of *Newsweek* someone had given me. In it, an article about the war had a map showing UN troop dispositions along the 38th Parallel. The article said the UN strategy apparently was to move to the border but not to violate it, so the North Koreans could ask for peace and we wouldn't have to invade. That sounded like a splendid idea.

By early afternoon, two of the trucks had had problems. One was our I Company kitchen truck. Eventually the men got it going again. Next was a truck from K Company. I told the I Company truck to go on, and I stayed with the K Company truck until some maintenance people arrived. They said it looked like a serious repair job, so I told them to stay with the truck overnight, and we'd send someone to guide them to our new location.

My driver and I, now by ourselves, hurried on to catch the convoy. We came to a built-up area, and to a sign, fashioned with typical GI humor, saying, "Welcome to Kaesong—Courtesy of the 1st Cavalry Division."

There was a square in the middle of town, where an MP directing traffic waved us on through. After we had gone two or three blocks, a disquieting thought hit me.

"Pull over," I told the driver. I took out my copy of *Newsweek* and found the war map, which showed Kaesong exactly on the 38th Parallel. In that case, it seemed, we should have turned left, toward the west; continuing straight ahead might very well take us across the Parallel into North Korea!

We turned around and drove back to the square, where I confronted the MP. "How come you directed me north just now?"

"Well, that was the way you were headed, Lieutenant. I just waved you on ahead."

"But didn't you have any instructions about a convoy from the 21st Infantry?"

"Nope."

"Well, let me talk to your sergeant."

The sergeant ambled over. Yes, he *had* been instructed to direct the 21st Infantry toward the west, but he hadn't relayed those instructions to the next man, since he assumed all of the 21st's convoy had passed through.

I turned to the first man and said, "How long have you been directing traffic?"

"About twenty minutes, Lieutenant."

"Did any vehicles besides mine go straight ahead?"

"Just one kitchen truck a while back . . ."

With a shock, I realized the invasion of North Korea might have just been launched—by our company cooks! I jumped back in the jeep and we again headed north. At the edge of town was an American outpost, where someone called out,

"Hey, Lieutenant. This is as far as you can go. This here's the front line."

"Has anyone else passed through?"

"Just one truck a while back. We tried to stop 'em but they didn't hear us."

"That was my mess truck. We're going to try to catch up and

bring it back. Make sure no one shoots at us when we come back in. We'll be seeing you in a few minutes—I hope."

We kept going. Suddenly everything seemed still, lonely, and frightening. What a dumb way this would be to get captured—or worse.

A bit farther along, we rounded a turn and came upon the I Company kitchen truck, pulled off to the right of the road in the shade of a Korean hut. The truck's tailgate was down, the stoves had been unloaded, and the cooks were bustling about. The mess sergeant saw me and walked over.

"Oh, hi, Lieutenant. We figured the company was on ahead, and you guys didn't realize how late it was getting, so we figured we'd just stop here and get started with supper."

"Sergeant, you are in *enemy* territory. We are in *North* Korea. I suggest you get that truck loaded quick so we can get the hell out of here!"

They did, and promptly. We streaked back for Kaesong and, to our relief, soon reached the safety of American lines.

On 10 October, the *authentic* border crossing was made by the 1st Cavalry Division, with Jack Bender's Reconnaissance Platoon leading the way. His hometown paper ran a front-page picture captioned: "A patrol from the First Cavalry division advances cautiously through an open field on the north side of the Thirty-eighth Parallel. The patrol commander, Jack Bender, of Bremerton, Wash., is at left foreground."

The accompanying story began:

> A Bremerton man led the spearhead of American troops which plunged over the 38th parallel into North Korea on the weekend. He is Lt. John A. (Jack) Bender.
>
> Bender, 25, son of Mrs. Kate Bender, 2009 Parkside Drive, led a platoon of U.S. troops and some South Korean volunteers over the line.
>
> A United Press dispatch stated that Bender headed his platoon of 41 U.S. troops and eight South Koreans as they crossed the line north of Kaesong. . . .
>
> Bender attended local schools and was graduated from the U.S. Military Academy in 1949. His wife, Lottie, attends William and Mary College in Virginia.

Jack's family, reading this, was understandably proud. Then, on an inside page of the same paper, they saw a column by *New York Herald Tribune* correspondent Marguerite Higgins with a headline which made them gasp: "1st Yank across 38th in New Push Was 1st to Die"

Her story led off: "With 5th Cavalry Regiment—The first American to die in North Korea in the new American push, was the first to cross the 38th Parallel. He was a young lieutenant who last night led a patrol across the parallel and prepared the way for today's crossing. . . ."

Her story named no names, but the family made the obvious connection. Banding together, they decided to keep Jack's mother from seeing the Higgins article. However, their conspiracy of silence never had a chance. Soon neighbors were calling Kate Bender to commiserate with her about Jack's death.

Amid agonizing tension, the family waited for the telegram they didn't want to see. Each ring of the doorbell brought a moment of terror. Days passed, however, and still there was no message from Washington.

As the 1st Cavalry pushed north toward Pyongyang, the 7th Cavalry Regiment, on the division left flank, circled west to the Yesong River to look for possible crossing sites. To their surprise, a combination rail-highway bridge was still standing, although the structure was heavily damaged and able to support only foot traffic.

A sizable enemy force, dug in on overlooking hills, was waiting on the far shore, and the division commander wondered if it might be a trap. Surely the NKs would have their mortars, artillery, and automatic weapons zeroed in on the bridge, and might even be ready to blow the structure once Americans ventured out on it.

Nevertheless, they had to make the attempt. The regimental commander believed capturing the bridge, which could open the route to Pyongyang, might even be comparable to the seizure of the Rhine River bridge at Remagen in World War II.

West Point '49er Bill Marslender's platoon was first across. Bill led the way, stepping carefully on the ties, not looking back, not even knowing if anyone was following, just hurrying forward. The NKs began shooting, with bullets pinging off the steel girders. Although some were hit, Bill and most of his platoon made it across.

The plan called for Marslender's platoon, after crossing, to fan out to the right. Engineers would come behind to strengthen the bridge, followed by the remainder of Bill's company and the rest of the battalion.

The platoon moved well to the right, to the point that Bill lost radio contact with his company commander. By this time he and his

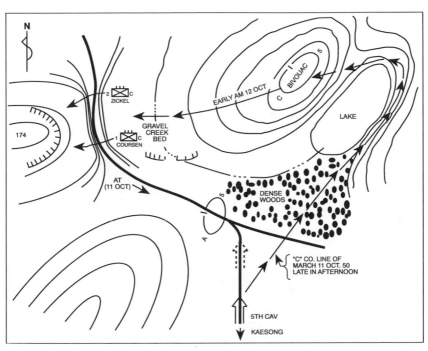

Attack on Hill 174, 11–12 October 1950

men were under heavy fire. As Bill was talking to one of his sergeants, the man was hit in the back by an enemy sniper. Then a second sergeant was hit. Although Bill couldn't reach his parent company, he was able to talk to battalion. He told them he couldn't stay where he was, that he was going to attack.

It was an emotional moment. Shouting "Garry Owen!" the war cry of the 7th Cavalry since the days of Custer, Bill led his men forward in a fierce attack, capturing the ridge to his front. Fighting continued throughout the day, with the battalion taking seventy-eight casualties.

That night the NKs launched a fierce counterattack, but it was beaten off, the bridge remained in friendly hands, and next day the drive continued.

On 11 October, a column of the 1st Battalion, 5th Cavalry, was stopped by small arms and antitank fire at a point where Hill 174 dominated a pass fifteen miles northeast of Kaesong. In late afternoon,

*Samuel Streit Coursen, Medal of Honor winner. Courtesy US Military
Academy Archives.*

C Company, with '49er platoon leaders Huck Long, Lew Zickel, and Sam Coursen, circled to the right so as to hit the enemy from the flank. They moved through a peaceful valley and past a small lovely lake. Lew Zickel was struck by its tranquil beauty. Charlie Company climbed an intermediate hill, but the going was difficult and darkness closed in. The unit was exhausted, for all practical purposes lost, and the company commander elected not to attack until the next morning. That night, as the platoon leaders gathered together, Sam Coursen said, "If anything happens to me, just tell the old lady I was a good soldier." Zickel and Huck Long exchanged glances and then kidded Sam about what he'd said.

Lew and Sam, fellow New Jerseyites, had first met in 1945 on the Governors Island ferry in New York harbor as they were en route to take the West Point entrance exam. Sam, a 6'4" gentle giant, had just graduated from Newark Academy, where he had made his mark as class president, president of the athletic association, and captain of the football team.

Once at West Point, Sam became known not just for his athletic ability, but for his easy-going nature, his capacity for friendship, and his fine sense of humor. Perhaps the highlight of his cadet career, however, came during CAMID (the Cadet-Midshipman joint training exercise), when he met Evangeline "Evie" Sprague, who had just graduated from college and was working that summer at a resort hotel. Sam and Evie were married soon after graduation, and just before Sam left for Korea, 9½-pound Sam, Jr., had been born at Fort Benning.

On the morning of 12 October, Charlie Company moved out amid a heavy ground fog. At the foot of their intermediate hill, they heard NK soldiers on their left, talking and digging in. Moving silently, C Company crept past the NKs and crossed over a gravel creek bed. At the base of 174, the company commander assigned platoon sectors and said, "I'll meet you at the top."

"Is that all you're going to tell us?"

"That's all I know!"

Meanwhile, other Americans attacked 174 from the south, and many of the defenders broke and ran. The situation was fluid as Charlie Company began climbing, reached the crest of 174, and kept going. As they started down the far slope, they began to receive fire from a hidden source to their right, and Coursen moved his men in that direction. They moved forward by rushes, passing a well-camouflaged emplacement which they thought was unoccupied.

One of the platoon members, seeking cover, entered the bunker, and found himself confronted by at least a squad of North Koreans.

Sam heard a shout from the trapped American, followed by a shot and a sound of scuffling. Without hesitating, Coursen went to the soldier's aid. The Koreans, perhaps ten or more, screaming and shooting, came after Sam. As they closed in, the wounded Coursen, no longer the gentle giant his classmates had known, fought savagely, like the tiger he had become. Sam grabbed his rifle by the barrel and began swinging it like a club. In the confined underground space, it became a fearsome weapon, and despite his wounds, Sam swung the rifle in powerful arcs, holding off the Koreans while his wounded comrade crawled to safety. One Korean after another was dropped, until at last Sam was overpowered by the force of numbers.

When the fighting ended, they found Sam's body, surrounded by seven enemy dead. The stock of Coursen's rifle showed the result of blows he had struck; several of the Koreans had died from crushed skulls.

The company was devastated by Sam's death, and Lew Zickel, who was not the only one in tears that day, vowed to tell the world of his classmate's courage. Many memorials preserve Sam's memory—the Lieutenant Coursen rifle range at Fort Benning, the Coursen Cup awarded annually at New Jersey's Baltusrol Golf Club, Newark Academy's Coursen athletic field, and poignantly, to those of us later stationed on Governors Island, the New York–to–Governors Island ferry named in his honor. On the passenger deck of that ferry was placed a framed copy of the citation accompanying the posthumous award, to Lt. Samuel Streit Coursen, USMA '49, of a grateful nation's highest tribute, the Congressional Medal of Honor.

"Lieutenant Coursen's action," General Ridgway later said, "and determination of purpose have earned him a place among the great soldiers of this and past wars."

A few weeks later, Evie Coursen wrote to fellow '49er widow Terry Hardaway, saying: "If Korea brings peace—and I pray that it may—the sacrifice that Sam and Tom and the others were forced to make is worth it for the world. But if it does not, then I am in despair. . . ."

Our company had gone into position in a fertile valley near the west coast. Somehow North Korean prosperity, compared with the devastated South, seemed terribly unfair, although we recognized that individual peasants were not the ones to blame.

On the march north, we had passed a light American observation plane that had crashed. Gib asked if I'd ever met John Watkins.

"Sure," I said, "he was with the battalion staff when I first joined the outfit. He was West Point class of '48—nice guy—real helpful when I was feeling so strange that first couple of days."

"Sorry to tell you this," Gib said, "but John was in that plane we passed. He and the pilot were both killed when it went down."

One morning, which up to that time had been uneventful, Corporal Lee, our interpreter, asked to see me. With him was a Korean farmer.

"Sir," said Lee, "this man says a couple GIs came to his village and took his two daughters away."

"Took them away? What for?"

"Well, they took them, you know, off to the hills someplace, so they could—well, you know. . . ."

"Why, that's terrible! When did this happen?"

"A couple of hours ago, I think. He wants an officer to come back with him to make the soldiers go away and not harm anyone."

"I don't blame him. I think we should do it. But how come he came to I Company?"

"Sir, he says he went to another company first, but no one paid any attention to him. Maybe they thought it was a trap of some kind."

"A trap? Why would they think that? Oh—you mean his village is to our *front*?"

"Yes, sir," Lee said. "I'm afraid so. But sir, I think he's telling the truth."

There didn't seem to be much choice. A half-dozen men had gathered around to see what was happening. I told all the curious ones to grab their weapons and come along. As we passed through my old 3rd Platoon area, a few more were added to our group, bringing the total to around fifteen.

We walked down a dirt road for about a half-mile, then turned onto a path leading into a peaceful green valley. I was beginning to feel a bit uneasy.

"Hey, Lee," I said, "tell him what will happen if he's leading us into a trap."

"Yes sir. I already did." Up ahead lay a score of mud huts with the customary thatched roofs. The farmer told Lee this was the place. We halted about fifty yards short of the village. Everything *appeared* okay, but. . . .

We split into three groups. I posted one group to the left of the trail, another to the right, and told them to keep us covered. The third group accompanied the farmer, Lee, and me on into the village and to a central clearing, where it seemed everyone in town had assembled. Lee began a lengthy conversation with an elder, who appeared to be the head man. The talk dragged on, punctuated by the guttural, explosive grunts which seemed an inherent part of Korean conversation.

Impatiently, I said, "Hey, Lee, what's he saying?"

"Sir, it's okay; they don't need us. The soldiers are gone, and the girls are back safe. No harm done."

Eventually we pieced the story together. When the soldiers forced the girls to come with them, the whole village had followed along. Then, up in the hills, with all the old people, children, etc., looking on, the GIs had understandably lost their ardor. Finally, in disgust, they had given it up as a bad job and taken their leave.

The two maidens were produced, bowing and smiling, to thank me for my interest. Then the head man and the girls' father, also bowing and smiling, asked Lee to express their gratitude to the kind lieutenant.

Lee explained that we came as friends and that no misconduct would be tolerated. At my suggestion, he then asked if someone would like to return with us to identify the soldiers. After another lengthy conversation, Lee said my offer, while appreciated, was being declined.

"But why? Don't they believe the soldiers would be punished?"

"Well, sir, they said they wouldn't be able to identify the men."

"Why not?"

Lee's moon-shaped Oriental face broke into a huge grin. "Sir, they say that all you Americans look alike!"

On 15 October, President Truman and General MacArthur met at Wake Island. During the meeting, MacArthur discussed the amphibious landing scheduled for 20 October at Wonsan. Marines at Inchon, and the 7th Infantry Division, which had been trucked back to Pusan, were already loading up for it.

By 20 October, however, thanks to a rapid advance by the ROKs, Wonsan was already in friendly hands, so an assault landing was more or less superfluous. Moreover, the Wonsan harbor was heavily mined, and it would be some time before a major effort from that direction could be supported.

During their meeting, Truman asked MacArthur about the likelihood of Chinese intervention. MacArthur assured him victory was won in Korea and said there was "little possibility of the Chinese coming in." The general went on to express his belief that "formal NK resistance" would end by Thanksgiving, in which case he planned to withdraw Eighth Army to Japan by Christmas.

Between 14 and 20 October, unbeknownst to MacArthur and

General Willoughby, his G-2, even as the Wake Island meeting was in progress, four Chinese armies were moving across the Yalu River from Manchuria into North Korea.

It had been two weeks since the ominous article by Marguerite Higgins had appeared, and in Bremerton, Washington, Kate Bender was becoming more and more frantic. Finally she sent a telegram to the Defense Department, mentioned the article, and asked for news of her son, Jack. A few days later a reply came from the Army adjutant general, saying an inquiry would be made.

Mike Wadsworth, dissatisfied with his job on the Fort Benning Weapons Committee, and perhaps influenced by the death of his friend Cec Newman, had volunteered for combat. After spending a preembarkation leave with his wife, Bette, and their infant daughter, he arrived in Korea on 25 October and was assigned as a platoon leader in Company E, 9th Infantry Regiment, of the 2nd "Second to None" Infantry Division.

Since early boyhood, Mike had been preparing for this kind of role. As a youth in Gadsden, Alabama, for example, Mike had received the coveted "Scout of the Year" award recognizing his leadership in scout activities.

Later, during plebe year at West Point, Mike's service career nearly ended when he broke his arm badly playing soccer. Little encouragement was given him that the arm would heal completely, and the medical authorities at West Point said he probably could not obtain a commission unless he regained full use of the arm. For three years, Mike spent off-duty hours at the station hospital and the gym trying to obtain the required usage of his arm so he might receive the commission he so earnestly desired. It was a happy day, in April of our First Class year, when Mike was told he would be commissioned with our class.

Now, joining his new platoon, Mike liked what he saw, and was particularly impressed with Henry Heissner, his platoon sergeant. Mike wrote home enthusiastically that he had "the best platoon in the best company in the division," and that his platoon sergeant was "A-1."

On 20 October, from our positions south of Sunchon, I watched an airdrop by the 187th RCT. Dozens of transport planes flew overhead, and far in the distance, we could see hundreds of parachutes, loaded with men and equipment, floating to earth. Among those making their first combat jump that day were my classmates Boyde Allen and Dene Balmer.

In a way, however, like the landing at Wonsan, the airdrop was anticlimactic. The South Koreans had already seized Sunchon, resistance in the drop area was negligible, and most of the NKs had already fled north, escaping the planned trap.

Apparently the enemy was in full retreat. At least I Company encountered no opposition as we moved north again and took up quarters in Sunchon itself. For Company CP, we commandeered the local constabulary office, which must have been a major headquarters for the NKs and their Soviet advisors. The place bulged with potential souvenirs—magazines and books in both Korean and Russian, flags, money, epaulets with assorted rank insignia, etc. Trying to use my two years of Russian language study at West Point, I thumbed through the Russian material and marveled at how the Soviets' UN ambassador continued to insist the Russians had no part whatsoever in this war.

After dark, we took off our boots and spread our sleeping bags. Suddenly from the next room, I heard a yell. A soldier there, starting to put down his sleeping bag, had shone his flashlight upon a gruesome sight—the body of a man who must have been executed shortly before our arrival. Evidently the man's hands had been tied behind his back, he'd been made to kneel, and then a pistol had blown off the back of his head.

Next morning there were reports of other atrocities. The townspeople said that before the soldiers had pulled out, they had shot many of those who were suspected of being anticommunist. At the edge of town, body after body—men, women, children, perhaps fifty in all—had been found piled into a mass grave.

Meanwhile, Brigadier General Allen, assistant commander of the 1st Cavalry Division, accompanied by his aide, '49er Jack Hodes, was trying to link up with the 187th RCT in an attempt to intercept a rumored prisoner train. Allen and Hodes, after jeeping through enemy-held terrain, found the train in a tunnel. Nearby, to their horror, they saw a large number of American bodies. According to a weeping survivor, who had escaped by pretending to be dead, prisoners had been taken from the train in groups, supposedly to be fed. Then they had been systematically killed. In one spot was a semicircle of fifteen dead Americans, many with rice bowls still in their hands, who had been shot as they waited to receive food. Altogether, there were sixty-six American corpses, not counting seven more emaciated bodies which were found lying on straw mats beside the railroad track inside the tunnel itself. These men had either starved to death or died from disease. Many had old battle wounds.

As we prepared to leave town, an old woman who'd been doing our laundry began to wail, begging us not to go, and saying the Communists would return and kill her for having helped the Americans. We assured her that other Americans would come to take our place, and that there was no way the Communists would be able to return. How little we knew.

Next day, I was told to report to Regimental HQ, where I'd be serving as liaison officer between our battalion and the regiment. Assuming the war was almost over, I welcomed the chance to see a bit more of the big picture.

Pyongyang, the capital of North Korea, had fallen to the 1st Cavalry Division. The division consolidated its positions, cleaned up, and began taking a well-earned rest. Some of the units even took the opportunity to set up projectors and show movies.

On 27 October, a few miles from Pyongyang, Beecher Brian, with his platoon of the 5th Cavalry, learned the war was now "official"— Bob Hope had arrived in Pyongyang to entertain the troops! At the proper time, Brian and his platoon loaded into jeeps to return to the company area so they could see the performance. About halfway back, however, Beech saw an armed civilian run into a building.

Ignoring the temptation to continue on to the show, Brian stopped the platoon and went to investigate. In the nearby buildings, they discovered dozens of weapons and realized they had stumbled upon a guerrilla headquarters.

Beecher, temporarily by himself, went into a small backyard and saw an NK disappearing over a wall. He fired his weapon and missed, just as he saw another NK duck down a hallway. This one Beecher chased, and following him into a room, he came upon about twenty men sitting with their legs crossed. Apparently he had come upon a staff meeting of some sort.

Brian, not knowing what else to do, pulled out his big .45 pistol, thinking perhaps it would look more threatening than his carbine. Although alone, he pretended to talk to people behind him. After about twenty seconds of this imaginary conversation, a couple of men arrived to investigate the shot he had fired. The prisoners were gathered up, the captured weapons were loaded into the jeeps, and the NKs were marched, with their hands over their heads, to the company area, whence they were sent to a POW collection point. Beech and his men never did get to see the Bob Hope show.

As we moved north, to Pyongyang and beyond, the Eighth Army Ranger Company, led by '49er Ralph Puckett, combed the hills searching for North Korean stragglers. From time to time, there were some minor skirmishes, but more often, the Rangers found the NKs quite willing to surrender.

Back in August, soon after his arrival in Korea, Puckett had been selected to form a Ranger Company. A colonel at Eighth Army, looking for an aggressive officer to put such a unit together and thinking a lieutenant fresh from West Point might operate with more daring than someone who had been shot at, interviewed Puckett for the job.

Ralph, former captain of the West Point boxing team, and fresh out of Benning's Jump School, welcomed the challenge and told the colonel, "I've always wanted to be Ranger, and if I had to, I'd even be willing to start out as a squad leader or rifleman!"

The colonel liked what he saw and told Puckett he had the job and should start recruiting the seventy-four men authorized for him, with the stipulation that he was to keep his hands off any trained riflemen; the fighting in the Perimeter was at its height, and there was a shortage of qualified infantry replacements.

His initial mission, Ralph learned, would be to infiltrate the "Naktong Bulge," a salient the NKs had pushed into the north-eastern side of the Perimeter. Back in Japan, Ralph talked to rear-area mechanics, clerk typists, and cooks, telling them he needed volunteers for "a secret and dangerous mission involving operations behind enemy lines." He was surprised how easy it was to fill his ranks, as eager young soldiers, thirsting for adventure, and with an unrealistic outlook on war, were quick to sign up.

Ralph had been delighted when his popular classmate Barney Cummings joined the company as a platoon leader. As a cadet, Barney had starred on the fencing team, winning an NCAA championship in his event, the foils. Academics, however, had been a struggle for Barney, and he had ended up as our class "anchor," last in graduation order of academic merit. Following tradition, on graduation day the very loudest cheer went up for Barney, last man to step forward for his diploma.

Despite his academic problems, no one ever doubted Barney's ability as a soldier, and our yearbook made the prediction that someday we would be "proud to say that General Cummings was our classmate." It wasn't too farfetched; many a class goat, such as George Armstrong Custer, last man in the Class of 1861, had gone on to wear stars.

Back near Pusan, Ralph, Barney, and others began training their fledgling rangers. By the time training was finished, however, Eighth Army had broken out of the Perimeter and the Naktong Bulge no longer existed. As the action moved north, the company was released from Army control, attached to the 25th Division, and given the job of rounding up enemy stragglers.

My living conditions as a liaison officer contrasted sharply with what I'd known in the rifle company. I was sleeping under canvas, eating from a tin plate rather than a C-ration can, and my only job was carrying a message to and from battalion once or twice a day.

Life seemed almost pleasant as the advance continued and we headed toward Sinuiju, at the far northwest corner of Korea, where the Yalu river formed the Korea-Manchuria boundary. To most of us, it seemed obvious that reaching the Yalu would mean the end of the war.

For the past week, there had been scattered contact with the Chinese Communist Forces (CCF), to include the capture of several CCF prisoners. Up the line, however, no one wanted to believe significant numbers of Chinese could have entered Korea without being detected. Then, as October ended, the ROK Divisions on Eighth Army's right flank ran headlong into massive Chinese formations. On 31 October, the 8th Cavalry Regiment was rushed forward to reinforce the besieged ROK 1st Division at Unsan.

Next day, 1 November, '49er Al Kendree, in G Company of the 8th Cavalry, had his platoon on a forward outpost. Fellow '49er Bob Springer, a member of the 99th Field Artillery Battalion, was with Al as an FO.

During the day, they saw crowds of Chinese occupying hills to their front. Bob requested permission to bring artillery fire on them, but permission was denied, even when an artillery liaison officer came forward and saw the situation. A report was circulating that negotiations were underway, so contact should be avoided. Added to that was a rumor that these were only peasants who had crossed the Yalu to safeguard their fishing rights. Throughout the day, despite their uneasiness, Al and Bob could only sit and observe.

That night, the CCF, firing signal flares and blowing bugles, horns, and whistles, launched mass attacks, wave after wave, putting the ROK 15th Regiment to flight and surrounding the 1st and 2nd battalions of the 8th Cavalry. Kendree's company commander radioed Al to pull back from the outpost, but "not back to where I am," since the Company CP was already surrounded.

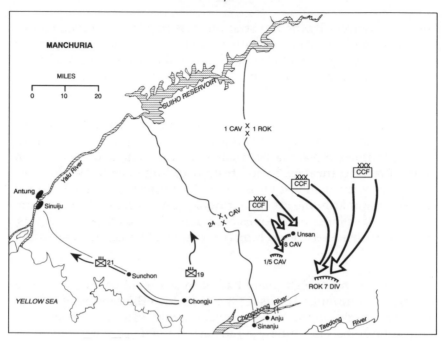

MANCHURIA

MILES

0   10   20

SUIHO RESERVOIR

Yalu River

1 CAV X 1 ROK
       X

Antung

Sinuiju

XXX
CCF

XXX
CCF

XXX
CCF

X 1 CAV
2A X

Unsan

8 CAV

1/5 CAV

ROK 7 DIV

21

Sunchon

19

Chongju

YELLOW SEA

Chongchong River

Anju

Sinanju

Taedong River

Chinese Intervention, 25 October–1 November 1950

In the darkness, Al, Bob, and their men left the outpost, took to the hills, and worked their way south. A day later, when they finally reached friendly lines, Al learned not only that his company commander was dead, but that he and Bob were the only officers from their outfit to make it back.

Men of the 8th Cavalry, who hours before had been thinking the war was almost over, were forced to retreat, often in disorder, and the result was disastrous.

The 3rd Battalion of the 8th Cavalry tried to cover the withdrawal. By 3 A.M. of 2 November, however, the situation was chaotic, organized resistance was impossible, and although certain small groups fought on bravely, eventually 3rd Battalion was overwhelmed. Before it was over, 3rd Battalion's commander was mortally wounded, and of the unit's eight hundred men, six hundred had either been killed or captured.

It was a sunny day, and in the far northwest corner of Korea, some fifteen or twenty miles from Manchuria, we were still unaware of the fighting east of us. Our mood was almost festive. From overhead, the pilot of a spotter plane called to us cheerfully, "Hey, you guys, I can see the Yalu!" We cheered.

Minutes later, the S-3 came rushing out of the Operations tent. "Pack up, everybody," he said, "we're moving out—south."

My first thought was that some sort of truce had been declared and we were being withdrawn. The truth, unfortunately, was that we too were under attack, and the CCF was trying to slice in behind our regiment to cut us off.

My driver, an articulate corporal named Broadhead, wedged our jeep into the column and we headed south amid traffic which soon became bumper to bumper. Mile after mile, hour after hour, we kept going, finally arriving at Anju on the south bank of the Chongchon River.

Next day I was busy delivering messages to units establishing a bridgehead just north of the Chongchon. Engineers had built two pontoon bridges as delicate but vital life lines. Each bridge was one-way, and all day long Broadhead and I crossed the river over one bridge, drove along the road paralleling the north shore, delivering map overlays, signal instructions, and various messages to units in the bridgehead, and then recrossed over the second bridge to receive further items for delivery.

Once we passed elements of the 19th Infantry, marching along the road in double column. When we came alongside E Company, I saw, leading one of the platoons, my classmate Leslie Kirkpatick. Kirk had been one of my closest friends since our precadet days at Lafayette, when he was a staff sergeant and student company commander, and I a buck sergeant and student platoon leader. Kirk, the ex-paratrooper from Alabama, tall, confident, personable, with combat experience from World War II, was everyone's pick as man from our class most likely to become a senior general.

I yelled, "It sure is funny to see a paratrooper doing all that walking!"

Kirk looked up, startled, then recognized me and his face broke into a grin. I jumped from the jeep; we pounded each other on the back, and I walked with him for a few minutes. We compared notes, and these days it seemed the main news was about the latest classmate to become a casualty. I said I had just heard that Bill Wilbur had been killed.

Kirk shook his head in sad acknowledgment. He and Bill had been in the same cadet company. We agreed that one almost dreaded meeting a classmate, since each time it seemed there was more bad news to share.

Kirk plodded along, looking weary, needing a shave, seeming more subdued than I had ever known him. His column turned off the road and headed for the hills. I wished him luck, climbed back in my jeep, and waved good-bye.

Later that day, Broadhead wandered into the S-2 tent and saw the latest map symbols.

"Hey, Lieutenant," he began, "what does a box on a map with four X's above it mean?"

Happy to show off my military education, I said, "Well, one "X" is a brigade, two a division, three a corps, and four an army, like the Eighth US Army that we're in, which would be shown on a map by four Xs."

"Well, I just saw, then, that the Chinese have four of those armies south of the Yalu. Is that possible?"

"It doesn't seem likely, Broadhead. But after all, *you* are the one who saw the map, so you know more than I do."

He looked a little disappointed in me. After all, lieutenants were supposed to be reassuring—or at least to know more than corporals.

9. CCF Intervention

4–29 NOVEMBER

The Eighth Army withdrawal had been fairly well executed, but to the '49ers involved, who saw only congested roads and jumbled units, it seemed more like organized confusion. Nevertheless, except for the disastrous losses suffered by the 8th Cavalry Regiment, Walton Walker's troops had come south in good shape. Now, however, the Chinese had the initiative. Eighth Army took up positions along the Chongchon and braced itself for the next Chinese move.

On the east coast, the 1st Marines and the 7th Infantry Division of Ned Almond's X Corps had both landed, joining the ROK units which had arrived overland. Initially, the plan had been for X Corps to swing west and capture Pyongyang. By the time everyone was ashore, however, Pyongyang had already fallen, so MacArthur, changing signals, told Almond to head north toward the Yalu.

On 4 November, Beecher Brian wrote home: "I wish there were some way for me to get this letter to you today. . . . I hear the news reported the 1st Cav in a terrific fight with the Chinese Commies and that some were cut off. That is actually what happened, but it wasn't the 5th Cav. It was one Bn. of the 8th Reg. I understand none of those people got out. We have now withdrawn across a river to the south. I sure hope power politics come into play now and get those Chinese out of here. It wasn't so much their strength as it was the fact we weren't expecting them. . . ."

North of the Chongchon, four 24th Division battalions were grouped into a Task Force under the command of Gen. Garrison "Gar" Davidson, the 24th Division's assistant division commander and a brilliant engineer, who for a number of years prior to World War II had also served as head football coach at West Point.

An hour or two after dark, someone came and said, "Lieutenant, they want a liaison officer. The Task Force Commander has a job for you."

Davidson, youthful looking and strikingly handsome, with a full head of silvery hair, was by himself in a room containing only a small table and a pair of folding chairs. The sole light came from a flickering candle. He motioned me to sit down, then said: "We have four battalions north of the river. Unfortunately they're not tied in together; there's just too long a frontage. So what we've got are four separate bridgeheads."

He pointed to the map. "Now see this road running parallel to the river. Have you been over it?"

"Yes sir."

"Good, because I want you to travel it again right now. Go to each battalion CP; I'm not sure precisely where they are, but they should be fairly close to the road. Tell them we've just received a report that the Chinese are headed this way. Chances are they'll try to reach the river during the night, maybe even try to cross it.

"I want each of those battalions to button up tight, and to run patrols from left to right. Here's a patrol schedule for them to follow."

"Yes sir."

"And be careful, Lieutenant. In between those battalion positions, there's no telling what you'll run into. Do you have a map?"

"No sir, but I'll try to get one."

"No, that'd take too long. Here, take mine. Talk to the people at each battalion and plot the location of their companies. Come see me as soon as you get back."

As our jeep pulled out from the CP, I told Broadhead to drive only with the dim, shielded "blackout" lights. We went a short way, with Broadhead muttering there was no way he could drive without headlights. Finally we went off the road. Our front wheels dropped into a shallow ditch and the engine stalled. Broadhead swore under his breath, started the engine, slammed the gears into reverse, and we careened back onto the roadway.

Broadhead grunted, almost in satisfaction. Guess *that* would show the dumb lieutenant you couldn't drive a narrow road without lights! We went on, the road curved, and Broadhead momentarily flashed the headlights to get his bearings.

"Don't do that anymore," I said.

"But sir—I can't see the damned road!"

"I know. Just go slow." Again we slipped off the edge, and I sensed Broadhead was sulking over my unreasonableness.

"Corporal, I think I'd better tell you something. Those hills to our right are possibly crawling with Chinese, and maybe they're on their way to this road. If we're going to be a target, let's not be an *illuminated* target!"

We kept moving, with no complaints now that Broadhead understood the problem. Eventually, with a good bit of luck, we found each of the units, plotted their locations on the general's map, and relayed our messages. Then, fortified with a canteen cup of black coffee, we headed back. Fortunately the return trip was uneventful.

Later that night, the Chinese made a coordinated attack all along the bridgehead line. Leslie Kirkpatick's E Company, four miles north of the river on Hill 123, was hit by a Chinese assault force which came from the right rear, apparently following field telephone wire. Cpl. Mitchell Red Cloud, an American Indian from Wisconsin, was first to give the alarm. After being critically wounded, Red Cloud wrapped one arm around a small tree to hold himself up, then kept firing his BAR at point-blank range, killing more than thirty of the advancing enemy, until he himself finally fell.

Kirk left his own foxhole to go to the aid of a wounded comrade, but he too was cut down. (Kirk received a posthumous Silver Star, and Red Cloud received the Medal of Honor.)

Grover Asmus, USMA '46, commanding F Company of that same battalion, was a particular friend of Kirk's. Some time earlier, Kirk had said to Grover, "If I get killed, please take my class ring and send it to my wife, Kitty." Grover was surprised by the request; it was as though Kirk had a premonition. They had already been through several firefights, but this was the first time Kirk had ever mentioned the possibility of being killed.

When the battalion moved forward on 7 November, Grover found Kirk's body. He was in a reclining position with his head resting on his helmet, looking as if he were asleep. Not fifteen feet away lay the body of Mitchell Red Cloud. Bodies nearby had been stripped; in Korea's brutal cold, American boots and clothing were highly valued. Kirk's body, however, had not been disturbed, and only his ring was missing.

On a nearby hill lay another group of stripped American bodies, also members of Kirk's company. One was a lieutenant with whom Kirk had been friendly. Grover eventually concluded that Kirk had also asked that officer to retrieve his ring, and after Kirk was killed, the lieutenant had gone to Kirk, placed his head on his helmet, and

Leslie W. Kirkpatrick. Courtesy US Military Academy Archives.

taken the ring. The ring had then been lost when the lieutenant's body was stripped. The Chinese, who may have seen the officer go to Kirk, may have suspected the body was booby-trapped. Hence, while others were being stripped, Kirk had been left undisturbed.

Unaware of all this, I was at the Task Force CP when a Graves Registration officer noticed my West Point ring and asked if I "knew a Kirkpatrick."

"Sure," I answered. "He's a classmate—one of my best friends. What about him?"

"Well, he was killed two nights ago. We just identified his body this morning." Too stunned to talk about it, I wandered off, alone and hurting.

Months later I met an officer who had been in Kirk's company. "Y'know," he told me, "Lieutenant Kirkpatrick was the finest officer I ever knew. He would have become a great general." Somehow it helped, knowing that someone who'd been with Kirk for even a short time had recognized his worth and shared my grief.

On 7 November, a telegram from the adjutant general arrived at the Bender home in Bremerton, Washington. It had been nearly a month since the family had seen the two stories, the AP piece saying Jack was first across the 38th Parallel, and the concurrent Marguerite Higgins column with its chilling headline, "1st Yank Across 38th in New Push Was First to Die."

It must have been with trembling hands that Kate Bender opened the telegram. The message was simple and to the point:

"REFERENCE IS MADE TO MY TELEGRAM OF 26 OCTOBER CLN A REPLY TO MY INQUIRY HAS BEEN RECEIVED WHICH DISCLOSES THAT YOUR SON SECOND LIEUTENANT JOHN A BENDER CMA 059317 CMA WAS NEVER REPORTED CASUALTY BUT PRESENT FOR DUTY AS OF 2 NOVEMBER = WITSELL ADJUTANT GENERAL ARMY = "

The Chinese Communist Forces had driven Eighth Army back beyond the Chongchon and, to the east, had slowed the advance of X Corps. Then suddenly, and mysteriously, the CCF, breaking contact and pulling back into the mountains, seemed to disappear.

GHQ in Tokyo, continuing to underestimate Chinese strength and determination, misread the situation. (Incredibly, 300,000 CCF had crossed the Yalu into North Korea without being detected.) A decision was made to push north once again.

For the past few weeks, Bill Marslender and his platoon of Charlie Company, 7th Cavalry, had received more than their share of danger-

ous assignments, as on the day when they were first across the critical Yesong River bridge.

In any case, when Bill's company commander asked him, on
11 November, to volunteer his platoon for a patrol, Marslender re-
spectfully declined. Volunteering would involve not just himself, but
also the men he led, and it didn't seem right. Consequently, another
platoon was selected for the patrol. The company commander, USMA
'45, was a good man, and between him and Marslender there was a
strong feeling of mutual respect. Nevertheless, Bill sensed the CO,
who would have taken the patrol out himself had it been possible,
was a bit disappointed in him.

Next day, the company jumped off in an attack against an objective some two miles away. Midway to the objective, a big ditch ran
across their front. When Bill and his platoon came out of the ditch,
they received heavy fire, and men began falling. The other platoons
had never left the ditch, and Bill's platoon, still a half-mile or so from
the objective, was effectively pinned down, unable to move either forward or backward. They were told to pull back to the ditch, but had
to wait for darkness to do so. Even then, it was impossible to bring
the dead and wounded with them, so Marslender sent the others
back, while he and the platoon medic volunteered to remain with the
wounded.

Next day the attack was resumed, rescuing both Bill and the
others. The same attack also found the original patrol platoon; all
were dead.

In the second week of November, the 335th Fighter Squadron,
at Andrews AFB outside Washington, was ordered to Japan and then
to Korea. Doug Bush, becoming more and more proficient in his hot
F-86 Sabre, was on his way.

By this time, '49er pilots were scattered around the world.
Fletcher McMurry, Bill Marslender's brother-in-law, was undergoing
B-26 Combat Crew Training at Langley AFB in Virginia; Gene Mechling (who had transferred to the Air Force the previous December)
was just receiving his wings at Williams AFB in Arizona; Dolph Overton was in England flying F-84s; Dick Schoeneman and Bob Makinney were flying F-86s at Victorville AFB in California; while Floyd
"Bo" Stephenson was already in Korea with the 27th Fighter Interceptor
Squadron.

A few days earlier, the Russian-built MiG-15 jet had made its
first appearance over North Korea. Swarms of MiGs had attacked US
propeller-driven planes near Sinuiju, and it was evident the United

States would no longer have undisputed control of the air. Whether destined for Korea, or already there, all '49er pilots knew the game had changed.

On 13 November, Mike Wadsworth, who had written home so proudly about his new command, calling it "the best platoon in the best company in the Division," led that platoon of Easy Company, 9th Infantry, up an enemy-held hill near Pugwon. When the top of the hill was reached, however, Mike and the lead squad were cut off from the remainder of the platoon by a heavy enemy mortar barrage. He immediately ordered a withdrawal to a position of cover, and although wounded himself by a mortar fragment, he stayed on the hill until all of the wounded had been evacuated. He then established a defensive position and refused to be evacuated for treatment until the next day, when the threat of an enemy counterattack had been diminished. His Bronze Star citation for this action credited him with allowing his company to hold its position with a minimum of casualties.

Jim Scholtz, whose massive frame had awed the tiny nurses' aides at Tokyo General, had recovered sufficiently by 15 November for him to return to duty. When Jim arrived back at the 5th Cavalry Regiment, one of the first people he saw was Joe Toomey, who now led the Regimental I&R Platoon. Jim offered his congratulations; being selected for the I&R job was well-deserved recognition. At the same time, both men recognized that Joe, who had seen heavy action as a rifle platoon leader, was going into a position which was every bit as hazardous.

Once again I was back with Item Company. The liaison position had been eliminated, and it was probably just as well. Since we were heading north again, I guessed I'd be of more use as a company exec.

We wondered why the Chinese had broken contact, and what we'd encounter once we moved out again. For the moment, though, we weren't worrying about such things. It was 23 November, Thanksgiving Day, and through a miracle of logistics, a full holiday dinner—turkey and all the trimmings—was being prepared by our company cooks. To help us celebrate, we even had some non-American guests. Two days earlier, as we passed the encampment of the British Commonwealth Brigade, two young Tommies had tagged along, saying they wanted to see some action before the "bloody war" ended.

All of us, including the two Brits, enjoyed the traditional Thanksgiving feast. Then, as we finished eating, two British MPs arrived, calling for their missing comrades. They assured us the men wouldn't be in any serious trouble if they returned promptly.

"Actually, sir," one of them said in his proper English accent, "it's a question of benefits. If one of them were to have something happen to him while he was off with you chaps, he'd be disqualified for survivor benefits and all that sort of thing. . . ."

The truant Tommies were produced, there were smiles and handshakes all around, and soon they were on their way. About that time a messenger from battalion came by, saying he had heard General MacArthur himself had been at our Regimental CP and had even said he hoped to have us all back in Japan by Christmas. It seemed unlikely, but it was such a lovely rumor that no one wanted to question it.

The day after Thanksgiving, Eighth Army once more started north. At first all seemed to go well, and in many units there was almost a buoyant mood. As part of the advance, Ralph Puckett and Barney Cummings, leading the 8213th Ranger Company, were out in front of the 25th Division as part of Task Force Dolvin.

Ralph and Barney, working with the cooks and clerk-typists they had recruited in Japan, had put together a fine group of highly motivated soldiers. Their unit, however, in size more like a reinforced platoon than a company, was ill-suited, by numbers or equipment, for company-type missions. The Rangers were authorized only seventy-seven men to begin with, and at the end of training they numbered only sixty-six. Attrition had reduced the total still further, and a mere fifty-two Rangers were on hand on the afternoon of 25 November, as the unit, supported by a platoon of tanks, was told to seize and hold Hill 205, some fifteen miles north of the Chongchon River.

The tanks, with Rangers riding on their back decks, started across frozen paddy fields en route to the objective. As they came into the open, they began receiving small arms and mortar fire from their right front. The Rangers dropped to the ground, and the tankers proceeded to button up. Puckett, angry with the tankers for not returning the fire, climbed back on the lead tank and pounded on the hatch with his rifle butt. The tank commander raised the hatch halfway. Ralph yelled for the tanks to start shooting, then leaped back down and called out, "Let's go!"

The enemy continued to fire as the Rangers started across a half-mile of open field. Barney Cummings, on the left flank, urged his men forward and was out in front setting the example. When the company reached 205, they formed a skirmish line, then climbed and reached the top without finding any enemy.

They began hacking away with their entrenching tools, scooping out foxholes in the frozen ground. Ralph and Barney moved from point to point, designating firing positions for the machine guns and BARs. Taking every precaution, Puckett left the hill and walked back to the Task Force CP to coordinate personally with the artillery officer. Together, they put together a fire-support plan "just in case."

It was a weird situation. The Rangers hadn't been told to expect any serious opposition, at least not until they went much farther. At the same time, there were all these reports of Chinese "hordes" coming south, and at a Task Force briefing Puckett attended, an intelligence officer had said there might be as many as twenty-five thousand Chinese nearby.

That night the shivering Rangers hunkered down, unaware that hundreds of Chinese were approaching. Ralph, Barney, and a radio man shared what served as a "command" foxhole. Shortly before midnight, a shower of sparks from grenade arming devices flashed in the darkness, and seconds later grenades began exploding all over their position. In the past, many ROK and American units had been easily overrun in just such an attack. Green troops often stayed well down in their holes, not reacting until it was too late and letting the enemy swarm over them.

In this case, however, the well-trained Rangers rose up and began shooting. Puckett called for artillery support, including flare shells. In the light of the flares, more Chinese could be seen running up the slope behind the lead squads. The artillery planning paid off, as round after round of 105 and 155 high-explosive shells crashed into the Chinese formation. Now that the attackers were clearly visible, the Ranger fire intensified, bodies began piling up, and at last the Chinese pulled back.

Ralph and Barney moved around the perimeter, counting casualties. So far there had been only six wounded, all of whom refused evacuation, saying they could still fight. Puckett was near the right of the perimeter when he heard bugles and whistles, indicating another attack was about to begin. He began sprinting back toward the foxhole he shared with Barney, and as he did so, he saw a trail of sparks from a grenade thrown in his direction. He remembered what they'd taught him at Fort Benning—if a grenade comes your way, throw yourself flat on the ground and the exploding fragments will miss you. He hit the ground, feeling confident and invulnerable; then he felt a searing pain.

Ralph made it to the foxhole and told Barney he'd been hit. "Where?"

"In the hip!" Then he began to laugh.

"What's so funny?" asked Barney.

"I just learned the people at Benning don't always know what they're talking about!" Despite Ralph's wound, for the moment the two classmates felt relieved, little knowing that the night's work had just begun and that they were under attack by a full Chinese battalion of about six hundred men.

Again there was a mortar barrage, followed by exploding grenades and a crowd of Chinese rushing forward. Once more the Rangers' steady fire, supplemented by supporting US artillery, beat them back. Over the next two hours, still further assaults were made, and rather than weakening, each attack seemed to become more determined. By this time, more and more Rangers had fallen, and ammunition was running low.

At 2:45 A.M., a fifth assault was launched. This one was the worst yet. It began with a long, intense, mortar barrage, followed by a shower of hand grenades from the leading Chinese squads. Ralph called for artillery support, but was told by the officer at the FDC that the howitzers were busy on another mission.

"We'll give you the fire as soon as we can," the man said. Puckett, on his knees, crouched against the wall of the foxhole, was bent over, shouting into the mike to make himself heard amidst the noise of battle. "We really need it now," he said. "We've just got to have it."

Just then two mortar shells landed a fraction of a second apart, exploding almost on top of the '49ers' foxhole. Ralph was wounded severely in both feet, his left shoulder, and left arm. His right foot was damaged so badly that he later had difficulty persuading the medics not to amputate it.

A few feet away, mortar fragments had also crashed into Ralph's classmate. Barney Cummings, class "anchor man," varsity fencer, and Ranger hero, had been killed instantly.

Ralph summoned his remaining strength, picked up his radio handset, and again called for artillery support. Once more he was told the guns were busy on another fire mission. With the casualties they had taken, there were gaps in the line, and the Chinese were beginning to pour through.

"It's too late," Puckett told the artillery officer. "Tell Colonel Dolvin we're being overwhelmed." The Rangers who were still alive were forced back. Two of them, Billy Walls and David Pollock, heard Puckett was wounded and went looking for him.

They found Puckett and asked if he could walk. "No, I'm hurt bad, you'll have to carry me." A few yards away, they saw a Chinese soldier firing a submachine gun burst into a foxhole to finish off another of the Rangers.

In the confusion, Walls slung Ralph over his shoulder, but after twenty or twenty-five yards, was unable to keep going.

"I guess you'll have to drag me," Ralph said. Walls and Pollock each took an arm and pulled him on down the hill. Puckett, fighting against the pain, kept saying, "I'm a Ranger, I'm a Ranger."

"Shut up, sir, or you'll get us all killed!"

They kept going. Wondering if Puckett was still alive and conscious, Walls asked, "Are you still with us?"

"Yes, I'll never leave you," Ralph said.

"We'll never leave you either, sir." Somehow they made it to the base of the hill, where the tank platoon was in position. A tank sergeant picked up Puckett and, as more shots were fired in their direction, put the wounded '49er on a tank and eventually got him to an aid station. All told, only nineteen of the fifty-two Rangers managed to get away. Ralph, who was awarded a DSC for his actions, spent the next year in a series of Army hospitals.

In his Pulitzer Prize-winning book, *A Bright Shining Lie*, Neil Sheehan related a bizarre footnote to this episode, wherein another man, John Paul Vann, would later tell the story of Hill 205 as though he, rather than Puckett, had been the Ranger commander that night.

On that same night of 25–26 November, Mike Wadsworth's 2nd Division platoon was ordered to dig in on the side of a slate-covered hill. It was less than two weeks since Mike had been wounded by mortar fire, but he'd been patched up and was back with his unit.

As best they could, Wadsworth's men scraped out shallow foxholes in the rocky, frozen ground. They split up the night into watches and waited, shivering, apprehensive, wondering if the rumors about returning to Japan by Christmas could really be true.

Mike tried to get some rest; nearby was his "A-1" platoon sergeant, Henry Heissner. About 3:30 A.M., Mike woke up, feeling uneasy, and heard a lot of chattering to his front. Words carried on the crisp night air, and Mike realized he was hearing Chinese. The alarm was given, and Wadsworth's platoon began firing, but the attackers were already so close that they were able to throw grenades into the American positions and then rush forward. Fighting became hand-to-hand, the Americans fought bravely, and the Chinese were starting to be pushed back. About that time, Wadsworth was standing erect, shouting to his own men and to the enemy as well, when he was hit in the chest by fragments from a bursting grenade. He refused to leave,

Fort Benning, Georgia. Maj. Gen. John Church, commanding general of the Infantry Center, congratulates Ralph Puckett as Puckett is awarded the Distinguished Service Cross for his actions as commander of the Eighth Army Ranger Company on Hill 205 on 25–26 November 1950. Standing next to Puckett is '49er Robert C. Sanders. Bob Sanders won both the Silver Star and the Bronze Star for Valor while serving in Korea in 1950–51 with the 65th Infantry Regiment, 3rd Division. Courtesy Col. Ralph Puckett (Ret.).

and continued to direct the action. Then, a few minutes later, he went down for good when a burst from a submachine gun tore into his chest and stomach.

By this time almost everyone on the hill was either killed or wounded. One of Wadsworth's devoted men, Corporal Brown, bravely carried Mike down the hill, put him into a jeep, and personally drove him through enemy fire to an aid station.

The CCF had laid their plans well. On this night of 25–26 November, as Ralph Puckett, Mike Wadsworth, and others were being attacked by swarms of Chinese, well-rehearsed assault forces hit all across the Eighth Army front in what became known as the Second CCF Offensive. In the east, the ROK II Corps quickly gave way, exposing the Army's right flank. In the center, the US 2nd and 25th Divisions suffered crushing defeats and began falling back, often in disorder. Only along the west coastal road, where my own battalion of the 21st Infantry had advanced virtually unopposed, did the Chinese fail to appear.

Item Company had gone into position on a frozen ridgeline well north of Chongju. On 26 November, we sent out a platoon-sized patrol which made little progress because of the snow and the rugged mountains. The next day's patrol, we were told, would have to go much deeper. The patrol leader selected for the job, grumbling about his bad feet and his diarrhea, took a "why me" attitude.

"What's the matter?" I said. "Do you want *me* to take the damned patrol out for you?"

"Yeah—that'd be great. And after all, you've been resting up as exec the last month and are probably in better shape than I am."

At first I couldn't believe he was serious. Then, when I realized he was, the idea started making sense. I *had* been feeling a bit left out of things, and this would be a chance to do something worthwhile. Also, I was worried about this particular lieutenant, and how he might react if his patrol ran into trouble.

Back at Battalion HQ, the S-3 showed me my patrol objective on the map. It was a broad valley, just south of Manchuria, and nearly fifteen miles to our front. A weird conversation then took place, during which it became clear those ordering the patrol felt this was something of a sacrificial mission to make the Chinese show their hand. I was instructed, perhaps as a salve to someone's conscience, to go out armed to the teeth and to return during daylight hours the same day I left.

The battalion exec, the S-3, the artillery liaison officer, the S-2 —all took turns briefing me on the route, the farthest point supporting artillery fire could reach, the requirement to bring along machine guns, mortars, and rocket launchers, and above all, the need to leave and return during daylight. They asked if I had questions, and I surely did.

"Is this a reconnaissance or a combat patrol? In other words, if I encounter any enemy, do I try to avoid them or do I fight them?"

"It's a recon patrol, Harry. But if you come across any enemy, we want you to knock them out."

That made no sense at all; neither did the answer to my next question. I told them about the rugged terrain in that sector, how our earlier patrol had averaged only a thousand meters an hour, and then asked, "Which takes priority—getting to the objective or getting back before dark? There's no way I can do both."

"We want you to go all the way to the objective, *and* we want you back before dark. That's all there is to it."

"Then can I forget about the heavy weapons and the extra men? If I take a couple of stripped-down squads, carrying just rifles and carbines, we might just be able to do it."

"No, we want you to go out in force, with at least fifty men. And bring the machine guns and mortars like we said."

We went around the track a couple more times, but I still couldn't get any straight answers, only wishes of "good luck" and exhortations to "be careful." Frustrated, I withdrew to a corner with Capt. John Burns, the artillery liaison officer. He more or less confirmed what I already suspected, that people were covering themselves by saying, "go out in force . . . carry heavy weapons . . . get back before dark," so they couldn't be blamed later if anything happened to me. They might realize I was being given conflicting, even impossible, instructions but that was *my* problem, not theirs, once they had relayed the orders from above.

Burns and I discussed artillery support, and I said I'd have to borrow a compass, since I'd lost the one I had. Listening nearby was a captain who had formerly commanded K Company. Recently a new man had taken over K, and this man had been given some sort of odd-job assignment at Battalion. The reasons were unknown, at least to me, although it was rumored there had been problems, maybe with battle fatigue, maybe with alcohol. I didn't know and didn't really care, except that now, for some reason, he decided to light into me.

"What do you want a compass for? Haven't you ever adjusted artillery fire?"

"Yes sir, I have."

"Where?"

"On the Naktong."

"Hell, if you think you need a compass, I don't believe you ever *were* on the Naktong!"

I turned to Captain Burns, who seemed embarrassed by the man's outburst. Softly, Burns explained one might adjust fire from prearranged check points, but that it *was* customary for the observer to use a compass, giving the azimuth from his own position to the target; so in effect I was right.

That seemed to make the captain even angrier. "Hell, these damned West Pointers. They think they're all such smart asses. What do they know about anything? They ought to teach them to walk before they start trying to run. . . ."

He didn't make much sense, and it was becoming apparent his problem wasn't with me, but stemmed from something deeper. I held my tongue and left; it didn't seem that further talk would solve anything, and I had enough problems of my own.

Back on the Item Company ridge, Gib and I decided on the composition of my "task force." I would have the 3rd Platoon, part of the weapons platoon, a machine-gun section from M Company, plus an artillery FO team, about sixty men in all. We would also pool our resources so I could have four radios with me and be able to set up relay stations as we went farther out. Larry Sullivan, platoon sergeant of the 3rd Platoon, would act as my second-in-command. I studied the map, plotted a route that would keep us mostly on high ground, and continued to puzzle over the confusing orders.

At last I reached a decision. We would comply with all the instructions about extra weapons, but only as we started out. There was no way we could stay in the mountains carrying all that extra load. Therefore, we would proceed from peak to peak, drop off our relay stations, and give each of them an overly generous security force for protection! By doing so, we could shed most of our heavy weapons and end up with a stripped-down "flying patrol" after all. It might be risky if we ran into a sizable number of Chinese, but if in truth we were a recon patrol, going out to develop the situation, I figured we could afford to trade firepower for mobility.

I briefed the squad leaders, told them we would get up an hour before sunrise and be on our way at first light. Then I suggested they get some sleep; it looked like a hard, cold day ahead.

On 27 November, with the Chinese attack in full gear, the 1st Cavalry Division was pulled out of Army reserve and set in motion. Jack Bender and his division recon platoon went into position on a hill behind the 2nd Division. Bill Marslender's company of the 7th Cavalry was near Sinchang, behind the ROKs, with Bill's platoon next to a road that came down from the north. The 5th Cavalry Regiment, which Jim Scholtz had just rejoined, was put on alert and made ready to move. When the move came, their route would be marked by Joe Toomey's I&R Platoon.

"Lieutenant, it's time to get up." It was Sullivan. I looked at my watch, peeked out cautiously at the blackness, and fought the temptation to close my eyes again. Slowly we came awake; men crawled from their bags and ventured reluctantly into the frosty dark. As we pulled ourselves together, I decided we had become waddlers rather than walkers. In my own case, for example, I had six layers of clothing above my waist: a T-shirt, woolen undershirt, OD shirt, GI sweater, pile liner, and field jacket. After draping binoculars over one shoulder and a bandoleer of ammunition over the other, pulling down the flaps of my pile "bunny cap," and picking up my weapon, I felt like an obese pack mule.

Breakfast consisted only of some tepid coffee sent forward from our mess section. There had been supply line problems, so not only would we miss breakfast, there would be no C-rations to stuff in our pockets. This meant, of course, there would be no eating until we returned from patrol, and even then it might be doubtful. We would just have to hope the supply people managed to push something forward.

Sullivan and the other noncoms gathered our patrol group together. I briefed them as well as I could, explaining about the radios and security teams we'd be dropping off, and then cautioned them we would be moving rather rapidly, so we'd be counting on each man to keep up.

We formed a column of two's and started off just as the sky began to lighten. Circling to the east, we came to a road that led generally north, followed the road up a gentle hill, and then descended into a broad valley. Once on the valley floor, we left the road and aimed northwest toward the ridge which was to be our patrol route. It looked forbidding.

A line of trees afforded us some cover as we crossed the valley, climbed a ridge, and reached the first peak. There we dropped off a radio man plus a few heavy weapons — ostensibly to guard the radio, but actually to lighten our load. We had gone but a few hundred more yards, when we met a group of refugees moving south.

"The Communists ran us out of our village," they told our interpreter. I showed them my map, which had both English and Korean lettering, and they pointed out their village.

"Who were these Communists, Koreans or Chinese?"

"Chinese — about fifty of them." We kept going, and a vague plan began to take shape. Perhaps we could move along the ridge and go into position above the village without being discovered. We could then bring artillery and mortar fire on the village and force the Chinese into the open. Then, from the ridge above, we could pour down fire with everything we had, and without being in much danger our-selves.

Suddenly the radio man ran up to me. "Sir, the relay station picked up a message for us."

The reception was good, and although Gib was talking to the radio relay, I could hear him directly. To my surprise, he was telling us to return. The patrol had been canceled.

There was a momentary feeling of disappointment. I couldn't explain it; certainly I was just as happy not to be going into danger. Then why the disappointment? Maybe it was that the refugees had given us an advantage. We knew where the fifty Chinese were; pre-sumably they didn't know about us. Now that we were turning back, that information had lost its value.

Then too, all the preparation and the walk up to this point had been wasted. Well, I thought, there must be a good reason. As we started back, someone asked, "Why are we turning around, Lieuten-ant? Do you suppose the war's over?"

"Beats me." Now that he had said it, though, that idea made as much sense as anything else. The more I thought about it, the more likely it seemed. After all, we *were* very close to Manchuria, and all along we had been saying that once we came this close to the border, the North Koreans and Chinese would probably call it quits. And what other reason could there be for canceling the patrol?

We reached the road, headed back the way we had come, and circled toward the I Company area. When we reached it, we found the company packed up and in a loose formation, ready to move at any moment. Gib called to me, "C'mon, Harry, get your men in col-umn. We've been waiting for you."

"Where we heading?"

"How the hell should I know? We're moving out; that's all they told me. I think the Chinese made a big attack somewhere. I'm sorry you can't take a break, but I can't help it. We're pulling out right now!"

We started walking. Back at the main highway, which was really just another two-lane frozen dirt road, we fell in with the rest of our battalion. It was noon before the first halt. The temperature had con-tinued to drop, snow was falling, and I was cold and hungry. The men seemed numb about the whole thing, which was a bad sign; some-how it would have been better if they had been griping.

Not knowing what to expect, but with a good bit of apprehen-sion, Jack Bender kept watching the road coming south from the 2nd Division sector. When Jack first came forward, his platoon had been supported by an attached British company. After the British had left, Jack had continued to send out patrols but so far had made no contact.

Their mission was mainly observation and early warning, but perhaps they could also provide some security to any retreating 2nd Division people. Once commo wires had been strung to his location, Jack strapped an EE-8 telephone to a tree near his own foxhole and called division to say he was in position.

Suddenly, to the north, they could hear firing. The sound of small arms, mingled with mortar shell explosions, grew closer. What they were hearing was the final portion of the tragedy described by S. L. A. Marshall in *The River and the Gauntlet*. Remnants of the 2nd Indianhead Division were fighting their way south along a valley road, while the Chinese, on dominating hills, continued to pour fire down on them. The first American unit, led by an engineer captain, approached Jack's position. Jeeps and trucks with shattered windshields and blown tires limped along, sometimes with one vehicle pulling another. Wounded men lay in the truck beds and on the hoods of the jeeps. The Americans, even those not wounded, looked dazed and beaten. A few men staggered along on foot, hanging on the vehicles for support. It was a pitiful, heartbreaking sight, especially since there was so little the recon people could do to help.

Jack cranked the EE-8 and called division to report the situation. The division chief of staff came on the line, and as they were talking, Bender heard the sound of approaching planes. At least the American column would have air support.

Looking up, Jack saw two Navy attack bombers, painted black, beginning their bombing run. Then, in horror, he realized *he* was the target!

Jack dove for his foxhole. The EE-8 handset was still in his hands, and as he scrambled, the wires were pulled loose, breaking the connection. When the planes pulled up, Bender got out of his hole and began reconnecting the two wires. As he did so, the chief of staff, not used to being cut off in midconversation by a mere lieutenant, cranked his own phone vigorously to ring Jack back.

Jack, holding the wires, was given the full benefit of the electrical charge. Gritting his teeth, he reconnected the phone and resumed the conversation. Just then the Navy planes returned for a second pass. Once again Jack dove for his hole, again breaking the connection. Once more he tried hooking up the phone wires, and once more he was given an electrical shock. After one or two more repetitions of this the chief of staff finally was given a full report, and the planes became convinced they were attacking a friendly unit.

The 2nd Division column continued to straggle south, and the recon platoon members gave what help they could. For the moment, the CCF opted not to pursue any further. Bender's platoon held its position, and after a time, they were sent on another mission.

Around 8:40 A.M. on 28 November, Joe Toomey and his I&R platoon left the 5th Cav HQ area near Pyongmyong to check out the road south to Sunchon. About an hour later, the regiment's 2nd Battalion, which included Jim Scholtz and his platoon of George Company, climbed into trucks and started along the same road.

As Toomey and his men reached a ferry crossing site of the Taedong River, they ran smack into a Chinese ambush. Almost before they knew it, they were completely surrounded. The platoon sergeant and two other men spun their jeep around, made a break for it, and managed to escape. Everyone else was either killed or captured.

The 2nd Battalion, alerted by the I&R platoon escapees, reached the ambush site just before noon. They dismounted from their trucks and deployed for an attack. Jim Scholtz had been back from the hospital barely two weeks; now he was in the middle of it again.

The trucks were turned around and told to try getting to Sunchon by another route. Fox Company, together with Scholtz's George Company, launched an attack but were unable to dislodge the well-prepared CCF. By late afternoon the battalion, despite taking seventy casualties, had made little progress. They sent for more ammo, evacuated as many of their wounded as they could, and resumed the attack. Finally the Chinese at the ambush site fell back, but to an even stronger position, where a full CCF regiment held two critical hills.

A company from the regiment's 3rd Battalion came forward to help, but it was no use. Joe Toomey's former company commander in I Company, out of loyalty to Joe, volunteered to lead a rescuing force to try bringing Joe back, but it would have been a foolhardy mission, and permission was denied.

Before it was over, more than two hundred men were either killed, wounded, or missing. After dark, Scholtz and the others, on foot, made their way overland by a bypass route, leaving the enemy in control of the road to Sunchon.

When Scholtz tried to find out what had happened to Toomey, someone said a group of prisoners had been seen being led away, and "one of them was very tall." That would have been Joe, the tallest man in our class. In the following weeks, the '49er grapevine passed the word around, saying Joe was probably a POW, and everyone felt sure he'd come out of it okay. Some two months later, Joe Toomey died in prison camp. No details of his death were ever learned.

On Thanksgiving Day, the 7th Cav had staged an award ceremony and the atmosphere seemed almost festive. Now, only a few days later, the Garry Owen troopers were shocked back into reality. Coming out of reserve, they had gone into position astride a narrow road east of Sinchang. The ROK unit north of them had given way, and there might or might not be any friendly units still remaining to their front.

The regiment buttoned up tight, with the 2nd Battalion left of the road, the 1st Battalion to the right, the 3rd in reserve. Bill Marslender and his men were on flat ground next to the road, on the left flank of his 1st Battalion.

Soon after the sun went down, it began to snow, and men who were already cold began to shiver still more. A little before midnight it stopped snowing, fog set in, and the temperature dropped even lower. All seemed still, and Marslender started getting into his sleeping bag to catch a little warmth. Suddenly, on the crisp night air, Bill heard the sound of a bugle. This was followed, within seconds, by more signals, from whistles and rams' horns, by shouts and by the roar of exploding grenades.

Almost before he could get out of his bag, Bill saw dozens of figures running into his platoon position. Organized resistance was already impossible as fierce hand-to-hand fighting broke out and men began heading for the rear. "Get back to the high ground!" Bill yelled.

They withdrew to the next ridge and began to regroup. Earlier, infiltrators had gotten behind the front-line companies, and soon not only the rifle companies, but both the 1st and 2nd battalion headquarters were under attack. The 3rd Battalion, which had been in regimental reserve, was committed in a counterattack, and the fighting continued throughout the night. Howitzers of the 77th Field fired round after round in close support, breaking up Chinese formations and inflicting hundreds of casualties.

Bit by bit, lost ground was retaken and the perimeter was restored, but at a heavy cost. In Bill's platoon alone, 11 men had been killed. Regimental casualties numbered 156, including 38 dead. However, the 7th Cavalry counted 350 CCF bodies inside the perimeter and estimated another 1,250 lay immediately outside.

Late in the afternoon of 25 November, artilleryman Dave Freeman was assigned as FO to Baker Company of the 187th RCT and told to report immediately to the company commander. Arriving at the company about 9:00 P.M., Dave was sent to the crest of Hill 171, east of Pyongyang, and told to check in with Sergeant Dumas, the platoon sergeant. The sergeant oriented Dave to the situation and told him where the enemy was located. Dave registered artillery on several points and then retired to his foxhole.

Later that night, Dave was awakened by small-arms fire and Dumas said he was heavily engaged. Freeman began calling for fire, and Dumas kept asking him to bring it in closer and closer. Dave knew it was close enough when a round landed between Sergeant Dumas, on the forward slope, and his own position on the crest. For an instant, Dave thought sure he had killed Dumas and his assistant, but fortunately they were hit only by flying dirt. Rather shakily, Dave suggested to the FDC that a hundred yards be added to the last volley.

Throughout the night, Dave remained on position adjusting fire. Finally the attack was repelled. Next morning, the ground in front of the position was found to be littered with enemy bodies.

Item Company had been walking for hours, and by this time the rubber boot shoepacs we'd been issued were a new source of complaint. The boots were good for warmth, but everyone agreed they were horrible for prolonged walking. During a temporary halt, our company medic, who had been with me in September when I was wounded, asked how my leg was holding up.

"The leg's okay," I said, "but thanks for asking. Right now, though, I'm too darned hungry to think about anything but food!" The coffee at breakfast was all I'd had for more than twenty-four hours.

With true generosity, he reached in his pocket and handed me three candy sour balls. They had been in a package from home he had received a few days earlier, and at the moment they looked mighty valuable. I popped one in my mouth and tried to make it last.

We kept going, and my earlier thought about the war being over seemed rather ludicrous. From all appearances, we were engaged in a full-scale retreat. The light was starting to fade when we next halted. What was to become of us? If we dropped where we were, we might be killed or captured; at the very least many would freeze. Nevertheless, by this time the idea of just settling to the ground began to have a certain appeal.

Presently several M-26 Pershing tanks came clanking up the road, and with engines roaring, stopped alongside our column. A lieutenant poked his head from the turret of the lead tank and yelled for us to climb aboard.

Pushing, pulling, handing up weapons and extra items of equipment, somehow we all managed to make it onto the tanks' back decks. We were jumbled together over the engine, where except for a couple of brackets on the turret, there was nothing to hold onto. The tankers said the mast of the radio antenna, the only thing resembling a handle, was strictly off limits, since a sudden jerk might break it off.

By the time all were loaded, we had a dozen or more on each tank, jammed together in a confused pattern. As the tanks began moving, we immediately had trouble keeping our balance. Two men were clinging to the projections on the turret; two more were hanging on to them; and the rest of us were just trying to balance each other. With all the weapons and other gear we were carrying, plus the jolting of the tanks, it wasn't easy.

We lurched back and forth, trying to steady each other so no one would fall off. I tried bending my knees like a skier, swaying with the motion of the tank. It worked for a while, but any sudden jerk by the tank still sent me off balance, clutching frantically for someone's arm.

An hour passed, then another. Noxious engine fumes were starting to make us groggy, and the engine grill on which we stood was becoming ever hotter from the prolonged running of the engine. Our boots' rubber soles acted as conductors, and we were getting a massive hot foot. Suddenly one of my feet would feel scorched; I'd lift it to let the boot cool, meanwhile struggling to keep my balance. Then I would put the boot down, and by that time the other foot would be burning. Others were doing the same, and we must have made a comical sight, a group of clumsy storks, standing on one leg at a time and clinging to each other for support.

About midnight we stopped for refueling. Five-gallon gas cans had been stacked alongside the road, and we formed a chain, passing the cans and pouring them one at a time into the near–empty tanks.

We loaded up again, the tanks lurched forward, and the same routine was repeated—men reeling awkwardly against each other, cursing the cold, cursing the engine fumes, cursing the heat of the deck. Twice the tank sergeant poked his head from the turret and scolded those clinging to the radio mast. They yelled back at him, suggesting what he could do with his mast.

Around 2:00 A.M., we passed through a town whose street was lined with simple shops, all of which were shuttered. Behind one or two of the shutters there seemed to be a faint glimmer of candlelight. By this time I was having to fight to stay awake. I felt cold, hungry, and wanted nothing more than just to close my eyes. Time passed.

My eyelids grew heavy and started to drift shut, causing me to lose my balance.

"Don't fall asleep, Lieutenant," a voice said.

"Mmm . . . okay . . . thanks," I mumbled.

My eyes closed again, and suddenly I was falling, pitching head-first over the side of the tank. Someone grabbed my legs, and for one horrifying instant I was dangling, with my head just inches from the rapidly turning track. Hands yanked me back and propped me upright. I thanked them; the nightmarish journey continued.

Around 4:00 or 5:00 A.M., while it was still dark, we left the road and turned into a snow-covered valley. The tanks stopped, and the crewmen shouted for us to dismount. I jumped to the ground, ran for the lead tank, and called for the lieutenant. Presumably his radio was working, and he was my only link—with anyone.

"What's happening?" I yelled.

"I don't know," he called back from the height of his turret, "but this is where we leave you. They said to drop you off here."

"But where are we? And where's the rest of my company?"

"I don't know. Get your men out of the way. We've got to get going."

The tanks backed and circled, then moved out toward the road from which we had come. The sound of their engines grew ever fainter and finally disappeared altogether. Men were milling about, muttering, questioning, grumbling.

I tried calling Gib on my radio, but could get no response. Jim Exley said, "It looks like you're in command, Harry."

"Mmm, yeah."

"Hey, what's going on, Lieutenant? Where are we? What's happening?"

All I could think to myself was, "How the devil should *I* know?" When I spoke, however, I tried to sound confident. "Never mind about that! For now the important thing is to take up some positions and 'circle the wagons.' First Platoon, go in on the left; Second Platoon, go up ahead to that first ridge and spread out; Third Platoon, you go in on the right. The Weapons Platoon will set up on that flat ground to the rear. The Company CP will be right where we're standing."

It was mainly bluster and bluff, but somehow they trusted me. In the darkness, I could hear the noncoms gathering their men and moving out, still grumbling, but at least feeling someone knew the big picture. Ha.

It was an eerie feeling, not knowing where we were or what was out in the darkness. Fortunately the feeling of isolation lasted but a few more hours. Soon after daylight, we were guided to a battalion assembly area. The kitchen and supply sections were already on hand, and the cooks even had some hot food prepared.

Evidently we had broken contact and escaped the Chinese trap. For a few hours at least, we were out of danger, and might even be able to relax.

10. X Corps Retreat from Chosin

29 OCTOBER–30 DECEMBER

At this point it becomes necessary to switch from a strict, chronological order when telling the story of '49ers in Korea. Just as Walker's Eighth Army and Almond's X Corps were operating independently of each other in November of 1950, their stories also become separated, with the chronologies running parallel and often overlapping.

The 7th Infantry Division had gone aboard ship at Pusan on 19 October, ostensibly to land at Wonsan and then, along with the Marine division, to drive west and capture the North Korean capital of Pyongyang. By 25 October, however, when the mines in Wonsan harbor had been cleared and the Marines were finally able to land, Pyongyang had already been captured by Walker's Eighth Army. At this point, MacArthur told X Corps commander Ned Almond to forget about Pyongyang and to head north.

The 7th Division, with twenty or more '49er lieutenants in its ranks, bypassed Wonsan and landed on 29 October at Iwon, some 150 miles farther north. First to land was the 17th Infantry Regiment, whose ranks included '49ers Hap Ware, Bob Fallon, Al English, George Orton, Reed Jensen, Bob Johnson, Bo Callaway (a future secretary of the army), and Pat Vollmer. The 17th Infantry, together with the 49th Field Artillery Battalion, was sent rushing north toward Hyesanjin on the Manchurian border.

On 31 October, at Pungsan, the 17th Infantry ran into heavy opposition, and the fighting went on for four days. During the action, Hap Ware was wounded as he led his men forward to secure a hill. He was evacuated by air to a hospital ship in Wonsan harbor, where he died on 5 November. To the members of Hap's company, it was a tragic loss, for in the preceding weeks, he had won the respect and affection of officers and men alike. The chaplain who conducted the memorial service for Hap wrote to Janet, Hap's young wife, saying: "The officers and men solemnly pledged to be better Christians and soldiers as a memorial to your husband."

Later, Hap's classmate, Paul Monahan, a member of the 7th Division Signal Company, came across a neatly lettered sign at the entrance to a 17th Infantry command post. It read: "CAMP WARE, Named in honor of LT 'Hap' Ware, KIA—Pungsan, North Korea, November 1950." Paul made a photo of the sign, thinking the ever-buoyant Hap would have smiled about being part of a memorial, but would also have been touched and pleased by the remembrance.

About the same time, Bob Fallon was also hit, suffering five bullet wounds. He was evacuated and eventually ended up in Washington as a patient at Walter Reed Army Hospital. While there, Bob wrote "It's Happening on Your Own Front Lawn" (see Appendix A), an essay that appeared in many newspapers and magazines, including the *Saturday Evening Post*, the *Reader's Digest*, the *Washington Star*, and the *Richmond News Leader*.

The other two regiments of the 7th Division, the 31st and 32nd, landed at Iwon on 3 and 4 November. For the first couple of days, local patrols were sent out, searching for any North Korean units which might remain in the area. Jack Madison and Joe Kingston's I Company of the 32nd Regiment was then given a unique mission. The company, crammed into boxcars, headed north on a train operated by North Korean civilians. Initially their route took them along the coast; they then headed westward, following the Ungi River valley and climbing ever higher until all around were the towering peaks of the Taebaek Mountains.

In the darkness and the snow, with the temperature continuing to fall, the train labored upward. Occasionally the wheels would slip on the icy tracks and the crew would have to dismount and spread sand. As they passed through a series of mountain tunnels, they were well aware that this was territory which had not been cleared of the enemy, and that every tunnel posed a threat. Finally they reached their objective, a hydroelectric plant near the Fusen Reservoir, which they were told to secure and to keep in operation.

Madison's platoon was given the mission of guarding the nearby village, home of the plant's workers and their families. Many of these people, having been warned about alleged American atrocities, had taken to the hills. However, when they realized they were not to be mistreated, they soon returned and were more than willing to keep the vital power plant in operation.

Jack, acting as a sort of military governor, decided to give the people a lesson in democracy and said an election would be held so the town could freely elect a mayor. The election was held, and somewhat predictably, the people elected the same Communist official who had formerly held that office. The man fully expected, as soon as the Americans learned his identity, that the price of victory would be summary execution. He was greatly relieved when he was left unharmed and allowed to remain in office.

With the power plant operating smoothly, it was time for I Company to rejoin the regiment. A truck convoy came for them, moving cautiously in weather of minus-20 degrees over icy, precipitous mountain roads which were little more than trails. On the way out, a trailer was lost as it plunged down a 2,000-foot cliff. Later, a truck overturned, severely injuring ten of its occupants.

Back with the regiment, I Company joined the column advancing from Samsu to the Yalu. In the lead was a platoon of K Company under Lt. Bob Kingston (no relation to Joe). The platoon ran into heavy resistance, and I Company was sent forward as reinforcement. I's commander, Capt. Jim Spettel, assumed command of the task force, which was reinforced with 81-mm and 4.2" mortars, two tanks, a bulldozer, and self-propelled AA guns. Overhead was a much-appreciated continuous air cap of Marine F4U Corsairs. After more heavy going, they reached the river, and on 28 November, Jack, Joe Kingston, and Bob Kingston were able to perform the hallowed ritual of relieving themselves in the Yalu, just to prove they were there.

On 25 November, X Corps issued an ambitious and highly controversial attack order, one which seemed to assume that the CCF opposing X Corps were of little consequence. The Marine division would concentrate west of the Chosin Reservoir, and a regimental task force from the 7th Division would replace the Marines east of Chosin. Both forces were to launch an attack two days later, on 27 November.

For the 7th Division, it became a scramble even to get in position within the two days allotted. Most of its units were a hundred miles away, at or near the Yalu. Consequently the units closest to the Chosin, two battalions of the 31st Infantry, the 1st Battalion of the 32nd Infantry, and the 57th FA Battalion, were designated Task Force MacLean (named for the 31st Regiment's commander) and rushed east of Chosin. First on the scene, and hence leading the way, was the 1st Battalion of the 32nd Regiment, led by LTC Don Faith, the man who had once asked Madison and Kingston if they were prepared to die. Three members of our class, Bill Kempen, Herb Marshburn, and Bill

Herbert Edgar Marshburn. Courtesy US Military Academy Archives.

Penington were platoon leaders in Faith's battalion. West Point '49 was also represented in the 57th Field, where Keith Sickafoose and Joe Giddings were both assigned and farmed out as FOs with the 31st Infantry, Joe with B Company, Keith with K.

The 3rd Battalion of the 32nd Infantry, meanwhile, including Joe Kingston and Jack Madison's I Company, became the last unit to get out of Samsu. (The ROK regiment that replaced them was almost completely destroyed.) On the second day of the withdrawal, Joe was told to take a jeep patrol over the mountains and to try making contact with Eighth Army. He made a valiant effort, but even the rugged jeeps couldn't cross mountains where there was no road.

Their unit, at the tail end of the column, and still separated, started back to the Hamhung area, at first on foot, and later on trucks. As they neared Hamhung, Jack was sent on ahead to find out where the regiment wanted I Company to go into position. When he asked about it at the S-3 section, there was a stunned silence, after which someone said: "You're asking about I Company? Why, we've written I Company off!" Jack was happy to report that the company was still intact and on the road, a couple of hours behind him. Upon arrival, they were quickly fitted into the perimeter.

On the night of 27 November, in subzero temperatures, massive waves of Chinese, blowing bugles and horns, launched simultaneous attacks on the Marines west of Chosin, on Faith's battalion to the east, and on the 3rd Battalion of the 31st Infantry a few miles to the south.

A and B companies of the 32nd, on the north side of Faith's perimeter, suffered heavy losses, including Marshburn's A Company commander, who was killed that first night. Next morning the battalion regrouped, called in an air strike, and punished the Chinese severely. Still the CCF held their position and prepared, once darkness fell, to resume the battle.

That same night, the CCF attacked the 31st Infantry and the 57th Field farther south, breaking through the rifle companies, then attacking the artillery batteries. Shortly before 3:00 A.M., Keith Sickafoose ran back to the artillery position to tell them the infantry was withdrawing to their rear. Thanks to Keith's warning, the artillerymen set up a perimeter defense and fought off the swarming Chinese.

Next evening, to the now-familiar sound of bugles and horns, the Chinese launched another ferocious attack, and once more the losses were heavy. Tragically, one of the killed was '49er Bill Kempen. As our yearbook put it, soft-spoken Bill, who "could always find time to talk about beautiful girls and fast horses," had been "liked by everyone." Now he lay dead in the snow.

Miraculously, Herb Marshburn was still unscathed. An artillery officer with A Company described that night by saying: "The Chinese stepped up their attack and made the mistake of trying to overrun Herb's machine guns. Herb put on a one-man show and proceeded to make a human parapet of oriental bodies in front of his guns."

On 29 November, Faith's battalion pulled back and joined the remainder of Task Force MacLean. During the day, Colonel MacLean was captured by the Chinese, leaving Faith in command of the now-surrounded Task Force. The CCF pressed their attacks, inflicting heavy casualties, and on 1 December, Faith gave the order to withdraw south so as to link up with friendly forces. The breakout proved to be an almost impossible task, as weary men on foot, accompanied by trucks carrying the wounded, headed along the reservoir's east shore in sub-zero weather. The CCF on surrounding hills poured devastating mortar and small-arms fire onto the hapless Americans, turning the column into a chaotic mass of dead bodies and burning vehicles.

At one point, Marshburn and that same artillery officer crept down a ditch together, only to be met by small-arms fire and a shower of grenades. Then they lost track of each other.

Lt. James Mortrude, a platoon leader from C Company, made it as far as a blown-out bridge. To advance beyond that point, it would be necessary to silence the enemy guns on Hill 1221. Just then, Mortrude and his men were joined by Marshburn and a group from A Company. As the two officers led their men forward, Mortrude was hit and temporarily knocked unconscious. When he came to, Marshburn told Mortrude he was bleeding badly and needed attention. Herb then offered to take all available men forward toward Hill 1221, with Mortrude following as soon as he was able. There was no way for them to know that by this time a full Chinese regiment was on that hill. Herb bravely led his men forward, but the enemy was waiting in force, and a few minutes later, the gallant Marshburn was killed.

In the next few confusing hours, both Colonel MacLean and Colonel Faith (who received a posthumous Medal of Honor) were killed. A few men managed to cross the ice and make their way to the Marine perimeter and safety, but the number who got away was pitifully small.

On the night of 29 November, as the troops east of Chosin were trying to break out from the Chinese trap, B Company of the 31st Infantry was made part of Task Force Drysdale, named for Lieutenant

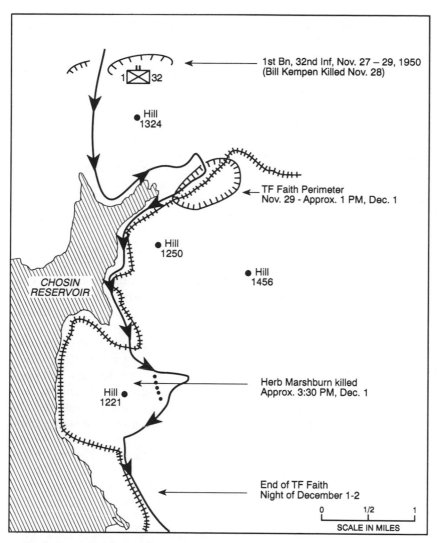

1st Bn, 32nd Inf, Nov. 27 – 29, 1950
(Bill Kempen Killed Nov. 28)

Hill 1324

TF Faith Perimeter
Nov. 29 - Approx. 1 PM, Dec. 1

Hill 1250

Hill 1456

CHOSIN RESERVOIR

Herb Marshburn killed
Approx. 3:30 PM, Dec. 1

Hill 1221

End of TF Faith
Night of December 1-2

0   1/2   1
SCALE IN MILES

Task Force Faith Breakout Attempt, 27 November–2 December 1950

Colonel Douglas Drysdale of the British Royal Marines. The Task Force, which included some of Drysdale's men as well as B Company, left Koto-ri with the mission of cutting through the Chinese and reinforcing the beleaguered US Marines at Hagaru-ri, some eleven miles away.

One of B Company's platoon leaders was '49er Al Anderson, who, before attending West Point, had played varsity football for two years at the University of Missouri, where he was an All-Conference tackle. At the Academy, Al had been a teammate of Doc Blanchard and Glenn Davis on Army's team that won the national championship. Also with B Company, as artillery FO, was Al's classmate and friend, Joe Giddings.

Just north of Koto-ri, B Company ran into a Chinese ambush at a spot that became known as "Hell's Fire Valley," and before it was over, the Task Force had been cut to pieces. Joe, acting more like a platoon leader than an artillery observer, did everything possible to help the company organize a defensive perimeter. Anyone who knew him would not have been surprised, for New Jerseyite Joe Giddings had always been a good man to have around, whether he was participating fiercely in intramural athletics, or laughing and playing his guitar at a company party.

The company took up positions, but soon men were falling as an enemy sniper placed himself in a spot from which he could fire into the company perimeter. Without hesitation, Joe left his own covered position to go locate the sniper, even though it meant exposing himself. He managed to knock out the sniper, but as he did so, Joe himself was mortally wounded.

Ironically, Joe and Bill Kempen, members of the same cadet company, had died within a few miles of each other without either knowing of the other's presence. (Don Gower and Joe Giddings had been together in Pusan as the 7th Division was loading up for the landing in North Korea. That was the last time they saw each other. Months later, Don met a Marine who had buried Joe's body in the frozen ground of North Korea.)

The Chinese continued to press their attack, and before it was over, more than a hundred men of B Company were either killed or missing. With over half the company down, and many of the survivors seriously wounded, complete disaster seemed imminent. At that point Al Anderson showed the kind of initiative which had made him a star on the football field. During the night, Al gathered what men he could find and formed them into a defensive perimeter.

Historian Roy Appleman described Al's next actions, for which he was later awarded a DSC: "Armed only with his .45 pistol, he set an example of leadership throughout the night. Twice he closed with enemy soldiers who entered his perimeter and killed them at arm's length, deflecting their weapons with one arm as he used his pistol in these close encounters. At 6:00 A.M. on 30 November, Anderson received orders to withdraw that part of B Company under his control. He led them back safely through enemy opposition to Koto-ri."

FO Don Gower was still with Lew Baumann and George Company of the 32nd Infantry when it landed at Iwon and proceeded north. Since they'd been two days behind the Marines at Inchon, and landed administratively at Iwon, they were never in a position to receive an amphibious invasion "arrowhead" for their Korean Service Medal. (Later they joked that they should get one to wear upside down to show they'd been driven into the sea by the Chinese.)

During their time in North Korea, Lew Baumann was constantly running patrols. On one of these, his group ambushed an NK militia detachment which included a paymaster carrying a large quantity of old-style North Korean money. They turned in the payroll, but each man kept a few "won" as a souvenir.

All this time, they had been living on B- and C-rations, occasionally supplemented by domestic apples or rabbit, and on at least one occasion, according to Gower, by a wild little saber-toothed deer. Consequently, when one of Baumann's patrols found a farmer who owned not only vegetables, but also many chickens, ducks, and geese, it used its "won" to trade with him.

A few days earlier, Lew had been told he was being considered as a possible aide-de-camp to General Hodes, the assistant division commander, whose son Jack, a '49er classmate, was in the 1st Cavalry Division. Lew said he wasn't interested, that he liked being a platoon leader, and he stuck to that, even when his regimental commander assured him it was a great opportunity and would be good for his career. This refusal piqued General Hodes's interest, so he came forward to meet Baumann in person, arriving at George Company while Lew was out on patrol.

Hodes was standing with the company exec when the unkempt, odd-looking patrol arrived carrying its newly acquired poultry.

"Which one is Lieutenant Baumann?" Hodes asked.

The embarrassed exec, shuffling his feet, said quietly, "Uh, sir, he's the one with the goose."

Hodes then questioned Lew, both to assure himself that the fowls had been purchased legally and to find out why Lew didn't want to be an aide. Once again, Lew explained that he liked being with troops and that he didn't think he was the aide type. The general, perhaps influenced by the goose slung over Lew's shoulder, said he understood.

When the Chinese hit the Chosin Reservoir area, Baumann's George Company was told by telephone that trucks would pick them up and take them south in the morning. Don Gower then received a call from his liaison officer telling him to leave George at that time and rejoin his artillery battalion at Samsu. Next morning Don and his FO crew drove north. It was not snowing, but snow had fallen and there were no tire tracks, which seemed odd. After awhile, one jeep with a wire team came from the north. The driver said they'd had to build a fire to warm the engine to get started, since there was nobody left in Samsu to give them a pull. Then they gunned it south.

Don and his party continued on, finally arriving at Samsu, which had empty foxholes filled with snow, lots of dangling commo wire, but no Americans. Moreover, the few villagers they saw looked rather hostile. They turned the jeep around and drove south. It was a long, lonely trip, with many anxious moments, before they managed to reach American lines at Sang-ni.

Months later, Don's liaison officer said he'd known Don should go either to Samsu or Sang-ni, because he knew the destination began with an "S," but it was so cold that he did not wish to leave the warmth of the hut he was in and go check the map, which was in his jeep. Thus, for a few unhappy hours, he'd made Don the northernmost American in North Korea. Although Gower did not shoot the liaison officer, the thought crossed his mind.

A few days later, Jack Madison wrote home:

Well, I suppose the war news looks pretty bad on the home front. Matter of fact, it looks pretty bad from over here. We had no trouble getting up to the Yalu, but the Chinese had different plans. We made a hasty withdrawal to the Hamhung-Hungnam area, where we are now. It was tragic to see our columns have to turn tail. On icy mountain roads we lost a terrific amount of equipment. As I rode along in my jeep on the 270 mile trip back to Hamhung, I saw tanks that had slipped over the sides and rolled into the bottom of a valley hundreds of feet below; 105's, 155's, prime movers, and 2½ tons by the dozens. They had to be destroyed because there was no time or equipment to get them back on the road.

While we were on our way back from Samsu . . . our 1st Battalion was hit by the Chinese and cut off, along with the Marines. We still have not received any detailed information on them, but they have suffered a terrific number of casualties.

Slowly, painfully, the Army and the Marines withdrew to Hamhung and the nearby port of Hungnam. On 16 December, Army forces demolished and abandoned Hamhung, then withdrew to Line A, above Hungnam. A strong defensive arc was established, complete with mines, barbed wire, well-planned fields of fire, naval gunfire support from offshore, and an almost continuous air cover. Although the CCF launched a few local attacks, no all-out effort was made to complete the destruction of X Corps. Perhaps they hesitated because of the strength of the new perimeter, or perhaps it was because the Chinese, according to one estimate, had taken over forty thousand casualties by this time, and half those remaining were suffering from frostbite.

When the time came for Jack Madison's platoon to withdraw from the perimeter, the relieving platoon leader, from the 65th Regiment of the 3rd Division, turned out to be '49er Art Underwood. The 65th was from Puerto Rico, and Jack sympathized with Art's communication problem. When Art wanted something done, he had to first tell the platoon sergeant, who then translated Art's words into Spanish so the troops could understand.

On 20 December, I Company rode LCVPs out from Hungnam and then climbed aboard the *USS Billy Mitchell.* As Madison and Kingston reached the deck level, one of the first things they saw was the Officers' Mess, where waiters in starched white jackets were carrying huge silver trays and serving strawberry shortcake. After taking their first bath in weeks, they put on the clean fatigues that had been laid out, murmured a prayer of appreciation to the Navy, and headed for the shortcake. It was a glorious form of culture shock.

That evening Jack wrote home again, saying:

> As we withdrew, we occupied the first Main Line of Resistance, and then, when enough people had embarked, we went to a second position and so on. The Chinese pushed us pretty hard, but we didn't have any real trouble keeping them off. . . . So here I am, still in one piece, out of North Korea, and I thank God I am. Some of my men were not so lucky. I lost one of my recoilless rifle squads—6 men—and my jeep driver. They went on a patrol with our 3rd Platoon and never made it back. . . . Joe is fine, and doing a real job. I've run into many classmates lately since we withdrew into so small an area. It is good to see each one of them.

By any standard, the evacuation from Hungnam was a remarkable feat. The Navy brought out 105,000 troops, 17,500 vehicles, and 350,000 measurement tons of cargo. They also crammed 91,000 Korean refugees onto the ships, although sadly enough, thousands more had to be left behind. By Christmas Eve, the withdrawal was complete and 200 drums of gasoline, plus the tons of explosives still on the beach, were detonated, creating an impressive fireworks display as the last ships pulled away.

West Point '49ers of X Corps celebrated Christmas with mixed emotions. They were happy to be clear of Hungnam and out of North Korea. At the same time, they realized X Corps had suffered a disastrous defeat, one of the worst in American military history.

11. Eighth Army Retreat

30 NOVEMBER–31 DECEMBER

As November ended, the CCF Offensive was gaining momentum and a dispirited Eighth Army was falling back, hoping to establish a defensive line near Pyongyang. In Tokyo, MacArthur met with X Corps commander Ned Almond and Eighth Army commander Walton Walker, after which he announced that massive Chinese intervention meant the beginning of "an entirely new war." GHQ and Eighth Army communiqués said the move north had caused the Chinese to tip their hand prematurely. In other words, the UN strategy had kept the CCF trap from succeeding and, in effect, had been a wise move.

Lieutenants on the ground recognized the proclamations as an obvious attempt to put the best face on a bad situation. No one was fooled; we had walked into a trap, been badly beaten, and were now in full retreat.

By this time more and more '49ers were in Korea, including nine bachelor engineers who had arrived from Okinawa. Ironically, engineer assignment orders had given married officers priority for Japan, where family quarters would be available. Hence, when hostilities began and units were rushed from Japan to Korea, married officers ended up in combat, while the bachelors, as George Stukhart put it, spent "three months in various important jobs, like counting fire extinguishers." George, Ed Townsley, and others, even back at Camp Stoneman before leaving the States, had tried in vain to have their Okinawa orders changed to Korea. Then, when they arrived in Okinawa, they found their proposed unit, the 76th Engineer Battalion, was shipping out and leaving them behind. Finally, in October, they had left for Korea. George ended up in the badly decimated 2nd Division, Townsley in the 25th Division. Harry Griffith, the Class of '49's First Captain, went to SCARWAF, the Air Force construction unit.

In November, soon after the appearance of the first MiGs in combat, the Air Force released a number of F-86 Sabres and F-84 Thunderjets for Korean duty. At San Diego, planes of the 27th Fighter-Escort Group were loaded aboard the carrier *Sitko Bay*, and two weeks later they were at Itazuke Air Base in Japan. By 5 December, '49ers Floyd Stephenson, Dave Barnes, and other pilots of the 27th Group were established at K-2, the airbase near Taegu.

About the same time, Doug Bush and the 335th Fighter Squadron, flying F-86 Sabres, arrived at Kimpo's K-14, near Seoul. In the next month, Doug was to fly ten combat missions as wing man for his squadron commander. It was exciting duty, but for ex-infantryman Bush there was also a frustration; because of its speed, the F-86 was unsuited for rendering close air support to men on the ground.

Floyd Stephenson (his family called him "Bo," but to most '49ers he was Steve), the son of a career Marine officer, had lived at a series of overseas posts and in the process had become a skilled linguist. The chargé d'affaires at the Mexican Embassy had in fact once remarked that Steve's Spanish was letter perfect, the best he had ever heard from any person whose native tongue was English. He was a good musician, a varsity gymnast, and a fine pilot, one who was understandably proud of his F-84 Thunderjet.

Tragically, on 13 December, a bare week after his arrival in Korea, Floyd Stephenson's F-84 went down, and Steve became the first Air Force member of our class to be killed in action.

Mike Wadsworth had been evacuated through medical channels, arriving in Japan about the same time that Doug Bush and Floyd Stephenson were shipping out. Sadly, his multiple wounds proved fatal, and on 3 December, in Osaka, Mike breathed his last.

Mike's platoon sergeant, Henry Heissner, wrote to Bette Wadsworth, saying:

> From the moment that Lt. Wadsworth arrived at my platoon while we were in a rest area I knew that I had received a prize. In no time at all he had shown by his leadership that he was the kind of an officer that you will follow to "Hell and back." . . . He was in most cases ahead of the scouts and on several occasions I had to remind him that it was his job to direct the platoon's actions and not scout for it. . . . I am positive that you must know that

he was really a wonderful type of person, and having had 4 previous platoon leaders in Korea and 13 in Europe during World War II, I honestly believe that he was my best and certainly had a great military future ahead of him. . . . I can justly say that I am glad to have been a member of his platoon, if even for a little while. . . .

While the 21st Infantry, including our own Item Company, was retreating on a line running along Korea's west coast, the Chinese were moving on a parallel line farther inland and periodically slicing in to attack the column both from the front and rear. Although I Company, near the middle of the column, had so far not been in direct contact, there were times when we could hear firing both ahead of us and behind us.

During a halt, I wrote a quick letter home. The mail orderly said he would keep it for me, but that he hadn't been able to forward any mail for days, and in fact was still holding a letter or two I had written the week before. His problem made me admit to myself what I had so far suppressed. We were more or less cut off. However, we kept going, to Sunchon, then Pyongyang, retracing the route we'd followed rather hopefully just a few days earlier. Finally it seemed we had broken contact; thanks to US mobility, we had been able to flee faster than the Chinese could follow.

After a week of retreating, we set up a defensive position and established our Company CP in an abandoned house. A few months earlier, that primitive hut might have repelled me, but now it looked snug and inviting.

Early next morning, the stillness was shattered by an explosion just outside our door. There was a yell, and we ran outside to see what had happened.

It was a freak accident. Some men from the Weapons Company had been sleeping on piles of rice straw in the courtyard. As they were getting up, a grenade must have fallen from someone's pocket. Then, shivering in the morning air, the soldiers had built a fire, using the straw as a base. The grenade had exploded, killing one man and wounding two others.

We worked our way south and were told we'd be going into permanent defensive positions, where we'd stay for the rest of the winter. The Chinese kept pursuing, moving mostly at night and hiding during the day. Orders came encouraging us, as we moved south, to burn any structures that might provide cover for the enemy.

Our convoy stopped alongside the road, and the new I Company sector was pointed out. It was exciting; finally we'd be able to prepare a solid defense, with good fields of fire, barbed wire, mines, and well-dug emplacements.

Just behind our new line was a large Korean house, tucked away in a peaceful valley. We commandeered it for a Company CP and told the occupants, a distinguished-looking elderly couple, they would have to leave. They moved about, sad, flustered, packing a few belongings into bundles. I asked the interpreter to tell them I didn't know what would happen to their house, but since we were going to be there a while, I'd do what I could to safeguard their possessions. The interpreter seemed puzzled. Why was the lieutenant bothering? What were these people to him? Still, he talked to them and transmitted my message. They bowed their appreciation and before leaving said something about their son, a doctor, who had studied in the States and was now working somewhere in South Korea. They had a young woman and child with them, probably the family of that son. Presently the old gentleman shouldered an overloaded A-frame; the younger woman strapped the baby on her back, and both women balanced bundles on their heads. Then off they trudged, a sad little group.

Although we had grown accustomed to refugees, the intimacy with this family—seeing them in their home, then seeing them forced from that home, made me feel especially depressed. After they left, I leafed through some discarded books, including some medical texts in English. It put that family and their son on a more personal plane and made the situation even more poignant.

We remained in our "permanent" position exactly one day. The Chinese had pulled an outflanking maneuver in another sector, and we again had to withdraw before they could cut us off. The company came down from the hills, assembled at the road, and waited for trucks to take us south. The 1st sergeant, who knew of the scorched earch policy, offered to go burn the house we had been occupying.

I thought of the elderly couple with the son who was a doctor. "No, let's leave that one alone," I said.

But I was too late. As I looked back, I could see a rising column of black smoke; someone had come behind us and torched the place. Maybe the legalized arson would keep some Chinese from finding shelter, but somehow I felt we had dishonored ourselves.

The plan to establish a defense around Pyongyang was quickly forgotten. The movement south was becoming more and more frantic. On the drive north, Bill Moore and his engineer unit had been builders, repairing roads, setting out floating bridges, often erecting fixed bridges. Now, as we retreated, they and other engineers became destroyers. Bridges, ammunition dumps, gasoline supply points, everything that couldn't be evacuated was blown up to keep it from the enemy. Although winter clothing had been arriving, a third of our division had yet to receive it. In some cases, men passed warehouses about to be blown and grabbed badly needed overcoats or parkas for themselves, sometimes having to plead for the demolition to be delayed so they could do so. Untold dozens, perhaps hundreds, of trucks, tanks, and artillery pieces were likewise destroyed and abandoned. It seemed like the end of everything for Eighth Army.

Beecher Brian's company of the 1st Cavalry Division was temporarily in reserve, and Beech, who had recently been promoted from platoon leader to company exec, wrote home: "We have sent out many patrols, but as yet we have contacted nothing but a few guerrillas. I feel that we will be moving tomorrow or the next day for sure. I hope we will be moving south and will soon load on boats to get out of here. I am at a quandary as to what is the long range strategical plan. They *must* be planning to get us out of Korea. I don't know what good we can do here. Well, we'll find out within the month what is coming off, if not sooner. . . ."

Item Company kept moving south, along the traditional invasion corridor toward Uijongbu and Seoul. This was the route the North Koreans had used in the first days of the war, and I presumed aggressors had come this way for centuries.

The trucks were unloaded, and Colonel Mac had all company commanders and execs join him on a bald hill near the road. The S-3 pointed out each company's sector, mentioning in passing that the 38th Parallel was less than a hundred yards to our front. Across the valley north of us, we saw a network of low ridges, and behind them a series of high, snow-covered mountains. Mac said he felt sure the Chincsc had already deployed in them.

Meanwhile, our artillery liaison officer, Capt. John Burns, was registering concentrations on potential future targets. An artillery shell crashed on the slope to our front. "Hey, Burns," someone said with a laugh. "watch those short rounds. Your gunners are supposed to be registering on those hills across the way—not this one!"

The S-3 continued pointing out positions. Another shell exploded in front of us. A moment later one landed off to the right and slightly behind us. "Hey, Burns, what in hell's going on?"

"I don't think that was ours. . . ." Before he could finish his sentence, there was a high-pitched whine followed by an explosion a few yards behind us. It had landed nearly in our midst.

"*That,*" said Colonel Mac, "was *incoming!*" Even as he spoke, we heard the shrill whistle of another incoming round. I dived for a nearby foxhole. Quick as I was, a lieutenant from M Company was even faster. He hit the hole first, and a split second later, I piled in on top of him. Round after round came screaming in, and we lay in the hole immobilized.

I said something to the lieutenant about what an inviting target we must have made—a group of officers, looking through binoculars and standing on the skyline big as life.

He agreed. Then he said, "Harry, you're hit!"

"No, I don't think so. At least I don't feel anything."

"You better check, damn it, 'cause you're bleeding all over me!"

Sure enough, I was dripping blood, but it was coming from my nose. When I landed, my nose must have hit his elbow, and now the blood was flowing steadily. It was worse for him than me, and cramped as we were, I couldn't do anything to stop it. After a few minutes things grew quiet. Cautiously we left the hill, this time making sure to stay low.

I asked my brother officer if he was going to write me up for a Purple Heart because of all the blood I'd dripped on him.

"Go to hell," he said.

On the morning of 23 December, Gen. Walton Walker visited our 24th Division HQ, conferred with Gen. Gar Davidson, then set off for the British Commonwealth Brigade. Walker's jeep was heading north on an icy road at breakneck speed when it collided head-on with a southbound South Korean army vehicle. The general was taken immediately to a nearby MASH unit, but was dead on arrival.

Back in Washington, Gen. Matt Ridgway was designated as Walker's replacement. Within a day, he was on his way, flying to the Far East in a four-engine Constellation provided by the Air Force. Ridgway had his work cut out for him. He later wrote that "the spirit of the Eighth Army as I found it on my arrival there gave me deep concern. There was a definite air of nervousness, of gloomy foreboding, of uncertainty, a spirit of apprehension as to what the future held."

Item Company's right flank touched the road leading south to Uijongbu and Seoul. Our left and center were on a series of low knobs. We bent our line back on the left, or as our West Point tactics classes might have put it, we "refused our flank," since there was no one on our immediate left.

Item's nearest neighbor, several hundred yards to the west, was a battalion of the 19th Infantry, where one of the platoon leaders was my classmate John "Rigger" Ragucci. It wasn't the first time Rigger and I had been neighbors. We both came from upstate New York—I from Syracuse and Rigger from nearby Auburn.

One of our squads set up on a finger-like ridge, which extended out from the left of our line. The jutting finger made a handy spot for an outpost; conversely, it also made a convenient pathway for someone wanting to come at us from the north.

They hit us on the second night. Around midnight, I was on the reverse slope behind a trench dug by former occupants, and had just crawled into my sleeping bag. Suddenly I heard scattered shots coming from the vicinity of the outpost, followed by the ugly hum of burp guns. Still in my sleeping bag, I rolled into the trench and landed heavily. More firing. Flashes from an automatic weapon. Confusion.

A voice came over the radio, "We've been hit! Some of the outpost is back in, but their squad leader is dead. We've got some wounded, and some others we can't account for. . . ."

The firing continued, and it was impossible to tell what was happening. More noise, a few seconds of silence, and then shots started coming my way. The Chinese, now on the former outpost position, were able to shoot down the length of our line. In the darkness, we hesitated to return the fire, since we might well end up shooting into our own men. Bullets were passing just above my head, and I hoped the enemy gunners could just fire *across* the trench and not *into* it. Automatic-weapons fire laced back and forth, including tracers which left a greenish trail. They arced through the blackness, and it was eerie to watch luminous bullets pass a few feet overhead.

Gib, a few feet away from me, was talking to our 3rd Platoon on the radio, but he wasn't learning much. For the moment, it was a standoff; even the platoon in contact wasn't sure who was where. Gib asked the artillery to fire an illuminating shell, then he and I crawled onto the forward slope so as to see the enemy's location when the flare opened. There was a rushing sound overhead followed by a pop. It was a fizzle; the flare ignited for a second or two, then went out. It was just as well, since it had been slightly behind us and would have shown us to the enemy rather than the other way around.

Our FO called for another flare and told them to increase the range. This one popped almost directly over our heads, and Gib and

I hugged the ground. Fortunately it burned only slightly longer than the first one.

"Damn it, tell them to increase the range and try again!" Gib said. There was a delay. The FO's conversation with the Fire Direction Center (FDC) seemed to be taking a long time. Gib, who was becoming more and more agitated, told him to shake things up.

"Sir, I've got a problem," the FO said.

"I don't care about your problem," Gib said. "Get us some flares up here!"

"Sir, the people back at the FDC say there's a shortage of flares. They want to know if it's a real emergency."

That did it. Gib grabbed the mike and started screaming: "We have a dead man up here. Do you want to come up and smell the blood? When I have people getting killed, I consider it an emergency! Do you want to argue about it?"

Finally we received another flare, this time where we wanted it, and it gave us a good sighting. Our left flank people started firing, keeping the enemy pinned down.

At this point, concealed by the darkness, most of the Chinese faded away, leaving only a handful to cover their withdrawal. Evidently this had been a probe to fix our location, not a full-scale attack. At first light, two squads, all that could use the connecting ridge, counter-attacked and regained the outpost position.

Next morning we sent out a reinforced squad patrol. They had gone less than two miles when they were fired on from both flanks. Two men were slightly wounded, but fortunately everyone made it back.

Obviously the Chinese now knew where we were. Maybe that meant they would avoid us. Maybe not. One thing for sure—they weren't fading away.

Soldiers of the X Corps, including the '49ers of the 3rd and 7th divisions, were happy to be clear of the Chosin Reservoir and Hungnam. Jack Madison, aboard the *USS General Billy Mitchell*, heard a variety of ingenious rumors, one of which said they were heading for San Francisco, where a banner reading "Welcome 7th Division" already hung from the Golden Gate bridge. Nevertheless, no one was surprised when their ship pulled into Pusan Harbor on 23 December. After unloading, and a bit of milling around, they traveled by train to assembly areas near Taegu. On Christmas Day, Jack wrote home: "We're set up in a nice warm schoolhouse. The turkey is in the stove, and we're all mighty glad to be here."

Soon they would be taking their place in the Eighth Army line, where they were sorely needed. The US divisions were badly weakened, the ROKs were in even worse shape, and the Chinese were massing for their next offensive.

My two closest friends were being transferred: Jim Exley was moving to the Heavy Mortar Company and Gib was going to Battalion Staff. Much as I'd miss them, I was glad they were escaping safely from a rifle company. They were wonderful guys; the Citadel could be proud of both of them. (Shortly thereafter, Gib left for a job in Japan at GHQ. He went on to a fine career as an infantry troop leader. Jim was killed a few months later, when the jeep he was riding in hit a mine.)

Ruff Lynch became acting company commander. Then, a few days later, he was transferred to Mike Company, where he would be their exec officer.

"But what about *this* company?" I asked Ruff.

"Bernie Porter will be taking over. He's due back today from the hospital." I didn't know Porter, but I remembered the name. He had commanded L Company at one time, then had become ill and been evacuated. Evidently he had now recovered.

To me it didn't seem right. Surely Ruff, who knew the men of Item better than anyone and had been with them from the start, deserved a chance to command them. I caught a jeep ride back to Battalion HQ and asked Colonel Mac if I could talk to him.

"Sure." He came off to one side with me; Lieutenant Colonel Evans, the exec, joined us.

"I wanted to talk to you about Lieutenant Lynch. Sir, he's a good man. . . ."

"We know that."

"And I think he could do a good job of commanding I Company. I've nothing against Bernie Porter, in fact I don't even know him. But I think Lieutenant Lynch deserves the chance at a promotion. Since he's a quiet kind of guy, and you haven't seen him that much, maybe you don't realize what a fine job he does. I hope you don't mind my speaking out on this."

"No, I don't mind," said Mac, "appreciate it, in fact. And we *do* know Ruff is a good man."

I accepted that because I wanted to. Still, I wondered if it was really true. I had no basis for comparison, but it seemed to me the battalion staff didn't spend enough time visiting the companies on line and getting to know the people. So how could they evaluate them?

Colonel Evans took over. "Harry, it's not a question of Porter being a better man, or of Lynch not being qualified. It's more a matter of seniority. When you've been around a little more, you'll understand that's the way the Army works. Porter has been a first lieutenant longer than Lynch; he has already commanded a company, and if he hadn't been evacuated a couple of months ago, he would have *already* been a captain. He deserved to get the next available company, which was Item. You understand, don't you?"

"Yes sir, I understand your reasoning. This is one time, though, when I think the seniority thing shouldn't matter so much."

"Well, the decision stands."

"Yes sir." That was it. I still didn't agree, however. On the other hand, while they might be wrong in basing their decision on seniority, I was wrong, too, for wanting them to reverse themselves so Ruff could have a chance at promotion. In combat, it seemed to me neither of these points should be decisive. Who could do the better job? Who could save the most lives? That was what counted.

After a brief good-bye to Gib, who was due to leave for Japan in a few days, I started back. The jeep brought me part of the way, and then, once more by myself, I began walking across the wide, bleak valley.

Suddenly a mortar shell exploded fifty yards north of me. Could it be incoming? Probably not, I thought. More likely it was a short round from one of our own units.

A second shell landed, this one nearer. I realized these *must* be incoming, and I began to walk more rapidly. Abruptly, I heard the whistle of still another incoming round, and I hit the ground. It crashed just a few yards behind me, and I could feel the concussion. Good grief, they were shooting at *me!* I began running for cover. Normally no prudent observer would waste long-range fire on a single individual. In this case, though, when *I* was the individual, it didn't matter whether or not the man was acting prudently—he had me scared as hell!

There was a dry streambed on the far side of the valley, heavily overgrown with brambles and thick underbrush. I headed for it as fast as my legs could pump. Once there, I dived into the thicket and burrowed out of sight. When the firing stopped, I began working my way north.

It was heavy going. I crawled along, pushing my way between bushes, branches, and vines. I was still shaken from the shelling, and probably affected even more by its having been aimed not against an area target, but against me individually. It was too personal. However,

I would have been even more shaken if I had known the horror that lay but a few yards ahead.

The former streambed provided good concealment, but it made a miserable pathway. At times it would be open, then it would close in again, and I'd find myself beating my way through underbrush and pushing aside branches which snapped back at me. The brambles were dense, and I had to move either on all fours or in a low crouch, my face close to the ground.

There it was. Just inches away, a hideous face was leering at me. But how could it be leering when it had no eyes? For where there should have been eyes, there were now just empty sockets. The mouth was open in a monstrous grin. I shuddered and jumped back.

The body, probably that of a Korean farmer, had been there quite a while, alone and undetected. Perhaps he, like me, had taken refuge in this streambed. In his case, though, the shelling must have continued until one final round had landed next to him and torn him apart. The body was even denied the dignity of repose. Caught in the thicket, it was suspended semi-upright in a ghastly simulation of life. Was there someone, somewhere, wondering about him and waiting for him to come home?

Giving the corpse a wide berth, I kept going. Soon I was out of the streambed, into the hills, and "home." Bernie Porter had already arrived at the hut we were using as Company CP. In the next few hours, he and I compared notes and became acquainted. Bernie turned out to be warm, outgoing, and knowledgeable. He asked solid questions about the people in the company, especially the key noncoms, and even suggested a few changes to improve our overall defense. Together, we walked the line and groaned in unison about the wide gap separating us from the 19th Infantry Regiment on our left.

The December weather grew ever more fierce, and we took over two houses in a draw just behind our position as a Rest and Recuperation center. Four Koreans, thankful for the chance to earn some won, set up large kettles in which they boiled our dirty socks and underwear. A schedule was set up so men could come down from the hill, get cleaned up, eat some hot food, change clothes, lie around for a few hours, and even play cards or read a paperback.

Disappointingly, several of the men didn't take their turn, preferring to stay on the hill and not be bothered climbing down. These were men who had surrendered to a terrible apathy, men who had been on line so long they felt an overpowering weariness of mind and body. Their stares were vacant and their speech was listless.

General Ridgway was beginning to make his presence felt. All units received a copy of a message which read:

> I have with little notice assumed heavy responsibilities before in battle, but never with greater opportunities for service to our loved ones and our Nation in beating back a world menace which free men cannot tolerate.
>
> It is an honored privilege to share this service with you and with our comrades of the Navy and Air Force. You will have my utmost. I shall expect yours.

Despite the brave words, Ridgway was discouraged by what he found when he visited the troops, later saying, "They were unresponsive, reluctant to talk. I had to drag information out of them. There was a complete absence of that alertness, that aggressiveness, that you find in troops whose spirit is high. . . ." Unfortunately, he might have been talking about Item Company.

A welcome mail call included several letters from my wife. She sounded depressed, having read in the papers about the 24th Division being nearly cut off, and having had no mail from me in nearly three weeks. Jeanne had been writing a daily letter quite faithfully; now she was saying she might stop writing until she heard something in return. The inference was clear—why keep writing if you suspected they were letters no one would ever see?

Others were receiving mail in a similar vein, and we all agreed the situation was hardest on the wives at home. Most of the time we were in no imminent danger and had no need to be apprehensive. The wives, however, had no such respites, no times when they could feel secure. Even when a letter came, it gave no assurance. It merely meant that eight or ten days earlier, when the letter was written, the writer had been safe. But as for the present day and hour? The wives never knew.

On Christmas Day, our company cooks prepared a proper holiday dinner, complete with turkey, cranberries, and all the trimmings. We set up a chow line and sent word for the men to come down in shifts, about a third at a time. After the first group had finished, I wondered what was delaying the second shift. Then one of the sergeants set me straight.

"Sir, the men don't want to come. They'd rather stay up on the hill, even if it means eating C-rations. It's just too much trouble for them to come down and then climb up again." Evidently the thought of a good meal and a break in routine, as long as it involved extra effort, held no attraction.

With some misgivings, I told the sergeants: "I'm *ordering* the men to come down for Christmas dinner. Pass the word and get the next group back here *right now!*"

Up on the hill, men were rousted from their holes and told to go down and eat. They came, somewhat reluctantly. A few seemed to think the order was strange, but the rest seemed not to care one way or the other. By the time everyone had eaten, and many had taken the opportunity to shave, they looked and acted much improved. That afternoon one of the men said to me, "That dinner sure was fine, Lieutenant."

"Good. Be sure to tell the cooks you enjoyed it."

"I will. And Lieutenant, thanks for *making* us come back for it. I feel a whole lot better."

For more than a month, the Chinese had been preparing for their Third Phase Offensive. The XIII Army Group, consisting of six armies, with nineteen divisions and fifty-seven regiments, was massed near the 38th Parallel. Our G-2 forecasters had a spotty track record, but this time they could predict with confidence: a major Chinese assault was anticipated within the next few days.

Bernie Porter spent the morning of 30 December at regimental headquarters, where he saw a number of correspondents. The gathering of newsmen was ominous; big things were expected to happen in our neighborhood.

When he returned in midafternoon, Bernie was accompanied by John Randolph, a young Associated Press correspondent who had landed in Korea only the day before. John questioned us with the enthusiasm of the new arrival, asking our opinions with a naive acceptance that was rather flattering. Being a good reporter, however, he knew the best stories lay not with the officers but with the enlisted men.

The daylight began to fade, and I told Randolph either Bernie or I usually went up on the hill at this time, since attacks tended to come just before dark. Randolph joined me as I began climbing the trail leading to our left flank, and we headed for a fire on the reverse slope, which with the coming of darkness was about to be extinguished. Several men had gathered around the flames to snatch one last bit of warmth. It made a dramatic picture—the snow, the flickering firelight, the unkempt bearded men with their weapons and bulky clothing.

Rather self-consciously, John said, "Gee, it's just like in the movies!" I guess it depended on one's perspective.

An hour passed. By now all fires were out and it was completely dark. I asked John if he was ready to head back to the CP.

"Well," he said, "I just heard some of these men are going to an outpost. Could I go too, just to see what it's like?"

"I'll tell you what it's like," I said. "It's cold and quiet and sometimes dangerous. And it's no place to visit just for fun."

"Well, I'd still like to go if I may, maybe for an hour or so."

"Okay," I said reluctantly. Since I felt responsible for him, I said I'd go along as escort.

There were four men assigned to the outpost; Randolph and I made six. Once we had cleared our own lines and were walking across the valley, the world seemed very still, very bare, very ominous. The only sound was the crunching of our boots on the snow.

Halfway to the outpost, I whispered to John, "Just about now, we're crossing the Parallel into North Korea." The outpost position was on a little knob, about a quarter-mile ahead of the line. We reached it without incident and the men silently took their positions. Time passed; it was getting colder, and our inability to move around made the cold even more penetrating.

I whispered, "Okay, John, let's head on back."

"Look," he said, "do you suppose I could stay out here?"

"Well, you can stay if you want, but I'm heading back," I said. "Don't forget, this squad will be here until just before daylight. Once I leave, there'll be no one to bring you back if you change your mind." He said he understood, and I figured I had fulfilled my obligation.

As I walked back, the trail suddenly seemed longer, emptier, scarier. It was an uncomfortable feeling to be in the dark, in no-man's-land, and by myself, and it also occurred to me I might soon be in as much danger from Americans as from Chinese.

A whisper came out of the darkness, "Who's that?"

"It's me—it's Lieutenant Maihafer."

"Oh, okay, Lieutenant. Come on in."

Relieved, I climbed a tiny rise and found the position, a two-man foxhole, housing an automatic rifleman and his squad leader. The hole was a good one, well dug, carefully concealed, and capable of covering anyone coming along the trail.

I climbed into the hole with the two men and we talked a bit in hushed tones, sharing confidences about nothing in particular.

Harry Maihafer and I Company KATUSA, December 1950.

The sergeant said, "I've got something here, Lieutenant." He reached into his parka and drew out a dark brown bottle with a Korean label.

In a sly, conspiratorial tone, he said, "How 'bout a drink of banana brandy?" I shuddered. Cold as I was, I still wasn't tempted; the stuff looked downright evil.

"No thanks," I said. He looked disappointed, almost hurt.

"Well, maybe a little one," I said. I put the bottle to my lips and took a cautious sip. It was sickly sweet and caused a burning rawness, almost making me gag.

"Mmm, good," I said, "that just hits the spot."

"Yeah," the sergeant said. Perhaps I should have forbidden liquor in a front-line foxhole, but what the hell.

Back at the CP, Bernie was getting messages from all sectors: from our own platoons, from units on our flanks, and from the rear. There were scattered reports of enemy patrols, but nothing of real significance.

John Randolph reappeared at our CP the next morning, tired, disheveled, but understandably proud of himself. He thanked us for our hospitality, we shook hands, and he left. (Later, one of the men received a clipping from a Chicago paper. It began: "Each night there is a tiny portion of North Korea which becomes American property. . . ." It mentioned some of the squad by name and said that during the night there had been a "stirring in some bushes near the outpost . . . a burst was fired from an American's automatic rifle . . . the stirring stopped. . . .")

As 1950 drew to a close, the UN forces were in a precarious situation. In Tokyo and in Washington, discussions were held about the coming CCF offensive and the very real possibility of our being forced completely off the Korean peninsula.

The US 24th and 25th divisions held positions on the 38th Parallel, with the 1st Cav, at reduced strength, in reserve behind us. Although X Corps had completed its evacuation from Hungnam, it was still regrouping in the Taegu area, too far to the south to help those of us on line. The 2nd US Division, which had lost so heavily at Kunu-ri, was still taking in replacements and was far from combat ready. That left the understrength ROK divisions to hold much of the line, and in their weakened state, they might well give way as they had in the past.

Intelligence reports seldom trickled down to a rifle company, but this time they were plentiful. We were told the Chinese were massed and their attack might come at any time. On 31 December, we sent our extra baggage to the rear so we could travel light in case of a hasty retreat. It seemed more and more likely this would be the night.

I wrote home and considered saying something such as "if anything should happen to me, just remember. . . ." Then I abandoned the idea; if something *should* happen, a telegram would already have arrived. If not, then the letter would just cause more worry.

"Guess I'll head on up to the 1st Platoon," Bernie said. "You stay here and mind the store." Remaining with me were the company headquarters people: two radio operators, a runner, and the mail orderly. I wondered how helpful they'd be in a fight, and I hoped the question was purely academic.

An hour passed; it was now fully dark. Inside the hut, our temperamental Coleman lantern had given out again, and we were relying on the glow from a tiny candle. One of the commo men went outside to stand guard.

There was a sound of gunfire from the 2nd Platoon area, on our right flank near the road. They called and said they had fired at something and received shots in return.

"Couldn't you see them?" I asked.

"I'm not sure," the platoon sergeant said. "One of the men thought he saw a few of 'em, but it was too dark to tell."

"What were they doing?"

"I think they were trying to get behind us. Maybe they're heading toward Battalion, or maybe back your way. You guys be careful back there."

"Yeah—okay. Thanks." I relayed the report to the battalion S-2, and told him one of us might be having some unwanted visitors.

In the distance I heard some crunching sounds. The man on the phone looked up and said, "Sir, the 1st Platoon says they're receiving mortar fire—Oh no!—"

"What is it?"

"Sir, they said Lieutenant Porter's been hit."

"Damn! How bad?"

"They're not sure. It's his leg; there's a medic with him, and they're putting him on a litter." I could hear more crunching sounds —closer. Some appeared to be falling behind us. I called Battalion, talked to Colonel Evans, the exec, and told him about Bernie Porter and about the incoming fire.

"I know about the fire," Evans said. "Some of it is even landing back toward us!" Somehow he made it sound unfair, as though the Chinese were breaking the rules by shooting at someone other than a front-line company.

An hour later, Bernie's litter arrived outside the CP. They set him down, and I knelt alongside to talk to him.

"How is it, Bernie?" I said.

"Not too bad, Harry. My leg burns like hell, but they gave me a shot of morphine and it's easing up."

"Is there anything I can do?"

"Could you get my musette bag and put it on the litter? It has some letters I want to keep, my shaving gear, and a few other things." I hustled back to the hut, found the bag, and brought it to him.

"Now, we better get you on back to the medics," I said.

"Yeah, I suppose so. Take care of the company—and take care of yourself, too."

"Sure, Bernie. So long." I whispered to the litter bearers about the Chinese patrol and told them to keep alert when they crossed the valley.

Moments later, Colonel Mac was on the phone. He asked about Porter, then said: "We're getting reports from other places, Harry. Looks like there's activity all over. Do you think you can hold?"

"Yes, I guess so."

"Well, we want you to hold, of course, but we don't want you to get overrun. Keep me informed, and if it looks like there's too much pressure, we may ask Regiment to let us pull back."

"If it gets too bad, Colonel, don't worry—I'll be calling!"

"Good. How about you yourself? Are you planning to stay where you are at the CP?"

"I think so," I said, "at least for now. Seems to me the main thing is to be where I've got the best commo with everyone."

"I agree," Mac said. Then he added. "Well, you've got the company, boy."

"Yes sir, I'll do my best. I hope it's good enough."

"I'm not worried. You'll do just fine." With the switch from Gib to Ruff to Bernie to me, I'd be Item's fourth commander in less than two weeks. I had wondered what it'd be like to have a company. Now I'd have my chance, but it sure wasn't the time or place I would have selected.

On New Year's Eve, as the Chinese launched their invasion of South Korea, the main effort was in the west, against the ROK 1st and 6th divisions. The ROK 1st Division crumbled almost at once, but the 6th Division managed to hold out for several hours. Then the dam broke and all three regiments of the 6th Division fled in disorder.

The Chinese plan called for them to effect their penetrations through the South Koreans and to avoid the Americans. However, through a miscalculation, one of their major assaults, which they thought would be against the ROKs, instead hit squarely against the US 19th Infantry Regiment of our 24th Division.

Heavy fighting ensued in the 19th Infantry's sector. Front-line platoons, one of which was led by Rigger Ragucci, fought tenaciously, but finally a penetration was made and the 3rd Battalion of the 19th Infantry gave way. At some point during the night, Rigger Ragucci became the latest '49er to die in combat.

The battalion S-2 said Item Company should prepare to send out a patrol. I called the 3rd Platoon and asked to have one of their squads report back to the CP. Next, Colonel Stephens himself was on the phone from Regiment.

"Hello, Maihafer, did they tell you about sending a patrol?"

"Yes sir."

"Well, here's the situation. To your left on the next ridge is the 3rd Battalion of the 19th. No one has been able to contact them; their own people can't raise them, and there's no response on the lateral wire running from their battalion to yours."

"Have they been overrun, sir?"

"We don't know. But that's what your people have got to find out. If they *have* been overrun, the Chinaman could be working his way south along that ridge. If he is, your patrol could run right into him, and we don't want that to happen, so have your men go across the valley, up onto the ridge, and then start working their way up to the 19th's position—cautiously."

The squad arrived at the CP, and their leader, Sgt. Juan Maldonado, checked in with me. I told him what was up, then asked if he would like me to talk to his whole squad.

"Yes sir, that would be good." Six of them had been waiting outside, some familiar dirty faces from my old platoon, plus some newcomers I didn't recognize. They crowded into the room, sloppy, disheveled, moving awkwardly in their bulky winter clothing and blinking at the candlelight.

"Men, here's the story," I said. "You've been picked to go on a recon patrol over to the 19th Infantry. Their 3rd Battalion is on our left, but there's no contact with them, and we need to know whether they're still on position."

The men stared at me; it still hadn't registered. I went on. "They may still be there, but it's possible they've been pushed off. In other words, you might run into some Chinese. I'm telling you this so you'll be extra careful."

Now it registered. They looked at each other meaningfully, then once more gave me their attention. Someone muttered a four-letter word.

I said: "I want you to detour *way* to the south before you cut across. Then take your time working your way up that ridge. If you run across any activity, just observe, then come back here and let me know what you saw."

Maldonado took over and indicated how they would proceed. He was a cool one, hadn't asked any questions, hadn't complained, in fact hadn't shown any emotion at all.

"Good luck, Sergeant."

"Thank you, sir." He turned to his squad. "Okay, let's go." They filed out into the night. I wondered if Maldonado realized why I had spoken to all the men instead of just to him. He was a good man, but somehow I had wondered if someone so untalkative would pass on all the men needed to know. Also, if they hit something, I wanted to be sure each of them knew where to report back.

Now it was a question of waiting. A long, tense, slow hour passed; then another. My imagination played tricks. The Chinese could be anyplace—to our front, to our flanks, even to our rear. At least it was beginning to appear they weren't going to hit I Company directly. Nothing was certain, of course, but since they had hit the other units early in the evening, and since their attacks would probably have been coordinated, chances were Item Company's position wasn't one of their main objectives.

Calls kept coming in from units up the line, including a query from the 19th Infantry HQ, wondering if we had heard anything from the patrol.

There was a noise outside. I tensed up, then relaxed as I saw it was Maldonado, returning with his squad. He came in and reported, still in the same expressionless monotone: "Sir, we went back quite a ways like you said, then crossed over onto that other ridge. We found a path and worked our way north until we got where that company of the 19th used to be."

"No one around?"

"No sir. No Americans, but we saw some Chinese."

"What were they doing?"

"I couldn't tell, but they was moving around, and we stayed away from them."

"Good. You didn't see any Americans, then?"

"Well, we saw some up on that hill, but the only ones we saw was all dead. So we came on back."

"Oh." What could you say to a man reporting the experience of finding they "was all dead"?

"Well, thanks, Sergeant. Sounds like you did a good job. Tell the men I said so, and tell them I'm glad you all got back safely. Now go get some rest."

"Yes sir. Thanks." He shuffled out. I called in the report, and that was that.

It began to get light, and no sunrise had ever been more welcome. The tiny CP group looked tired; their eyes were red from lack of sleep, but they were starting to smile a little.

I said: "Guess we're okay for another day. Thanks for your help. Let's break out the C-rations and have some breakfast." Item Company was weary, a bit shaken, but still intact—and 1951 had arrived.

12. Attack and Counterattack

1 JANUARY–31 MARCH 1951

Eighth Army's plan, in the event of a Chinese breakthrough, was to fall back to a line midway between the 38th Parallel and Seoul. However, the utter collapse of the ROKs made it impossible to set up and hold an intermediate position. Reluctantly, Ridgway ordered a general withdrawal. Eighth Army would break contact, fall back to the Han River, and establish a bridgehead around Seoul.

On New Year's Day, it became evident that our 21st Infantry Regiment had been fortunate. The 19th Infantry on our left and the 2nd ROK Division on our right had been hit hard and taken many casualties, but so far the 21st Infantry had been relatively untouched.

In midmorning, Colonel Mac sent Ruff Lynch back to take over the company. That was fine by me. Ruff said, "I told Mac he ought to leave you in command."

"Hell, Ruff, there's no way I could keep this company; I'm too junior. I'm just happy Mac named you. Congratulations."

"Shoot, I still think it should have been you. After all, I'm just an ol' sergeant who was lucky enough to get a commission. But you— you're a West Pointer. I told Colonel Mac it'd look good on your record to command a company."

"I appreciate the thought," I said, "but I'm happy the way it is." And I meant it.

The Chinese pressure continued to mount on either side of us, and later that day we received orders to withdraw. We pulled back just before dark, walking across the valley to a road where trucks were waiting. As exec, I rated the No. 2 company jeep, and I rode alongside the driver in the right front seat. In the back was Mess Sgt. Tom Nelson, together with "Jeeves," a Korean kitchen helper who doubled as interpreter.

The convoy moved slowly. Trucks, tanks, and jeeps, often bumper to bumper, crawled southward in the subzero darkness. On the shoulders of the road a parallel evacuation was taking place—a sad, swarming, endless column of pathetic refugees. Women old and young carried huge bundles on their heads; many also had babies strapped on their backs. Men and boys bore even heavier burdens; most of the men had overloaded A-frames on their backs, causing them to bend well forward as they walked. Prominent among the refugee stream were the elders—the "papa-sans." These venerable seniors carried no loads other than the dignity of their years. Their status was indicated by the traditional black horsehair hat, and while they might be old, they carried themselves with a fierce dignity.

Once, as our column was halted, a papa-san, standing on the shoulder of the road, shouted at refugees walking some distance away along a narrow, elevated dike.

Jeeves explained that the elder had said, "Road down here!" Evidently the old gentleman was annoyed they had yielded the highway to the Americans, feeling it should be shared. After all, it *was* their road! Out of respect for the elder, the column changed course and wound its way back to the highway.

From the back of the jeep came the soft voice of Sergeant Nelson. He spoke deliberately, as though he had been framing the question in his mind and wanted to say it right.

"Sir, what's to become of us?"

Assuming the question was rhetorical, I just shrugged and said, "I don't know."

There was a pause, and then Nelson slowly said, "Gosh, if even the wheels don't know what's going to happen, how can the rest of us be expected to know anything?"

The "wheels"? Maybe, from Nelson's perspective, I *was* a wheel of sorts. At the moment, however, I surely didn't feel like one.

The first two days of January were crisp and clear, which was a blessing for the Air Force, or more correctly, for those of us relying on air support to slow down the pursuing Chinese. Both from Japan and from bases in South Korea, hundreds of sorties were flown, many of them by recently arrived pilots of USMA '49.

Meanwhile, the imminent loss of Seoul also meant the loss of nearby Kimpo Air Base. Doug Bush's F-86 squadron was relocated from Kimpo to Itazuke Air Base in Japan.

On 3 January, as many of the ROK divisions continued to crumble, Ridgway realized the entire Eighth Army was in danger of being cut off. He gave the order to abandon Seoul and to fall back south of the Han River.

With a major withdrawal underway, engineers such as Monk Kurtz, Terry Powers, and Ed Townsley were charged not only with destroying unneeded supplies, but also with blowing up bridges once the last friendly units had cleared. Jack Hayne, whose antiaircraft platoon was guarding Suwon Air Base, wondered if he should blow up the large supply of bombs abandoned by the Air Force, and he was happy when his engineer classmate, Harry Griffith, arrived to do the job.

Our regimental position on 3 January put us on the right flank of IX Corps, again with the 19th Infantry on our left and the 2nd ROKs on our right. Late that day we moved again, and once more it was a move marked by darkness and confusion. We passed through Seoul, whose streets were empty except for the jammed lines of military vehicles and the ever-present refugee stream.

On the edge of town, the column came to a full stop in a narrow, deserted street. Just ahead were the Han River and a single-lane bridge, whose decking rested on rubber pontoons. Huge chunks of ice, floating in the dark waters, kept bumping against the pontoons. MPs were keeping vehicles well spaced, telling each driver to maintain his interval and to proceed at a crawl. If anything happened to tie up the bridge, it would be bad news for all of us still on the north bank.

Alongside the road, a group was huddled around a tiny fire. I walked over and introduced myself to an engineer captain who seemed to be in charge and who said my convoy was in for a long wait. We commiserated with each other about the confusion, the cold, and the painful agony of massive retreat. His job, he said, was to dismantle the bridge once the last friendly vehicle had crossed.

The captain said he sincerely hoped the last American reached his position well ahead of the first Chinese. I agreed with him, wished him luck, and walked back to my jeep.

Finally it was our turn to move. Slowly the driver steered onto the wobbly pontoon span, and we eased our way across. The Han, which had appeared so ominous while we were waiting to cross, now became an ally as we looked back from the far shore.

Next day we were still moving, along narrow, icy roads, and still competing with civilian refugees for space. By evening we were in yet another village. For security, we had to make sure the houses con-

Men of the 19th Infantry Regiment, 24th Division, retreat ten miles south of Seoul, 3 January 1951. US Army photo.

tained only women, children, and old people. Taking two men with me, I opened the door of the first house and a sea of scared faces turned my way. The room was perhaps twelve feet by fifteen feet, but some twenty or more people were jammed into it. In one corner a woman was moaning. An old lady jabbered at me shrilly, and I backed out.

"What was she saying?" I asked the interpreter.

"She say 'woman having baby,' men go away!"

A baby? Remembering the birth of my own child a few months earlier, my heart went out to the poor woman. Maybe we could help.

"Hey," I said to the jeep driver, "let's go to Battalion and see if we can get Doc." We took the company jeep and jolted down a snowy trail to Battalion HQ.

"Doc," I said, "how about coming with me? There's a lady back at I Company having a baby."

"Okay, why not?" He seemed happy for a chance to practice his trade on someone other than a battle casualty.

"Why don't I come along too?" said Father Cook.

"Sure, Father. Happy to have you." We piled in the jeep, the doc with his medical kit, me with my carbine, Father Cook with a cloth bag filled with rice. Back at the company area, I led the way to the house. We opened the door, and once again startled faces turned our way. The interpreter explained we had brought a doctor, but an old woman got up and gently gestured us out. Men—even doctors—were neither needed nor wanted; women, not men, were the experts when it came to having babies!

Father Cook stepped forward and offered his bag of rice. The old woman took it and was profuse in her thanks. Next morning we were on our way again. I wondered about the women and children, and especially about the woman with the new baby.

"Oh, didn't you hear, Lieutenant? That whole group was on the road at dawn, including the new mother. She had her baby strapped on her back and was hiking right along with the rest of them."

Some thirty miles south of Seoul, supply people, working frantically, moved sixteen trainloads of supplies out of Suwon. Nevertheless, the Suwon railyards were still crammed with immobilized engines, loaded boxcars, and thousands of refugees who had gathered hoping for transportation farther south.

The 14th Engineer Battalion, as a result of their many demolition missions, was out of explosives. Consequently, the S-3 sent Bill Moore and his platoon of Able Company back to Suwon to search the railcars for supplies.

Bill and his men pushed their way through the refugees and began searching the cars. There was a cheer when one of their first discoveries turned out to be several cases of beer.

"Let's first find the demolitions," Bill said, "then we can come back for the beer."

They kept searching and eventually located a train filled with several kinds of ammunition as well as the TNT and plastic explosives they needed. As they began unloading the demolitions, they saw smoke, and someone said a fire had broken·out.

Climbing on top for a better look, Moore saw flames leaping from a nearby boxcar. In horror, he realized the fire would soon spread, blowing up the ammunition, the explosives, and finally the entire train.

Bill and his men, recognizing the need for a prompt departure, were unnerved to the point that they even ignored the beer! They called to the massed civilians that the train was on fire and would start exploding at any moment. The refugees either didn't understand or didn't believe what was said. Few of them made any effort to get clear.

Moore and his platoon drove out of the railyard, and a half-mile out of town, just beyond the crest of a hill, they stopped and waited. About ten minutes later, the ammo began to explode. It was a noise such as they had never heard, as though several squadrons of B-52s had simultaneously dropped their bomb loads on a confined area. Emerging from the flames, the smoke, and the pyrotechnics, and intermingled with the roar of the explosions, Bill could hear the refugees yelling, screaming, and moaning. It was a sound, and a moment, he would never forget.

In military terms, Eighth Army had "broken contact." Somewhat mysteriously, the Chinese made no effort to sustain the pursuit and, for the moment at least, seemed content to consolidate their position north of the Han.

The North Koreans to the east, however, including numerous guerrilla units, remained more active. During one action, Beecher Brian's company of the 5th Cavalry Regiment attacked a stronghold and managed to capture about fifty men, all of whom were in civilian clothes and trying to look like neighborhood farmers.

Beech talked to a huge, tough-looking ROK who was attached to their battalion S-2 section, and they discussed whether or not some of the captives might in fact be true civilians. After a time, the man walked over in front of the group, all of whom were either sitting on their haunches or kneeling. All eyes were on him when he suddenly came to attention and screamed a command in Korean. Except for one old man, the group sprang to its feet and stood at rigid attention. The ROK then barked a series of commands, left face, right face, and a couple of about faces. The group complied smartly. Then Beech saw them, one by one, realize they had been unmasked. No longer could they play the role of innocent farmer. The old man was released; all others were dispatched to a POW enclosure.

Item Company was in a blocking position behind an outpost line, and for the moment all was quiet. One afternoon I was summoned to Battalion HQ, where I reported to Lieutenant Colonel Evans, the exec. With Evans was a middle-aged Korean civilian.

"Sorry to bring you all the way back here, Harry, but I thought we'd better get this thing cleared up. This man says soldiers from your company stole his ox."

"There must be some mistake," I said. "I'd have heard if the men did something like that."

"Well, I hope so. After all, this is a fairly serious matter. One animal may not sound too important to us, but for a Korean, when that ox may be his most valuable possession. . . ."

"Yes sir, I understand. But really, he must have the wrong unit. Even though we haven't had any fresh meat for a long time, I just know men in our company wouldn't do that."

"Mmm. Well, he seemed pretty clear on where the unit was located, and it sure sounded like your kitchen area. Let's ride on up there."

We hopped in the colonel's jeep. Evans rode in front with the driver; the farmer, an interpreter, and I squeezed in the rear. As we traveled forward, the farmer and I traded suspicious glances.

We pulled into the I Company mess area. The mess sergeant hurried over, saluted, and said, "Good afternoon, Colonel. Welcome!"

"Good afternoon, Sergeant," Evans replied. "We just wanted to look around a bit."

"Yes sir," said the sergeant, "we're glad to have you. And you're just in time! How about—for each of you—a *nice steak?*"

I winced.

Colonel Evans favored me with an icy stare. I shrugged my shoulders and looked to the heavens.

"Steak, you say?"

"Yes sir! We bought an ox this morning, butchered it, and tonight the company is gonna eat steak!"

Evans challenged the word "bought," but the sergeant insisted it was true. After considerable sputtering, the explanation emerged. The "sophisticated" lads of I Company had, in effect, been sold the Brooklyn Bridge.

A delegation, hungry for fresh meat, had taken up a collection and gone shopping at the nearest village. They saw a likely animal and indicated they wanted to buy it. A Korean standing nearby said he would sell if the price was right. After considerable haggling, a bargain was struck, and the proud soldiers led away their trophy. The seller, evidently a stranger who happened to be in the right place at the right time, then pocketed his profits and disappeared. Some time later, the rightful owner had come looking for his ox, been told the soldiers had taken him, and had followed the trail to I Company.

"How much to make it right?" I asked. The farmer named a figure which seemed high, but the interpreter assured me it was a fair price.

"Okay, men, pass the hat again. It looks like we get to buy this creature twice," I said. They groaned but complied. Even the colonel and I chipped in, both of us laughing at the "shrewd Yankees" who had been taken in so handily by a Korean con man.

January of 1951 was a time of transition. Thanks in large part to the magnificent leadership of Matthew Ridgway, Eighth Army was turning a corner. As the year began, we were an exhausted, dispirited group with a defeatist attitude, weary of the war and fully expecting to be driven out of Korea. Ridgway, however, managed to inject new spirit into the Army. Soon commanders at all levels, many of whom were new men handpicked by Ridgway himself, were looking for ways to regain the initiative.

That same month also marked a transition for members of USMA '49. Most who had arrived the previous summer had entered combat either as platoon leaders or forward observers. Many of those, too many, were no longer with us, and those of us who remained were no longer shavetails at the bottom rung of the officer ladder. We were veterans, wearing the silver bars of a first lieutenant, and were moving to new positions, perhaps to utilize our experience, or perhaps merely to give us a break.

In I Company of the 32nd Infantry, for example, platoon leaders Jack Madison and Joe Kingston were being moved to new jobs. Jack became the company exec, Joe an assistant S-3 at Battalion.

Beecher Brian took over the 5th Cavalry's I&R Platoon, the unit Joe Toomey had once led. It was well-deserved recognition, just as it had been for Joe, but Beech accepted the job with mixed emotions. He would be the unit's seventh platoon leader within five months.

Lou Messinger, who had been wounded while with the 8th Cavalry Regiment, went to a Psychological Warfare (PsyWar) outfit at Eighth Army. Jim Scholtz, from the 5th Cavalry, became a liaison officer to the 1st Marine Division. Bob Ritchie, who had been a platoon leader in the 5th RCT, was moved to the regiment's Heavy Mortar Company.

Lew Baumann, for the moment, and by choice, remained a platoon leader. At one point he was offered a transfer to the 2nd Division. Since the 2nd Division had lost so many officers, he'd undoubtedly become at least a company exec, with a good chance of soon having his own company. Lew declined the questionable opportunity, reasoning that any unit he joined would be one which had been badly mauled and was now filled with replacements fresh from the States.

West Point '49er artillerymen, meanwhile, who had been serving mostly with front-line companies as FOs, were coming down from the hills and rejoining their firing batteries.

My relaxation period ended abruptly as our entire battalion went on a long-range patrol as part of Ridgway's plan to regain the initiative and reestablish contact with the enemy. We started out in trucks, prepared to dismount and fight on foot if we encountered any Chinese. Slowly we proceeded north, with no sign of enemy activity, in fact no sign of life at all—only a dazzling, empty whiteness. After a few miles we halted so men could stamp their feet, flap their arms, and somehow try to maintain circulation.

Again we started. A few miles farther on, we passed through a defile, with low hills on either side of the road, a perfect spot for an ambush. All of us studied the hills warily. However, nothing happened, either then or during the remainder of the morning. After we had gone about twenty miles, an order came for us to turn back. Evidently the Chinese were farther north than we had thought, which was fine by us.

Since our motorized patrol had uncovered no enemy to our front, it was decided we should move up to fill the void. Accordingly, our battalion proceeded about ten miles north to positions near Yoju. Two of our rifle companies set up abreast; a third company, which was to be rotated every few days, went father out to serve as an advanced outpost and patrol base.

The 7th Division had also moved north to reestablish contact. Before they left their assembly area near Taegu, however, their corps commander, Gen. Ned Almond, had ordered a full-field inspection to ensure they were properly equipped. Jack Madison's weapons platoon was turned out around 5:00 A.M. and shivered in the cold until 10:00 or so, when the corps commander arrived in a heated ambulance-type vehicle.

When he came to Madison's platoon, Almond's only comment was that the mortars were painted an improper shade. Jack, who had scrounged the paint from the Marines, felt he was lucky to have any paint at all.

Later in January, Jack wrote home: "Much action of late. . . . couldn't send out mail for five days . . . bitter cold . . . frozen feet big problem. . . . we're getting some replacements; our rifle company is authorized 241 [men] and we were down to 109. . . ."

Ruff Lynch, who had just returned from a meeting at Battalion, said, "Harry, I think I've got a good deal for you. General Church, the division commander, is going back to the States. A new general is coming in, and each regiment was asked to recommend an officer who might make him a good aide. Colonel Mac talked to Colonel Stephens, and they want to nominate you."

Ruff and I discussed the pros and cons of such a move. Tactfully, Ruff emphasized the benefit to my career and didn't make too much of the more immediate advantage—that people at a division headquarters seldom had bad guys shooting at them. Nevertheless, we both recognized it was a factor which had a good bit to be said for it.

That evening, at Battalion Rear, I discussed the aide-de-camp opportunity with the S-1, who acted as my host for the night. He produced a bottle and we sat up late, drinking and sharing confidences. As I crawled into a borrowed sleeping bag, my head was spinning, and not only from the unaccustomed drinks. It was flattering to have been singled out for an important job, but questions and self-doubts kept arising.

The threshold question was whether I truly wanted to leave Item Company and sever some of the closest ties I'd ever known. Now that leaving was a possibility, I began realizing how much that lowly company and I had become a part of each other.

My driver and I left Battalion early the next morning, back along the main road, passing Diamond, the 21st Regimental CP, and following melodramatic-sounding signs to Danger Forward, the 24th Division forward CP.

We were there by midmorning. The driver pulled into the headquarters area after being waved on by a crisp-looking MP in a lacquered helmet.

The installation made quite a contrast to the grubbiness of the front lines: many tents, many vehicles, many signs, everything neatly aligned. My I Company jeep and I suddenly seemed out of place, like country folks in the big city. I ignored the urge to turn and go back where I "belonged."

At the G-1 tent, a captain came forward and said, "Hi, you must be the officer from the 21st. Colonel Stephens called about you yesterday. The interviews were just about closed; candidates from the division artillery and the other regiments were here a couple of days ago, but Big Six said to hold everything."

"Well sir, I was pretty far forward and. . . ."

"It's okay. Colonel Stephens explained, said to forget the other interviews, he had someone picked who could do the job fine. Actually I'm not interviewing you; that'll be done by General Bryan, the new CG. At the moment he's meeting with General Church."

An hour or so later, I was introduced to General Church, the outgoing commander, and to General Bryan, his replacement. General Church, who had been with the 24th Division from the beginning, was short, wiry, leathery-looking. Brig. Gen. Blackshear "Babe" Bryan, on the other hand, a former varsity tackle and later assistant football coach at the Military Academy, was *big.*

"Do you want to be my aide?" he boomed.

"Yes sir," I heard myself say. Fortunately he didn't ask why; I would have had trouble framing an answer. The general asked for a brief summary of my background, and I mentioned my pre-Academy enlisted service in the Air Corps, followed by West Point, service schools, and Korean duty since August with the 21st Infantry.

"What class were you at the Academy?"

"'49, sir."

"God, that makes me feel old!" said Bryan, who had been class of '22. After a few more questions, I returned to the G-1 tent. That afternoon I was told I had the job. I moved three days later, just in time to witness a change-in-command ceremony presided over by the new IX Corps commander, Gen. Bryant E. Moore, who had been West Point superintendent during our final year. General Church received a Distinguished Service Medal and a sincere "Godspeed." General Bryan received a second star, command of the 24th Division, and the services of a green but willing aide-de-camp.

As February began, both Eighth Army and the CCF were planning offensive action. In keeping with Ridgway's desire to regain the initiative, Eighth Army, in what was optimistically named Operation Roundup, began to press north against an enemy who sometimes fought stubbornly and at other times seemed to melt away. In the

Elements of Companies C and K, 35th Infantry Regiment, 25th Infantry Division, keep a sharp lookout for movement in the Communist-held area. US Army photo.

western part of the line, UN troops by midmonth had once more recaptured Inchon and even reached the banks of the Han River.

Meanwhile, many of the CCF forces had moved to the central sector, where masses of Chinese had gathered in preparation for what would be their Fourth Phase offensive. In that sector, X Corps had launched an attack, the early stages of which saw Americans fighting well, overcoming ambushes, making good use of supporting air and artillery, and inflicting heavy casualties on the enemy.

The ROKs, however, continued to disappoint. Whenever they were attacked by significant numbers of Chinese, the poorly trained and poorly led South Koreans usually crumbled without warning. As an experiment, X Corps decided to bolster the ROKs by putting certain American units in direct support of South Korean divisions.

In the central sector, the 187th RCT was made available to strengthen X Corps and to back up the South Koreans. As Operation Roundup began, the 1st and 3rd battalions of the 187th attacked northeast of Wonju to secure a line of departure for the ROKs. During the attack, '49er Steve White, a platoon leader in Able Company of the 187th RCT, was seriously wounded and had to be evacuated.

For the operation itself, Support Force 21, containing artillery plus an infantry battalion from the 38th Regiment, was attached to the 8th ROK Division. One of the infantry platoons was led by Tom Byrd, a tall, soft-spoken '49er from a small town in Georgia.

On 11 February, when the Chinese launched their offensive, the 8th ROK Division gave way almost at once, streaming south in disorder and creating a huge gap in the line. Many American supporting units, including Tom Byrd's company, were overwhelmed by the Chinese masses flowing south. On 12 February, Tom was listed as missing in action.

As part of the same action, the 674th Airborne Artillery Battalion of the 187th RCT had been sent north to support the ROKs. Jim Coghlan, normally an FO with I Company of the 187th, was given a new assignment and told to take his FO party to the 27th ROK Regiment. On the way, Jim stopped at his battalion headquarters to pick up fresh batteries. Jim's battalion commander suggested he stay at Battalion overnight, saying the situation looked "a little unsettled."

Next morning their fears were confirmed as panic-stricken ROKs came stampeding down the valley surrounding the artillery positions. Mindful of the vulnerability of roadbound towed artillery, the US units remained in place, dug in, and commandeered as many crew-served weapons as they could from the retreating ROKs.

By midafternoon, Chinese units appeared on the surrounding hills, and the batteries started receiving long-range sniper fire. Fortunately, 187th RCT infantry elements arrived about that time to extricate the artillery.

The paratroopers assembled at a road junction around 4:00 P.M. and considered the two routes back into Wonju. One led west to Hoengsong, then south into Wonju; the other went mostly south and bypassed Hoengsong. In view of the Chinese breakthrough, neither route was considered secure. Jim, not knowing at this stage of his career that lieutenants were meant to be seen and not heard, mentioned to the battalion CO that he had come north recently with the 3rd Bat-

Jim Coghlan. Courtesy Col. James J. Coghlan, Jr. (Ret.).

talion over the latter route. Fortunately, the decision was made to head that way. Otherwise they would have been trapped, and presumably decimated, in what later became known as Massacre Valley.

After dark, the paratroopers moved out, with Jim and his FO party going ahead as road guides for the turn off to Wonju. With MPs arriving just as C Battery rolled past, Jim and his party hooked on to their own battery for the rest of the night. It was a nerve-racking ride, but the southern route proved to be free of enemy forces.

When the 187th RCT neared Wonju, it started picking up soldiers from other units and learned that the CCF, in addition to shattering the 5th and 8th ROK divisions, had broken through US elements to the north. Then, as C Battery was going into position, a captain and four soldiers from the Netherlands Battalion arrived and told how their battalion commander had been killed that night by CCF troops disguised as ROKs.

Next morning Jim and his party returned to I Company, and on the way ran into '49er Jack Hayne, who was reconnoitering positions for his quad-50s at the Wonju railyard. Jack gave Jim directions to I Company, located near a railroad tunnel, and shortly after they parted, the CCF gave Jack a close call with a heavy concentration of 120-mm mortar fire.

Jim, Dave Freeman, Ward Goessling, Dene Balmer, and Boyde Allen were all members of the 674th on 14 February as it took part in the famous "Wonju shoot." Aerial observers detected two CCF divisions boldly massed for a daylight attack. Coordinated fire from both division and corps artillery crashed into the Chinese formations, inflicting thousands of casualties. Hour after hour the ghastly slaughter continued, but the Chinese kept moving forward, in the words of one reporter, "like ants on a sidewalk climbing over the crushed bodies of those who had gone before." Nearly five thousand Chinese lay dead, and perhaps three times that number had been wounded, before the Chinese finally broke and fled north. Even then, close air support continued to punish the Chinese, taking over where the artillery could not reach.

Proud artilleryman Jack McDonald, a member of the 1st Cavalry's 99th Field, sent home a *Stars and Stripes* with an AP story saying that "for years, artillerymen will tell the story of the 'Wonju shoot' that turned the whole tide of battle Thursday on the central front," calling it the "dream of every Red Leg." (Coincidentally, the story was written by John Randolph, the man who had spent his second night in Korea on my Item Company outpost.)

For a few days, the weather turned warmer, the snow melted, and heavily traveled dirt roads became nearly impassable. Jack Madison wrote home that mud was "a tremendous problem . . . gooey and sticky, [getting] into everything and onto everything and really difficult to deal with." However, he added that they were "on a roll," that morale was improving and people were beginning to feel optimistic.

On 17 February, two days prior to his twenty-fourth birthday, Beecher Brian was sent on a contact patrol with his I&R Platoon. With him in his command jeep, just behind his two light tanks, were the driver, a radio operator, and a Korean interpreter. Suddenly, as they moved along the narrow road, Beech's vehicle hit two mines almost simultaneously. There was a violent explosion, and Beech was blown into the air, flying over the hood of his jeep. He grabbed his helmet with both hands and tried to perform one of the smooth tumbling rolls we'd learned in cadet gym class. It didn't work; with a crack, he landed flat on his back and the breath went out of him. Up ahead, the tanks began firing their machine guns at the surrounding ridgelines.

Despite the pain, Beech tried to do about four things at once — catch his breath, see what the tanks were firing at, reach some kind of cover, and stop moaning. His first thought was that the jeep had been hit by a flat trajectory gun of some kind, and he expected more fire. Within seconds, one of the other jeeps drove up, and Beech asked them to look after the Korean interpreter, who had a back injury. The driver and radio operator were shaken up but not badly hurt and were able to continue on with the patrol. By this time, Beech's foot, which had been severely mangled, was hurting badly.

Within a few minutes, Brian was back at a battalion aid station, and although he didn't realize it, he was also on his way home. He was routed through a series of hospitals, first to Taegu, next Yokohama, then Honolulu. Finally he landed at Letterman Army Hospital in San Francisco, where he spent the next eighteen months waiting for his foot to heal. Because the ankle had failed to fuse properly, Beech was fitted at Letterman with a permanent brace on his right foot. He felt rewarded when he was told he could return to active duty. However, his happiest reward at Letterman came in the person of Florence, his charming physical therapist, whom he courted and wed while he was still a patient.

By late March, Lew Baumann was the only platoon leader in George Company of the 32nd Infantry who had not been hit. Starting with Curt Anders, all the others had become casualties, and at Battalion it was decided that Lew needed a break. Consequently, orders were cut making Lew the battalion motor officer.

Baumann wanted to stay where he was, but the CO was adamant. It wasn't long before Lew became convinced he wasn't really needed at the motor pool. Not only was the S-4 really in charge, the motor sergeant was an exceptionally able man ("biggest crook I ever knew — a real Sergeant Bilko in spades") who had things well under control without Lew's interference.

After two weeks of feeling useless, Lew went AWOL from the motor pool and rejoined his old platoon, just as they were engaged in a firefight, one which fortunately turned out successfully. A few days later, recognizing that Lew truly wanted rifle company duty, his CO sent him to F Company as exec, with a promise that he'd soon be in line to take over the company.

On 24 February, Bryant E. Moore, the IX Corps commander, was visiting General Myers, 24th Division Artillery CG, whose aide was '49er Jim "Whitey" Whitmarsh. When Moore left the CP, his helicopter hit some wires on takeoff and tumbled back into a river. He was pulled out, shaken but apparently okay, and went into General Myers's van to dry off and rest for a moment.

A few minutes later, Moore was dead of a heart attack. Nearby, at 24th Division HQ, I may have been the first '49er other than Whitey to hear the news. On behalf of all our class, I said a silent prayer for the man who had been West Point "Supe" during our First Class year. I'm sure Whitey did the same.

Each day General Bryan left the CP early to visit front-line units. His visits had many advantages, not the least of which was that other commanders were also leaving their CPs and spending more time up on line. The general's personal attention also had the division *looking* much better; most of the 24th Division's soldiers were now clean shaven, wore their helmets, even had neater uniforms. While accompanying him on one such trip, I ran into my redheaded classmate Bob Ritchie. Bob and I had been in the same division for several months, but this was the first time we'd seen each other, and inevitably our talk turned to classmates who'd been killed, including pilot Floyd Stephenson, who had been in Bob's Western High School graduation class in D.C. back in 1944.

As the CCF Fourth Phase Offensive wound down, the 187th RCT reverted to Army reserve and returned to its assembly area near Taegu. Nearby was '49er Jack Burckart, whose antiaircraft artillery (AAA) platoon was guarding the Eighth Army CP. Another familiar face in the area was Air Force classmate Charlie Byrne, who was flying B-26 night photo-recon missions. Rumor had it that after he exposed all his film, Charlie would recut the fuses of his leftover five hundred–pound pyrotechnic flares to ensure surface bursts, then make bombing runs on targets of his own selection.

The 187th RCT's reserve role created an opportunity for additional training, part of which covered the workings of the air-ground operations system and which was conducted by none other than the well-traveled Doug Bush. When his squadron went back to Itazuke,

Maj. Gen. Blackshear M. Bryan visits one of his 24th Division units, summer 1951. On far left is Bryan's aide-de-camp Harry Maihafer.

Doug had fretted at the lack of activity and had volunteered for ground duty as a forward air controller (FAC). His first assignment had been with a ROK unit, and as might have been expected, he had been living dangerously. The day after he completed his tour, the entire control unit with which he had been serving was wiped out. Now, conducting these training classes, Doug was back with his first love, the parachute infantry, the type of unit in which he had served during World War II.

The day started with General Bryan saying he wanted to visit the 21st Infantry. On the way, we were joined by Colonel Stephens, who told the driver to head for I Company.

I Company? I feared General Bryan was in for a shock when he saw those dirty faces, muddy uniforms, and scraggly beards. As for helmets, I remembered only a handful in the whole outfit. This could be embarrassing.

I whispered to Stephens, "I Company, that's the one I was in."

"Oh, is that right?" he said, showing little interest. I wondered why we were visiting Item. Had there been some action? If so, how many casualties had there been, and who were they? We turned down a narrow road and came to an open field where soldiers were standing in ranks. It was my old company, Item, and not only did they look clean, they even had helmets!

Staff officers from 3rd Battalion stood near the edge of the road, all except for the S-3, who was in the center of the field. The company was given "present arms"; General Bryan returned the salute. Then the order was given for "order arms" and "parade rest." The general turned to me and said, "Go on, get out there."

Hesitatingly, I walked on the field, where the S-3 motioned for me to stand facing him. He began reading a citation in a formal, "parade ground" voice, and only then did it dawn on me that the inspection trip, the formation, the whole thing—was for my benefit. In a daze, I heard the reading and recalled Gib saying something about recommending a decoration for my actions the day I was wounded.

The S-3 finished the reading. General Bryan, with a broad grin on his face, came forward and pinned a medal to the pocket of my field jacket.

"Guess we surprised you that time," he said.

"Yes sir, you sure did," I said in a small voice. The company broke ranks and crowded around, laughing, congratulating, shaking my hand. I felt very awkward and self-conscious, but it was a moment I'd always treasure.

Operation Ripper, an advance all across the Eighth Army front, was launched on 7 March. Almost immediately, the 7th Division was into rugged mountain terrain, where roads were little more than muddy trails, and where supplies had to be either airdropped or brought forward by Korean bearers.

In L Company of the 32nd Infantry, Bill Penington's platoon was given the mission of attacking "Square Rock" Mountain. Although Bill's twenty-fifth birthday was still a month away, he was by this time a true veteran platoon leader. He had won a Bronze Star shortly after landing at Inchon, in the words of the citation "displaying outstanding leadership and bravery as he aggressively led his platoon against

Elements of Joe Kingston's K Company, 32nd Infantry, advance toward their objective, CCF-held Hill 671 northeast of Chae-jae, 12 March 1951. UN troops are dropping white phosphorus in the background. US Army photo.

the enemy without regard for his own personal safety," and as one of his men put it, he seemed to have the knack for "making the right decision at the right time . . . whether in combat or in reserve."

As they climbed Square Rock Mountain, Bill's platoon ran into heavy fire, and it became necessary to withdraw far enough to allow artillery fire to be brought on the objective. Bill, although he was personally in an exposed position, signaled his men to pull back while he himself stayed behind to provide covering fire. Moments later he was killed.

One of the men wrote to Bill's wife: "Your husband meant a lot to the boys in his platoon and to all of the officers of this regiment. . . . It was through his great heroism that many of us are here today to tell the story of Square Rock Mountain, the place where he so gallantly led his men and lost his life trying to get his men back to safety. . . . I know that we men who are here today because of his gallantry will never forget what he did up there that day."

West Point '49ers Joe Kingston and Jack Thomas were nearby, Jack in fact as a member of the same company. Together, they mourned, and with a heavy heart Joe obtained Bill's class ring and mailed it to Bill's wife, Mary, whom Bill had met while he was attending the infantry course at Fort Benning. They had been married the previous July, a scant month before Bill left for overseas.

Sincere, idealistic Bill Penington had understood the risks of infantry combat, but he believed in what he was doing. Not long before, he had written home: ". . . if anything should happen to me, realize, as I do, that neither mine nor the other daily sacrifices being made in Korea are for any but a very worthy and important cause."

To the west, units had crossed the Han River to outflank Seoul, and eventually the enemy withdrew from the capital so as to avoid being cut off. When Clay Buckingham forded the Han with his M-46 tank platoon, it became a "near thing," as at one point the water became deep enough to pour into the driver's hatch.

Clay passed through Seoul, which by this time resembled a wasteland, and moved north to his unit's assembly point. Next day brought another water barrier, but this time Clay was not so fortunate. As his tank tried to ford a swollen stream, Clay suffered a broken ankle, causing him to spend the next few weeks in a Yokohama hospital.

Action continued on the central front, and Chunchon, a road hub eight miles below the 38th Parallel, became the next important objective. Confirmed paratrooper Matt Ridgway decided an air assault on Chunchon might cut off and trap sizable numbers of CCF and NK troops.

The 187th RCT back at Taegu was alerted for Operation Hawk, an airdrop on Chunchon. Assembly areas were blocked off by barbed wire; equipment was prepared for heavy drop; and C-119 and C-46 troop carrier planes began gathering at K-2.

Doug Bush, having completed his tour with the ROKs, was back in Japan with his F-86 squadron when he learned of the planned air assault. For Doug, a veteran of World War II combat jumps in Europe, and still a paratrooper at heart, there was only one thing to do. He requested, and was granted, a thirty-day leave so he could jump with the 187th RCT and act as their forward air controller.

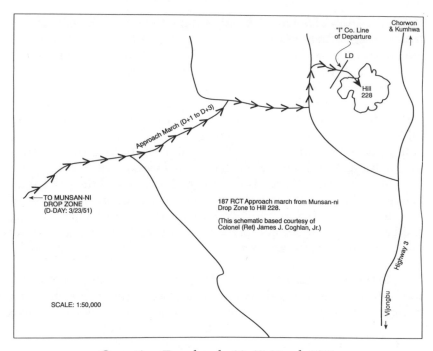

Operation Tomahawk, 23–27 March 1951

Meanwhile it was learned that the enemy had pulled back, Chunchon was deserted, and an airdrop in that area would be meaningless. Ridgway canceled Hawk and selected another objective, this time Munsan-ni in the I Corps sector. The new operation, named Tomahawk, was set for Good Friday, 23 March. Two drop zones (DZs) would be used, one north of Munsan-ni, the other south. The southern DZ would be a linkup base for an armored task force coming from the south, and only the 1st Battalion of the 187th RCT would land there.

Unfortunately, shortly after takeoff the lead plane in the 1st Battalion serial, carrying the battalion commander, FO Dene Balmer, and others, developed mechanical problems and had to abort. Back at Taegu, the plane's occupants transferred to a spare C-119 and once more headed north.

Meanwhile, the main body began landing, and the 1st Battalion serial, now missing its leader, bypassed their planned DZ and, by mistake, began unloading on the same DZ as everyone else. Jim Coghlan, Dave Freeman, and Ward Goessling, FOs with the 3rd Battalion rifle companies, got the green light and began jumping shortly after

9:00 A.M. Jim, exiting from the right-hand aircraft of a five-plane Vee, expected to see empty sky to the east. Instead, the air was filled with parachutes.

The DZ became rather chaotic as unscheduled troops and equipment crowded in upon the first wave. Fortunately the troopers encountered little opposition, and soon the area was secured.

A bit later, the C-119 carrying the 1st Battalion command group arrived over the southern DZ. They were surprised to see it empty, but assumed the troops must already have cleared the area and moved on, so down they jumped, an unimposing assault force of only twenty-nine men. Soon they were greeted by small-arms fire from the surrounding hills. At this point Dene Balmer became a key player, providing both artillery and communications support until a rescuing company arrived several hours later.

On D+1, 24 March, the RCT assembled at dusk for what became a rainy and physically demanding foot march over the trail leading east to Highway 3, the Seoul-Uijongbu-Chorwon road. The 3rd Battalion, as rear guard, alternated between halts and rushes to compensate for the accordion-like movements of the column ahead of them. All but the lead elements repeatedly slithered off the trail that preceding troops had turned into a morass.

By 26 March, D+3, Item Company of the 187th RCT was approaching Hill 228, a dominant hill mass pockmarked with Chinese foxholes and overlooking Highway 3. Item's FO, Jim Coghlan, on nearby high ground, began adjusting some "on call" artillery concentrations, when who should arrive but Doug Bush and his FAC party.

"I want to direct some air strikes against that hill," Doug said. "Can you mark it for me with some WP?"

Jim, happy to oblige, adjusted several 105-mm white phosphorus rounds to mark the fighter-bombers' targets, and Doug guided in the airstrike. A few minutes later, more '49er coordination took place as Coghlan exchanged fire-support data with fellow FO Dene Balmer.

Dave Freeman, moving forward with his own FO party, saw Doug Bush guiding in the air strike. They waved to each other, as Dave thought what a pleasure it was to see a real pro in action.

Item Company was ordered to attack 228, and the company deployed in the classic "two up, one back" formation, with Jim's FO party and the company command group just behind the lead platoons. The company jumped off, crossed a dry rice paddy, and started up the slopes of 228. Despite the air and artillery preparation, the well dug-in Chinese were able to lay down a heavy volume of small arms and mortar fire, intermingled with a shower of grenades from foxholes on the

Dave Freeman. Courtesy Col. James J. Coghlan, Jr. (Ret.).

lower slope. Men began falling, but Item pressed on through the scrub vegetation, the most effective weapons being hand grenades dropped into each foxhole.

It began getting dark, Item Company was almost to the crest of 228, and losses had been staggering. For Operation Tomahawk, the company had been brought close to its authorized strength of 214. On this day they had already taken 84 casualties, including all four platoon leaders, and the only officers remaining were the company commander and Jim Coghlan, his FO. Although not wounded, even they had taken hits in their clothing and equipment. In Jim's case, a bullet had split the boot leather over his toes but had left the sock intact.

Doug Bush, meanwhile, had seen the casualties being brought

to the rear, and had heard—incorrectly as it turned out—that Item had lost all its officers. He told his radio operator to stay behind while he himself went forward to "observe the results of the air strikes." Presumably Doug knew the situation was critical and was going up to help, no doubt feeling an officer might be needed to assume command and rally the troops.

Doug Bush's whole life had been marked by risk-taking, adventure, and success. This was surely the case, as told in the first pages of this book, when soon after graduation he boldly called on Army Chief of Staff Omar Bradley. His luck had always held, whether he was jumping in Normandy, competing in West Point athletics, or piloting his F-86 over North Korea. If he felt invulnerable as he climbed the slopes of Hill 228, it was understandable.

As Doug made his way forward, a Chinese mortar round came screaming down, and a single fragment penetrated under his right arm. He died before anyone could get to him. Under the cover of darkness, his body was carried down from the hill. In his pocket they found a small Bible.

His classmates also believed in Doug's invincibility, and next morning, when Jim Coghlan and Dave Freeman heard what had happened, their natural reaction was disbelief.

Next day the 187th RCT continued the attack, and by 30 March, having secured their objectives, the paratroopers were relieved by elements of the US 3rd Division. They then returned to their assembly area near Taegu.

13. Spring Offensive

1 APRIL–30 JUNE

By 1 April, Ridgway's Eighth Army was deployed more or less along the 38th Parallel, and for all intents and purposes, South Korea had been restored to its prewar status. During Operation Ripper, US troops had advanced some seventy miles. However, the enemy had withdrawn rapidly and with a minimum of casualties. Consequently, Ridgway judged Ripper to have been but a "qualified success."

Back in Washington, senior officials, including President Truman, were wondering if the restoration of South Korea meant the time was ripe to pursue peace talks. First, however, prudence indicated a move to more defensible ground. As a result, Operation Rugged, an advance across the Parallel to Line Kansas, was set in motion.

Meanwhile, the Chinese continued to augment their forces in North Korea, and the massive troop buildup was an alarming indication of still another all-out offensive.

For the past several months, Ernie Denham had been at Fort Benning teaching marksmanship. After the basic course, his initial orders, like those of his friend Cec Newman, had been for Hawaii. However, since Ernie's wife Gloria was about to give birth, Ernie had been pulled off shipment and retained on the Benning weapons committee. By the spring of 1951, however, Denham was on his way—to San Francisco, Tokyo, and eventually Taegu, then on to the 21st Infantry Regiment of the 24th Division.

Ernie pondered the fact that he was the fourth infantryman from A-2, his former cadet company, to arrive in Korea. By this time the other three, Cec Newman, Mike Wadsworth, and Rigger Ragucci, had all been killed.

The 21st Infantry had been in heavy fighting, and Ernie was told he could catch up with them as they came falling back along a certain road. Ernie stood, with a pack on his back, at the edge of the road. The regimental commander saw him and pulled over.

Denham introduced himself, and the colonel said: "The S-1 is in the jeep right behind me. Tell him to assign you to the 1st Battalion. Then catch B Company when they come by. They've lost all their officers, so you're their new commander."

Bob Ritchie, after being a rifle platoon leader, had been transferred to the 5th RCT's Heavy Mortar Company with the thought that it would be safer. A similar transfer had taken place when Citadel graduate Jim Exley, my brother platoon leader in I Company, had gone to the 21st Infantry's mortar company. Ironically, both men were killed about the same time. Bob died on 3 April after being wounded in action near Hyon-ni, and Jim was killed instantly when his jeep hit a mine.

When his boss, General Allen, went home, Jack Hodes took off his aide insignia and once more donned the crossed rifles of an infantryman. Since 23 February, Jack had been leading the 2nd Platoon of F Company, 8th Cavalry. A month and a half later, on 7 April, he was seriously wounded and evacuated to Japan. (That summer, while I was on R&R, I visited Jack at Tokyo General. Later I mentioned the visit to General Bryan, who knew General Hodes, Jack's father. Bryan expressed great concern about "Hank's boy," and the way he said it made me realize the closeness and intimacy of the peacetime Regular Army.)

For the past several months, Jack Hayne and his platoon of the 76th Anti-Aircraft Battalion had been guarding a series of airbases up and down the Korean peninsula. In early April, his unit was assigned to K-2 Airbase near Taegu, where he ran into Dave Barnes, his plebe-year roommate. Dave was a pilot in the same 27th Fighter-Escort Group that Floyd Stephenson had been in when he was lost back in December, but while Floyd had been lost soon after arriving in Korea, Dave by this time had flown many missions, enough to earn a Distinguished Flying Cross (DFC) and five Air Medals.

Dave's tent was about a hundred yards from Jack's CP, and Jack couldn't understand why Dave called one day through at least five switchboards (Air Base to Eighth Army to an intermediate board to Jack's battalion, Jack's battery, and finally to Jack). It would have been quicker just to shout. In any case, Dave asked Jack to come by as soon as possible, since there was a visitor who wanted to say hello.

Jack trotted on down to Dave's tent, opened the flap, and a hand reached out of the shadows to greet him with a "Hiyah, Jackson. How you doing?" It was Dave's dad, Air Force general Earl Barnes, USMA '25, on a weapons evaluation trip to Korea.

Jack Madison wrote home about this time that, after a month of heavy fighting, the 32nd Infantry was back in reserve where they could receive some replacements, get cleaned up, and "even eat some hot chow—a real luxury." He added that Joe Kingston was now commanding K Company and "doing a real fine job."

Whenever senior visitors came to our division, General Bryan felt obliged to escort them while they were in the area, even though he might have preferred doing something else. (He once joked that there should be a two-star general to manage the division, and a three-star general to run the visitors' bureau.)

On 12 April, there was no question about his being on hand to greet his visitor, for the VIP was none other than Secretary of the Army Frank Pace, Jr. Accompanying Pace were several senior officers, including Army Commander Matt Ridgway.

General Bryan and I, along with several others, met Pace's party at the division airstrip. We went first to "Doughboy," the 19th Infantry Regiment, then proceeded to "Domino," the CP of the 5th RCT. Soon after we arrived, a call came to the regimental switchboard asking for Frank Pace. The operator's initial response was that there wasn't anyone in the 5th RCT by that name. Fortunately the error was caught, and moments later Pace was informed that Eighth Army Chief of Staff Lev Allen had been trying most urgently to get in touch with him.

The switchboard connected Pace with General Allen in Taegu. Allen was relaying a message from Washington.

"Read that to me once more, Lev," said Pace. "I don't want to relieve General MacArthur upon one reading."

Despite a hailstorm which had arisen, Pace took Ridgway outside and said: "General Ridgway, it's my duty to advise you that you are now the supreme commander of the Pacific. General MacArthur is relieved."

"I can't believe it, Mr. Secretary," Ridgway said.

"I can't either, so I'll repeat it. You are now the supreme commander of the Pacific; General MacArthur is relieved."

Those of us nearby had no idea what was going on. However, when the secretary cut short his visit, and he and Ridgway rushed back to the airstrip, we all knew something must be up. Ridgway looked as though the weight of the world was on his shoulders. In a way, that may have been how he felt. (A delayed cable message had botched the original plan, which was for Pace to be in Tokyo and personally to inform MacArthur. What would he have done if the cable had arrived on time? "No problem," he later joked. "Presidential order. I'd commandeer the first plane and fly to Tokyo. Being after hours, I would have gone immediately to General MacArthur's quarters. I'd have taken the order, rung the doorbell, and shoved it under the door and run like hell!")

On 19 April, Douglas MacArthur delivered his emotional, "old soldiers never die" farewell speech to a joint session of Congress. People across the nation voiced their outrage over the manner of MacArthur's dismissal. At the same time, when he said "there is no substitute for victory," implying that the war should be expanded, the American public felt uneasy.

That uneasiness would have been far greater had they known the ominous situation on the battlefield. Enemy troops in North Korea now totaled 475,000, with another 478,000 in reserve in Manchuria. The CCF and NK buildup was in preparation for their coming Fifth Phase Offensive. Peking and Pyongyang radios openly boasted that this was the assault which once and for all would "drive the aggressors back into the sea."

Operation Dauntless, a cautious advance toward the Chorwon-Pyonggang-Kumhwa "Iron Triangle," had begun on 11 April. General Van Fleet, who had assumed command of Eighth Army on 14 April, was continuing Ridgway's plan, by which the move north would continue even though the new enemy offensive was imminent. The concept was for friendly forces, once the enemy attack began, to withdraw to planned defensive positions, meanwhile using both artillery and air to inflict maximum casualties.

Enemy resistance stiffened as UN forces approached the Iron Triangle. It was obvious the spring offensive was about to begin, and prisoner reports gave 22 April as the probably target date. More and more reports confirmed this, and based on the interrogation of a prisoner captured that day, General Bryan called Corps around 7:00 P.M. on 22 April, predicted the offensive would begin in about two hours, and said, "I think this is what we have been waiting for."

That night the Chinese hit in force. Artillery poured thousands of rounds into the human waves, but still they came on. Tactical air was also busy flying close support missions, and '49er pilot Dave Barnes was soon in the air. On this first day of the Chinese offensive, and only two weeks after that visit from his dad, Dave's plane went down and he was taken prisoner.

As a cadet, Dave, one of the brightest members of our class, was always ready to help those less gifted. Those who knew him best appreciated his sense of humor, his cheerful nature, his love of classical music and good books. It was hard to picture him as a POW. Two months later, on 20 June, Dave Barnes died in prison camp.

As midnight arrived on 22 April, Joe Kingston's K Company of the 32nd Infantry was strung out along a 3,400-meter front, occupying a ridgeline whose dominant feature was Hill 902. For this impossible frontage, Joe had some three hundred men at his disposal. This included his own King Company (now close to authorized strength, thanks to recent replacements plus hospital returnees), a weapons platoon from M Company, the regimental I&R Platoon, and a platoon of 4.2" mortars in direct support.

By the light of a full moon, men on the company outpost saw North Korean soldiers creeping past them. The outpost began firing, thereby alerting the company and also causing the enemy to back off momentarily. Several times enemy squads rushed the outpost position. Each time they were beaten back, and finally, during a lull, the outpost force, along with their six wounded, rejoined the main body.

Kingston called his CO, the 3rd Battalion commander, and said it looked as though a main attack was building, with 902 as its principal objective. He asked permission to pull in his flanks and said he might be needing reinforcements.

"Do what you have to," the battalion commander said. "I'm three hours away from you. There's nothing I can do to help, so you're on your own."

Joe, angry at this unhelpful comment, handed the radio handset to his first sergeant, saying: "There's no point my talking to those people anymore. If anyone calls, *you* talk to them! Meanwhile, tell the company exec what's going on, and ask him to bring forward any available men and extra ammo."

Kingston left his CP, which had been turned into an aid station, and headed up on line. Seeing the masses that had bunched for the attack, he realized this might be the day he "bought it."

Soon the NKs came on in waves. The main attack hit where Joe had positioned the heavy machine guns from M Company. The guns opened up, spitting out a volume of rapid fire, piling up dozens of bodies, and breaking the momentum of the initial charge. Artillery and mortar fire also began tearing into the massed formations. Still they came forward, with courage worthy of a better cause. The first assault waves had weapons, either burp guns or rifles; succeeding waves were armed only with sacks of grenades; and finally came unarmed soldiers who tried to equip themselves with weapons dropped by those who had fallen.

Kingston's 1st Platoon was led by former sergeant Boyle, an outstanding soldier who had won a battlefield commission and was now a second lieutenant. During one assault, the 1st Platoon, through sheer weight of numbers, was forced to give ground and Boyle was killed.

Kingston organized the men around him, including some of the 60-mm mortar people who had fired all their ammo, and told them to fix bayonets. Then he led them in a fierce charge to restore the position.

Joe moved up and down the line, urging, encouraging. "Whenever those guys start screaming," Joe told his troops, "you scream right back at them!"

By 4:00 A.M., hundreds of enemy bodies were stacked in front of the King Company position, but more and more enemy, perhaps the greater part of the NK 45th Division, were continuing to mass on the slopes of 902. Kingston's men had been firing steadily, and by this time some of the Americans had been reduced to using captured enemy weapons and ammunition. The situation was improved somewhat when Lieutenant Rogers, the King Company exec, arrived with more ammo, plus thirty to forty reinforcements. Some were replacements getting a memorable introduction to their new unit, others were rear area cooks, drivers, or KATUSAs Rogers had rounded up.

Around 5:00 A.M., King Company had been forced back from the crest of 902, when a young soldier, on all fours, tugged at Kingston's pant leg and said he was a runner from A Company.

"We've been told to reinforce you. The company commander needs to know where to fire his mortars, so he wants you to come back and coordinate with him."

"You go back and tell your CO where I am, and if he wants to talk to me, he can just come up *here!*" Joe shouted.

A few minutes later, Lieutenant Colonel Gillis, commander of the 1st Battalion, appeared out of the morning mist along with his artillery liaison officer, '49er Don Gower.

"How can I help you, Lieutenant?" Gillis asked.

"Sir, I need some men up here who can fight!" Gillis called the A Company commander and told him to "give Kingston whatever he wants."

Shortly a platoon from A Company came hurrying up the hill. Joe had them fix bayonets and told them they were going to retake the crest of Hill 902. Up they started. Joe, with the lead elements, turned to say something to the man next to him, and as he did, a bullet hit the soldier squarely in the left ear. Blood began to flow, and the man went down.

The attack continued, up over the crest of 902, and at last the enemy fell back. Although the action continued four more days, with the remainder of the battalion coming up on line, the enemy attack had been blunted. King Company now occupied an area which initially had been the responsibility of only its 1st Platoon.

Joe Kingston's King Company, while killing several hundred of the enemy, had suffered seventeen dead and fifty-five wounded, plus another five killed and seventeen wounded in the attached units.

For the action of 22–23 April, Joe's outfit was awarded a Presidential Unit Citation, and Corps Comdr. Ned Almond, in a commendation letter to Kingston, said that A and K companies had "withstood the brunt of the enemy's determined attack and held intact the shoulder of the X Corps . . . [a] prompt and decisive action . . . felt throughout the X Corps front."

In the IX Corps sector, the 6th ROK Division collapsed, with soldiers abandoning equipment and fleeing in panic. This opened a huge gap in the line, and the Chinese poured through. American units were shifted to plug the gap, more losses were suffered, but eventually Eighth Army's front was stabilized. As the Army withdrew to successive positions, artillery and air continued to pound the attackers.

The period 22–30 April, saw some of the war's bloodiest fighting, with UN forces suffering some 7,000 casualties. CCF and NK losses, meanwhile, reached staggering totals as their massed formations were decimated by US air and artillery. Within this nine-day period, enemy casualties reached the appalling figure of 70,000. One wondered how long the Communist leaders would be willing to sacrifice their men so ruthlessly.

In May, '49er pilots Dick Schoeneman and Bob Makinney sailed from San Francisco, headed for the replacement depot at Fuchu, Japan. From there, Bob was assigned to F-86s in the 4th Tactical Fighter Wing at Kimpo, and Dick was assigned to F-80s in the 51st Tactical Fighter

Wing at Suwon. First, however, Schoeneman went to a Wing Training Base at Tsuiki, Japan. From there, Dick flew his first combat mission, despite never having dropped a bomb or fired a gun from an airplane in his life.

General Van Fleet expected the next Chinese assault would be directed at Seoul. In mid-May, however, the main thrust came against ROK divisions in the east. Once again the ROKs collapsed, exposing Eighth Army's right flank. The US 2nd Division, on the shoulder of the penetration, fought tenaciously, and eventually the line was held. Eighth Army poured in additional forces, mounted a counterattack, and the Chinese began falling back.

In the central sector, where the 24th Division was engaged, Jack Arnette, a member of the 21st Infantry's Easy Company since the fall of 1950, was wounded on 27 May. Stu Martin, another '49er, had also been in Easy Company for a time. Stu, who'd been with me at Fort Knox, had, like me, been an armored officer "converted" into an infantry platoon leader. He had now left the infantry, however, and was serving with the 6th Tank Battalion.

A few days later, on 1 June, Joe Turley, fighting nearby with Able Company of the 19th Infantry as part of the same operation, was wounded and evacuated.

On that same day, '49er Bill Mueller took off on a bombing mission in support of the current Eighth Army offensive. Bill, who hailed from East St. Louis, had been an Air Force sergeant before entering the Academy and was now a pilot with the 343rd Squadron of the 98th Bomb Group. During the mission, Bill's plane went down, and he became another '49er to die in combat.

By mid-June, having commanded Charlie Company for nearly three months, Ernie Denham had learned a great deal about those he led. One of his favorite characters was 1st Sgt. Henry Cecil, a tall, Gary Cooper–like maverick whose background included an almost-forgotten chapter of Army history.

In the Depression year of 1933, when the Army's budget was cut to almost nothing, a weird economy was proposed whereby soldier prisoners would be released from the Fort Leavenworth stockade provided they agreed to leave the continental United States and not return. Cecil, one of these men, had gone to Hawaii, joined the Hawaiian National Guard, and fought in the Pacific during World War II, after which he remained in Hawaii with the 24th Division.

In Korea, Sergeant Cecil and the platoon sergeant of the weapons platoon, the only two remaining from the original C Company, had formed their own irregular "army" out of likely Koreans they had first fed, then trained and recruited. By this time the weapons platoon had nearly a hundred additional KATUSAs.

During the June offensive, Denham's company was given the mission of attacking and seizing a forbidding height known as Granite Mountain. A narrow ridge led to the top, which meant only one platoon at a time could make the assault. After an artillery preparation, Ernie sent his 1st Platoon up the mountain. Before long they were met by small arms, grenades, and a thunderous mortar barrage. The platoon, after taking some twenty casualties, was finally forced to fall back.

More artillery was fired, and a new assault was launched by the 2nd Platoon. This time the attackers got a bit farther up the ridge, but they too, in the face of heavy fire, withdrew after suffering heavy losses.

An air strike was brought in against Granite Mountain. Then still more artillery concentrations were fired. The Chinese, however, were still on position, and once again the final brutal phase, closing with the enemy, was a job for the infantry.

Ernie realized there could be no more "after you, buddy." If another platoon went up that hill, it had to be "follow me!" Denham was with the lead elements as the 3rd Platoon worked its way up the ridge. As they neared the top, Ernie could make out the well dug-in positions. A hand would come out of a hole, a grenade would come flying, and the hand would disappear. From another hole a head would pop up, a burp gun would fire, and the head would pull back. Despite the bullets, and the exploding grenades, the men of Charlie Company continued to inch forward.

In school, we had learned the doctrine of final protective fire, the all-out "shoot everything but the kitchen sink" when the enemy reaches a certain point. To his regret, Ernie now had a chance to see it demonstrated. In one terrifying crescendo, a volume of mortar and artillery fire descended on the lead elements. The explosions, one after another, made a continuous crunching roar.

A screaming shell from a 120-mm mortar exploded just inches behind Ernie, tossing him into the air. He landed about thirty feet forward, with his head pointed downhill. One of his legs was mangled, the other was literally blown off.

The survivors fell back, which was the signal for a Chinese counterattack. Still dimly conscious, Ernie saw white sneakers running past his face. His first thought had been, "Will I die?" Now it became, "Will I become a POW?"

Ernie lost consciousness, but had he been awake, he would have heard the yells of 1st Sgt. Henry Cecil, leading a charge with the ragtag KATUSA irregulars of the weapons platoon. The Chinese fell back, giving the irregulars a chance to carry Ernie back down the ridge.

At the base of Granite Mountain, Ernie was laid alongside the other casualties. A Navy doctor, on detached service with the Army, came down the line performing triage. Who needed immediate treatment? Whose treatment could be delayed? Who was beyond hope?

When the doctor came to Ernie, he just shook his head and moved on. Ernie, although unconscious, seemed to be floating outside his body. Physically, he had been on his back, facing the sky with his eyes closed.

Yet, in an out-of-body experience, he looked down, saw the doctor moving down the line, even saw his own face. When the doctor came to him, shook his head and moved on, Ernie wanted to cry out that he was still alive. Next, Ernie felt himself to be in a dark tunnel, at the end of which was the brightest light he had ever seen. He proceeded, or perhaps floated, down that tunnel and as he did so, Mike Wadsworth, his friend who had been killed back in December, said: "Come on, Ernie, follow me. It's not so bad." Later, Ernie wondered if he had seen Mike, only heard him, or just sensed his presence.

For some reason the doctor doubled back, put his stethoscope to Ernie's chest, and detected a faint heartbeat. Although he still felt there was little or no hope, he decided to administer plasma so there'd be at least some small chance of survival. The doctor thought Denham looked vaguely familiar, although in his present condition he was hard to recognize. Actually the two had met some weeks earlier, and Ernie had even bought the Navy man a drink. Much later, in a Tokyo hospital, Ernie met the doctor and learned the story of the "doubling back."

It was hardly a subject for humor, but even so, Denham could smile as the doctor said, "Maybe, if you hadn't bought me that drink. . . ."

Today, remembering that dark tunnel, Ernie says, "I know if I ever enter it again, I'll never return."

In mid-June, Clay Buckingham's tank platoon supported the 65th Infantry as it fought in the Iron Triangle area near Chorwon. During one operation, Clay's tank hit a mine, breaking the track. Seconds

Point men of Joe Kingston's K Company, 32nd Infantry, advance along a snow-covered forest trail toward the final ridge of Hill 671, northeast of Chae-Jae.
US Army photo.

later, the mine explosion was followed by an antitank round that wounded Clay's driver. Clay and the others bailed out of their disabled tank, and as they did so, the tank behind them was hit by another antitank round. That tank's commander, hit in the head, was killed instantly.

Clay rounded up some nearby men. Working with them, together with his own crew, he became an infantry troop leader for the next several minutes. They managed to take out the antitank guns, after which Clay and his crew were able to repair their damaged track. Their tank could live to fight another day.

As part of the same offensive, the 32nd Infantry Regiment of the 7th Division was also operating in the Iron Triangle area. The 3rd

Battalion of that regiment was given the job of attacking one of the highest peaks in Korea, the infamous Hill 1073. This was a key piece of terrain, dominating an area east of Kumhwa, and well dug-in Chinese had every intention of holding it.

Joe Kingston and Jack Madison, who'd been together from the start, were still with that 3rd Battalion, Joe commanding King Company, and Jack as an Assistant S-3 at Battalion. For a time, Madison had also commanded a company, until, to his disappointment, he'd been replaced by a newly arrived captain.

Finally 1073 was captured, but not before a struggle which involved heavy hand-to-hand fighting. A few days later, on 18 June, Kingston was told to take his men still farther north on a company-sized patrol.

By this time, most commanders agreed with Ridgway, who felt terrain was meaningless and that the main goal was to inflict punishment, killing North Koreans and their Chinese allies until the enemy realized aggression could not succeed. Tentative diplomatic truce feelers had already started, and it was clear the war of maneuver was winding down.

Despite all that, or perhaps as a consequence, each side was still trying to seize good defensible terrain, ground which could be fortified and held indefinitely. Kingston's patrol on 18 June was part of that effort.

Up to this point, Joe had been amazingly lucky, emerging without a scratch, despite having had several close calls. On this day, however, he had a premonition something bad was going to happen. The night before, he'd had a dream of being wounded, and as they started out, Joe told his exec, "I think I'm going to get hit today."

As the patrol worked its way forward from 1073, it ran into trouble. Chinese on high ground poured fire into King Company, driving Kingston's men back toward friendly lines. The last man wounded was Joe himself, by a bullet which entered his shoulder and then plunged downward into his lungs and liver.

Back at Battalion it was Jack Madison who had the task of calling for a Medevac helicopter. Once he'd done so, he left the CP and hurried up the ridge. Jack met up with Joe's litter team, saw where the bullet had entered Joe's shoulder, and shaking his head, noted there was no exit wound. Joe, still fighting mad, was complaining about considerable pain lower down on his right side.

They carried the litter to an open place which could serve as a helicopter landing pad. For part of the journey, Kingston had high-paid litter bearers, his battalion commander, his regimental commander Colonel Mount (our former West Point tactical officer), and his division commander, Gen. Buddy Ferenbaugh.

They placed Joe in the helicopter's external patient carrier pod, and through the tiny viewing window, Madison could see his face. Joe was losing color and was in obvious pain.

The battalion commander turned to Madison. "You go up there and take over King Company." Jack complied, and as he climbed the hill, he wondered if he'd ever see his friend again.

On 18 June, the day Kingston was wounded, *Newsweek* carried an article headed "West Point's Toll." The class of 1951 had just graduated, and *Newsweek* noted that for USMA '51:

> the Korean casualty lists provided gloomy reading. They showed that one-half of the Army lieutenants from the preceding two classes had been rushed to Korea and that one-third of this half had been killed or wounded, or were missing in action. Of the '50 Pointers, 17 were killed, 30 wounded, and 8 missing. Of the Class of '49, 22 were killed, 30 wounded, and 7 missing. Although Pointers are outnumbered 20-1 in Korea by non-Point officers, nearly 100 of the 530 officers killed have been Academy graduates.
>
> This is no surprise to old soldiers. In every American war, Pointers have suffered more than their share. Their Korean casualty rate might become the highest in history. . . .

While the article said the figures were no surprise to "old soldiers," they weren't surprising to young ones either. Though the tally was high (and would climb still higher), we knew proper combat leadership inevitably placed one in harm's way. We didn't like it, but we accepted it, and we also deeply resented it when a senator from Alabama was quoted as saying there should be an investigation, since the high number of West Point casualties showed something must be seriously wrong with West Point training.

Only minutes after being placed in the helicopter, Kingston was back at a MASH unit and on an operating table. (Today he's convinced the two wise-cracking surgeons he met were the models for Hawkeye and Trapper of the *MASH* TV series.) They went to work after telling Joe the bullet had hit his collarbone, had been deflected downward to puncture a lung, and had then lodged in his liver. They needed to operate at once, and if they didn't, he'd probably die. "Of course you may die anyway," one of them added cheerfully. Joe managed to sass them back, then passed out. Although the surgeons were unable to retrieve the bullet, the operation was successful and his condition was stabilized.

A week later, Kingston was flown to the Swedish hospital ship *Repose* in Pusan harbor, where X-rays showed the bullet was shifting. More surgery was performed, and after several difficult probes, the doctor told Joe, "If you can stand it, I'm going to take one more look." A few seconds later, he placed the bullet in Joe's hand.

Diplomatic truce feelers had now been coming from both camps. The Soviet ambassador to the United Nations, while claiming not to speak for Peking, indicated a desire for a peaceful settlement "at the earliest possible moment."

On 25 June, more or less in response, President Truman said, "We are ready to join in a peaceful settlement in Korea now, just as we have always been. But it must be a real settlement which fully ends the aggression and restores peace and security to the area and to the gallant people of Korea."

Additional overtures were made, through both public and private channels. Evidently both sides recognized that a clear-cut victory, even if possible, would be far too costly. On 29 June, following carefully crafted instructions from Washington, General Ridgway addressed an invitation to "the Commander in Chief, Communist Forces in Korea," saying, "I am informed that you may wish a meeting to discuss an armistice providing for the cessation of hostilities and all acts of armed force in Korea, with adequate guarantees for the maintenance of such armistice. . . ."

Peking responded some thirty hours later, suggesting talks to be held at Kaesong, on the 38th Parallel, between 10 and 15 July, 1951. The fighting was still going on and people were still dying, but at least it was a start.

14. Stalemate

JULY 1951–JULY 1953

Truce talks might be pending, but the war went right on. Ridgway and Van Fleet decided to keep up the pressure, feeling anything less might be interpreted as weakness. UN negotiators wanted the world, and especially the Communists, to know they were coming to the table as bargainers, not petitioners.

Operations in the Punchbowl area of eastern Korea, and in the Sobang Hills near Kumhwa, resulted in heavy fighting but caused very little change in the battle line. Meanwhile, commanders at all levels were becoming concerned about stateside talk of "bring the boys home at once" and its possible effect on combat esprit and aggressiveness. Obviously, if peace was imminent, no one wanted to be the last man to die.

On 1 July, elements of the 3rd Division attacked to seize Hill 717 in the Iron Triangle area near Pyonggang. Clay Buckingham was in the lead tank as Task Force Hawkins, several miles behind enemy lines, tried to cut off an enemy escape route. When the column came to a large expanse of flooded rice paddies, Clay volunteered to find an alternate route to the objective, and in the words of his Bronze Star citation, "he led his platoon forward, dismounting in the face of small arms fire to guide the tanks through a difficult stream bed and skillfully deploying them to place maximum fire on the enemy. He also reconnoitered a road in the area to see if it was mined, and heedless of the hostile artillery fire, probed until he found the road safe."

Bill Moore's engineer platoon was on hand as a "peace camp" was established at Munsan-ni to support UN negotiators. Both sides had agreed to meet at Kaesong to discuss the agenda, and the UN team, headed by Adm. C. Turner Joy, might have to travel along a certain dirt road. Accordingly, Moore was given the job of reconnoitering the road and checking it for mines.

As per an agreement, the engineers put white flags on their jeeps and left their weapons behind, all except for the bayonets they'd use to probe for mines. For the first few miles, all went well; fortunately the road had never been mined.

Just short of Kaesong, as Bill's platoon came to the Imjin River, they were greeted by a burst of small-arms fire. On the far bank was a group of Chinese soldiers. Evidently the shots had been their way of telling Moore not to come any farther. A Chinese officer, who spoke a bit of English, called for the American officer to come over and talk.

Bill thought, "What the heck, I guess I should." With some apprehension, he crossed over. Clearly this was as far as he needed to go. From this point forward, the Chinese would be responsible for the road. The officer's English vocabulary was quite limited, but at least it was better than Bill's nonexistent Chinese. With some difficulty, they managed to exchange brief "pleasantries," and Bill returned to his platoon.

At this point the officer called for Bill to come back so they could talk some more. Bill decided this was a ploy to have the Americans lose face.

"No," Bill shouted, "if you want to talk some more, you come over here." This the officer refused to do, so Bill and his men, mission accomplished, returned to Munsan-ni. In many ways, that junior-officer encounter, reflecting American firmness in the face of Chinese manipulation, was a foreshadowing of the coming truce-talk frustrations.

With the ground fighting slowing down, added attention was given to the air war, and more and more '49er pilots were playing a part. Early in July, Dick Schoeneman, who'd been flying his F-80 missions out of Japan, was transferred to the Korean airbase at Suwon. With Dick, in the same 16th Fighter Squadron, was '49er Phil O'Brien.

Suwon saw a minireunion of sorts when engineer Ken McIntyre, Dick's plebe-year roommate, arrived to resurface the airstrip. They laughed, but were impressed, as Ken's "playkit" arrived—a full asphalt plant packaged like a giant erector set. Somehow Ken managed to assemble the plant and resurface the runway successfully.

Also arriving in July was Gene Mechling. A month earlier, Gene had finished the Fighter-Gunnery school at Nellis AFB. Then, after spending a joyful second honeymoon at Laguna Beach, he had shipped out, eventually ending up at the K-2 airstrip near Taegu. At K-2, Gene joined the 9th Squadron of the 49th Fighter-Bomber wing, an F-84

Gene Mechling, 1951. Courtesy Col. Eugene B. Mechling, Jr. (Ret.)

Thunderjet outfit. With him at K-2, also in F-84s, was D. D. Overton, who would eventually fly more missions than any other '49er.

As Gene prepared for his first mission, he was told about the many things he might see. However, the old hands predicted that on that first mission his main concern would be survival and he "probably wouldn't see a damned thing." An F-84, with a thousand pound bomb on each wing, was especially sluggish in the heat of summer. After takeoff, more than one pilot had crashed into "Bust-your-ass Hill," a saddleback ridge just off the runway. (In the following year, the 49th Wing, through combat losses and accidents, would lose some seventy-five planes—a 100 percent turnover.)

For an extra boost on takeoff, the F-84s were using JATO, jet assisted takeoff. As they roared down the runway, the pilots would activate the JATO, not only giving them extra power, but also spewing out a dense cloud of steam and smoke. On his first mission, Gene was in the last flight to take off. By the time he and his wingman began their takeoff run, there was a dense cloud from all the JATO emissions, providing an extra thrill as this very first mission, although in daylight, began with what in effect became an instrument takeoff in zero visibility.

Before volunteering for Korea, D. D. Overton had been flying F-84s in England. At K-2, it developed that D. D. had more F-84 time than the rest of his squadron put together. The original group, after completing a hundred missions, were all rotating home about the same time. The new arrivals, mostly National Guardsmen, had very little jet time. Soon D. D. was made squadron operations officer, a job normally reserved for a major. Then, when the squadron commander broke his arm, D. D. ended up leading the squadron, or sometimes even the group, when his turn came to fly a mission.

Ever since he'd landed in Korea, Jack Madison had been corresponding steadily with Arden Hennig. As the months passed, their letters had become increasingly affectionate, and finally the two decided to get married upon Jack's return.

Jack had been commanding King Company ever since Joe Kingston was wounded. In late July, when the company went into reserve, Jack asked his battalion commander for permission to go see Colonel Hennig, whose artillery headquarters was in Seoul.

"A pass so you can visit some artilleryman?"

"But I want to ask for his daughter's hand in marriage."

"I must admit that's not only an unusual request for a combat zone, it's probably the best I've ever heard!" said Jack's boss.

Back in Seoul, Jack called on Colonel Hennig. The colonel remembered Jack slightly, but was obviously puzzled about the visit. Nevertheless, Madison accompanied Hennig over the weekend, and on Sunday evening, after a good meal, Jack decided the time was right.

"Sir, Arden and I want to get married."

Jack Madison (left) and 32nd Infantry staff officers selecting positions along Line Kansas, summer 1951. Courtesy Col. John H. Madison, Jr. (Ret.).

After a rather chilling pause, Hennig looked at Jack. "You're a rifle company commander, right?"

"Yes sir."

"Well, Lieutenant, *when* you get back, and *if* you get back, and *after* Arden finishes college, we might discuss this situation further."

Happily, Jack *did* get back, he and Arden *did* get married, and as this is written, the two are about to celebrate their fortieth wedding anniversary. Years later, Jack's father-in-law, by then a retired major general, told Jack that on the evening in question something he'd eaten had disagreed with him and he was suffering from terrible indigestion!

Dick Schoeneman, after completing twenty-five missions, was sent as a Forward Air Controller (FAC) with the 9th ROK Division. This was a unit which twice had bugged out, and Dick was just as happy when most of his FAC time was spent in a training area north of Seoul. Front-line duty with certain ROK divisions could be hazardous to one's health.

When he returned to Suwon, Dick learned the wing was converting to F-86s. His old unit was being disbanded, and most of the pilots were being reassigned. Dick, with previous F-86 experience, was one of the few to be retained in the wing.

The new F-86 unit, with a nucleus of people and planes from Selfridge AFB in Michigan, contained many World War II veterans, including such famed aces as Colonels Francis Gabreski and Bill Wisner. Their arrival, plus the increasing MiG presence in North Korea, caused a change in tactics. The leaders started operating as they had in World War II, with big wing formations.

Early in the F-86 operations, Dick was with the wing at about the latitude of Pyongyang, when they met head-on, at the exact same altitude, a massive flight of MiG-15s. If asked immediately after the incident, Dick would have said there were at least a hundred MiGs. The meeting was a total surprise to both parties, and with a closure rate of over six hundred knots, neither side had time to do anything but exert a death grip on their triggers. The next few seconds seemed an eternity. Both formations wheeled around and engaged in what Dick recalled as a Disney cartoon of a cat and dog fight in a big ball complete with dust cloud. As far as Dick knew, there were no losses on either side, mainly because everyone's primary attention was devoted to avoiding a midair collision with so many planes wheeling around.

With truce talks underway, the battle line had more or less stabilized. Our front-line units dug in and fortified their positions, putting out barbed wire and mines, filling sandbags, sending out patrols to learn what lay to their front.

Lew Baumann's Fox Company was on a key ridge line. The Chinese were in position two ridges away. In between lay an intermediate knob-shaped hill which kept changing hands. Often the Americans would seize the hill, hold it during daylight hours, then withdraw. The Chinese would occupy the hill at night, then either pull out before first light or remain with a token force and fall back when the Americans attacked.

This routine was maintained with such regularity that, during early August, Lew was able to use the intermediate hill as a training site. One by one, Lew coached his new lieutenants as they maneuvered their platoons, changed formations, deployed for an assault, seized and occupied the knob, then later withdrew to home base.

Perhaps it was some higher-up wanting to be aggressive. In any

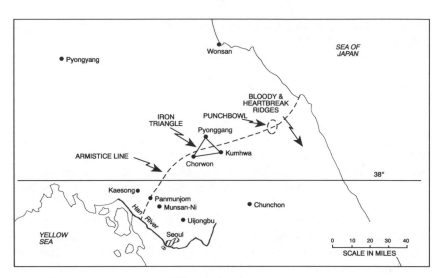

The Armistice Line

event, on 20 August, Lew was called back to Battalion HQ and ordered
to make a reconnaissance-in-force with Fox Company. He was to seize
the intermediate hill, cross a valley north of it, then probe to see how
strong the enemy was on the high ridge beyond that valley.

"Colonel, I *know* the enemy is over there," Lew told his battalion
commander. "I've been out on that knob at least three times and
watched them. I can't give you a head count, but I'm certain they're
over there in strength. While these peace talks are going on, they're
not bothering us and we're not bothering them. I think it's *crazy* to
go over there. All you're going to do is get a bunch of people hurt and
beat up."

The order was reaffirmed, and Lew repeated his protest. "I want
to offer my objections! This is *not* the thing to do. It's not going to
do any good to run a rifle company over there, and we're just going
to get the hell beat out of us!"

The colonel's patience had run out. "Lew," he said, "if you don't
want to do it, I'll get someone who can."

"Sir, I'm not going to walk away from my company when they're
about to get hammered. I'll do it, but I want you to understand; I'm
doing this under protest."

Lew returned to his company and made his plans, including fire
support, how they'd seize the intermediate knob, and the formations
they'd use.

Next day, 21 August, Baumann was with the lead platoon as they headed along a trail leading to the intermediate hill. Suddenly they noticed there were trip wires on the trail. This was a new development; evidently the Chinese had decided the knob was worth defending. The booby trap was disarmed and word was passed for everyone to stay off the path.

When they neared the knob, they began receiving fire, causing the lead platoon to hold up. Lew deployed the other platoons, then gave orders for a coordinated grenade assault, followed by a general advance. They swept over the hill and down the far side. The Chinese by this time had pulled back.

A mortar round exploded just short of the knob, followed by a second one just beyond. Obviously enemy mortars were ranging in. Then, in the distance, Lew heard a number of muffled thumps as a series of mortars were fired, one after another. Seconds later the barrage landed, and the entire hill seemed to erupt. Exploding shells crashed along the Fox Company position. One round landed about three feet to Lew's right, blowing him off his feet and throwing him against a nearby stump. He shook himself, got to his feet, and began calling on the radio for counterbattery fire. As he did so, his right leg gave way. He fell to the ground, tried to get up, and suddenly realized he couldn't stand.

The radio operator came running up. "Lieutenant, you've been hit! There's blood on your trousers. There's even blood on your hand."

"You better call the exec and have him come forward," Lew said. Unable to walk, Lew crawled forward to the crest of the hill, and when the exec arrived, told him he'd have to take over and lead the company into the meatgrinder.

Minutes later the medic arrived. He slit open Lew's trousers and said, "Lieutenant, you've been hit bad. I don't think any bones are broken, but you've got a pretty big hole in your right leg."

"How many casualties have we taken?" Lew asked.

"Well, the 1st Platoon leader is hit, and there must be at least six to eight more people dead or wounded up here, either from fragments or small arms."

The exec reported the situation to Battalion. "We've run into a small firefight which has escalated into something bigger. Fox 6 is down. Fox 1 is down. And we've taken additional casualties." About five minutes later, Battalion called with a message. "Scrap the operation. Bring 'em back."

To Lew, the evacuation, over a series of trails and ridges, seemed to take forever. In addition to the leg wound, there was shrapnel up and down his arm. The pain was becoming intense, and Lew kept repeating to himself: "I'm not going into shock. I'm not going into shock. I'm going to keep my composure. I'm not going to die on this damned hill."

At one point, they set Lew's litter down, and in horror, he saw they had placed it directly on top of a trip wire. How the men carrying him had missed the wire he'd never know. Lew reached over, gingerly disarmed the booby trap, then called out: "Hey, you guys, remember we said to stay off this trail when we came this way the first time. So stay off it going back!"

Eventually the litter bearers brought Lew to a space open enough to accommodate a Medevac helicopter. As the helicopter approached, a chaplain on the scene decided to help by marking the landing site with smoke. Unfortunately what he thought was a smoke cannister turned out to be a white phosphorus grenade. The WP exploded, spewing forth a spray of hot fragments. Men on litters frantically began to throw off their blankets to avoid the burning particles. Fortunately the casualties no longer had their weapons. If they had, someone, including Lew, might have been tempted to shoot the well-meaning but bumbling man of the cloth.

At last the chopper landed, Lew was "entombed" in the carrier pod and on his way. Before long he was being well cared for in a hospital in Japan.

On 23 August, two days after Baumann was wounded, the Communists walked out of the peace talks, claiming a US plane had bombed the Kaesong neutral zone. The charges were investigated and proved to be unfounded. Nevertheless, the talks were suspended for two full months, during which time the UN representatives insisted on Panmunjom, rather than Kaesong, as the meeting site. For once the Communists yielded, and on 25 October the talks resumed—at Panmunjom. Fighting continued unabated during the recess and names such as Heartbreak Ridge became part of US military history. Severe punishment was inflicted on the enemy, and General Van Fleet estimated that Communist losses from all causes during the recess were approximately 234,000. During the same time frame, UN casualties numbered 60,000, of whom 22,000 were Americans.

Back at home, people were reading about new US casualties and fierce fighting over seemingly inconsequential ridges. With US casualties in Korea now totaling nearly 100,000, American public support for the war was fading rapidly.

One of Gene Mechling's first missions was also one of his most memorable. Three wings, perhaps 150 planes, accompanied a dozen B-29s as they hit enemy airfields around Sinanju. Since it was a daylight raid, they fully expected to encounter heavy flak and many MiGs.

Word for the mission was received rather late, so Gene and the other pilots had to scramble quickly in order to get airborne. The runway was slick, and during the takeoff run, two of the F-84s collided, causing their external fuel tanks to rupture and burst into flames. Firetrucks and bulldozers managed to clear the runway, after which the other F-84s took off.

Because of the fire, there'd been a delay in assembling, so Gene and the others, not wanting to let down the bombers they were supporting, proceeded north at full throttle. By the time they arrived in the target area, the bomb run had already started, heavy ground fire was being received, and the sky seemed full of MiGs.

According to Gene, there were planes going every which way, parachutes, planes on fire, calls of "Mayday," all combined into an incredible melee, "the damnedest thing I'd ever seen." Gene was number-four man in a flight of four, protecting his leader while the leader looked for something to shoot at. All at once a MiG came screaming across Gene's nose. With no time to aim, he just pulled up and fired, hoping the MiG would fly through his line of flight. There was no way of knowing whether or not the shots took effect.

Before the mission was over, there'd been heavy losses, not only of fighters, but of some nine of the twelve B-29s. Fortunately some of the nine managed to crash-land in friendly territory. However, this level of attrition caused a rethinking of tactics, and understandably, this turned out to be the last daylight B-29 raid of the war.

In the fall of 1951, word came from Washington that all units should be integrated. Accordingly, the 64th Tank Battalion, an all-black outfit with mostly white officers, sent about 80 percent of its members to other units and received white replacements in return. Clay Buckingham, who had been with the 64th Battalion ever since it landed, was truly saddened as he said good-bye to the black soldiers who, during the past year, had fought so loyally alongside him. (No one could doubt Clay's devotion to the men of the 64th Battalion. Several months earlier, when he returned from his stay in a Yokohama hospital, Clay reported to the division replacement company in Seoul and was told he'd be going to a regimental tank company rather than back to the 64th Battalion. Clay thanked them, found a truck heading north, and made his way home to the 64th Battalion before the replacement company knew what was happening.)

By November, Jack Thomas and Jack Madison, both commanding companies in the 32nd Infantry Regiment, were overdue for rotation. Nearly everyone else who'd landed at Inchon in September of 1950 had sailed for home by this time. Thomas and Madison, although they were at the top of the rotation list, had been recommended for promotion, and they had both extended, hoping their captaincies would come through. Ironically, although many companies were being commanded by lieutenants, Eighth Army promotions to captain were frozen because of an overall surplus in that grade. (Prior to this, seventeen '49ers—ten infantry, 5 artillery, 2 engineers—had become captains before the freeze went into effect.)

One morning, as he looked out from his company position, Madison nearly had his head taken off by a round from a Chinese recoilless rifle. He picked up the field phone and called Jack Thomas.

"They almost got me this morning, Jack. I think it's time we got out of here."

"I agree," said Thomas. "We've been pushing our luck." Their regimental commander, Col. Louis Hightower (a tactical officer during our cadet days), urged them, almost in a fatherly fashion, to hang on until their promotions arrived. A month later, with promotions still frozen, they decided they had waited long enough. With apologies to Colonel Hightower, they started for home.

I too was heading stateside. Serving as an aide to General Bryan had been a great experience, but enough was enough. After a few broad hints on my part, my understanding boss said it was time I got back to my family. My replacement was '49er Goble Bryant, who'd been serving in the 11th Field Artillery Battalion of our division. I felt honored that Goble was the man replacing me, and I knew he'd do a fine job. Goble and General Bryan had much in common. Not only were they both artillerymen, each had been an Army football star and each had served for a time as an assistant coach at the Academy.

Finally it was time to leave. General Bryan thanked me warmly for my services, rewarded me with a Commendation Medal for my time as aide, and I was on my way.

The trip over had been all "rush-rush." Getting home, however, was more like "delay-delay." At one of the way stations, the Japanese port city of Sasebo, I was reunited with several friends, including Jack Madison, and learned my new assignment—the Training Division at

Fort Dix, New Jersey. Then came a Pacific crossing on a lumbering World War II Victory ship, followed by a tedious five days (Fort Lawton, Washington, to Camp Kilmer, New Jersey) as a troop train commander. Understandably, the prolonged anticipation made the December reunion with Jeanne and our baby all the more wonderful.

That same month, the *USS Gordon* sailed from San Francisco carrying '49ers Hayes Metzger, Bob Black, Murray Williams, and Clint Norman. Each of the four would see action as a company commander. (It was easy for Hayes to remember the trip's duration. It took twenty-two days, during which he lost twenty-two pounds!) For Hayes and others, the nature of the war had changed; there would be no more headline-making events, such as the landing at Inchon, nor any sweeping maneuvers on a grand scale. Both sides were dug in, in trenches almost resembling those of World War I. Every piece of ground would be hotly contested and paid for in blood as Americans did battle on obscure hills given identity by names like Porkchop or Old Baldy.

Even at Fort Dix, I was constantly aware of the war. More and more '49ers were heading to Korea, as were most of the Fort Dix trainees. Often I heard news of various classmates, but some stories, such as Fletcher McMurry's, Hayes Metzger's, and Dolph Overton's, I didn't learn until much later.

As mentioned earlier, Fletcher McMurry had married Bill Marslender's sister Linda after having roomed with Bill and Roger Kuhlman for all four cadet years. In March of 1952, Fletch said good-bye to Linda and to their infant son named in Kuhlman's honor. Arriving in Korea, he joined the 8th Bomb Squadron. A few days later, like his classmates Chuck Reed, Tom Bullock, and J. P. Hawn, Fletch was flying night intruder missions against targets in North Korea. Then, late at night on 19 April, 1952, Fletch's heavily loaded black B-26 crashed shortly after takeoff and was swallowed up by the Yellow Sea.

For some reason, Fletch wasn't wearing his West Point ring on that last mission. When Linda received Fletch's personal effects, she remembered that surgeons had cut off her brother's ring after he'd been wounded in the hand. In a poignant footnote to the story, Linda gave Fletch's West Point ring to her brother Bill.

In late July of 1952, Hayes Metzger, commanding Charlie Company of the 23rd Infantry, was told to prepare his company for a coordinated night attack. Hayes's experience was somewhat typical, in that for some time he had occupied a well-fortified entrenched position, with ample supplies and good fire support, some of it from a mortar company commanded by Murray Williams. The supply channels had worked so well, in fact, that when the regimental commander asked Hayes if he needed anything, all Hayes could think to say was that they never seemed able to get any lighter fluid.

For three days, Charlie Company practiced for the coming attack on terrain similar to the objective area. Then they ran patrols to learn the best routes to their objective. Shortly before the attack, as tension was mounting, Hayes saw an unfamiliar figure crawling up the trench toward him. It was the warrant officer who handled regimental PX supplies. From the pained expression on his face, it was obvious the man was not at all happy about having to visit a frontline rifle company.

The warrant thrust a small paper bag into Hayes' hands and said, "Thanks to you, I got chewed out. Here's your damned lighter fluid!"

Hayes laughed at the irony of the situation, then thanked the man, who was wasting no time in making his departure. On 1 August the attack jumped off in the rain, and under cover of darkness, crawling through mud, Charlie Company got within fifteen feet of the Chinese position before being detected. At that point the enemy began throwing grenades, and heavy firing erupted from both small arms and mortars. The fighting intensified, and by the time the objective was secured, more than two hundred Chinese bodies covered the area. In the action, Charlie Company suffered four killed and fourteen wounded. Hayes, one of the wounded, was evacuated to an aid station, where he was patched up by a young dentist who had been pressed into emergency service, then further evacuated to Pusan and eventually to the Swedish hospital ship anchored offshore.

About the time Hayes Metzger was wounded, D. D. Overton was completing his tour in F-84s. He had flown 102 missions, had bombed railroads, dams, trains, cement plants, and power plants. He had gone to the front to be with ground troops, had flown the T-6 "Mosquito" spotter plane, been with the Navy on the carrier *USS Valley Forge*, visited the Marines at Pusan (where baseball great Ted Williams was flying), and hit Pyongyang three times in one day amid the heaviest flak anyone could remember.

All this should have been enough for anyone. D. D., however, wanted a chance to fly the hot F-86. With an assist from his CO, he received permission for fifty additional missions with an F-86 unit. At Suwon, he joined the 16th Fighter-Interceptor Squadron led by Col. Ed Heller, a top pilot who'd become an ace in Europe during World War II.

Jet ace Dolph "D. D." Overton in cockpit of his F-86 Sabrejet, following completion of his 49th F-86 mission and his 151st overall Korean combat mission, January 1953. Courtesy Dolph Overton.

Over the next several months, D. D. flew a variety of F-86 missions, had several close calls, encountered many MiGs, and possibly damaged a few of them. It was on 21 January, 1953, however, during his forty-sixth F-86 mission, that he was credited with his first aerial victory. He spotted a flight of four MiGs, attacked one of them, and scored hits on the wing and tail section. The MiG turned to the right, began trailing black smoke, spun out of control, and was last seen going straight down. Just three minutes later, D. D. attacked a second MiG, his shots sending it out of control and into a steep dive, with fuel streaming from the right wing.

Amazingly, D. D. then shot down MiGs on each of the next two days, making it four aerial victories within a three-day period. On 22 January, as reported in General Orders, "he initiated a diving attack on one of a flight of two MiGs . . . scoring hits on the wings, fuselage, and tail pipe sections. The enemy aircraft was observed to crash into the ground and explode near Uiju." His fourth victory, on 23 January, also occurred near Uiju.

On the following day, D. D. flew F-86 mission No. 49, or overall mission No. 151. On that day, 24 January, he was called to be on a sweep flight led by Colonel Heller, who would fly the No. 1 position. Heller's wingman, in No. 2, was a pilot named Smith. The No. 3 element lead would be Major Herrick, the new squadron operations officer. Overton would fly No. 4 as Herrick's wingman.

D. D. was a bit upset at having to be a wingman, since he had only two more missions to fly and needed one more MiG to reach the magic number of five. Heller, whom D. D. considered one of the greatest, pacified him, saying he needed Herrick back in one piece and D. D. had better see to it or he'd "stuff his ragged tail up his exhaust pipe." D. D. came back with a sassy response, at which Heller, slapping him on the back and grinning, said that was no way to speak to a superior officer. In high spirits, the two of them walked together out to their planes.

They proceeded directly to the Yalu. Soon they were in the middle of a large flight of MiGs. Heller and Herrick became separated, and suddenly D. D. and Herrick were all alone. They managed to get behind two MiGs. Herrick shot down one, D. D. shot down the other, and they returned to base. Overton felt on top of the world. He had five MiGs to his credit, and after one more mission he'd be on his way home.

It was fifteen years before D. D. again saw Colonel Heller, who was shot down in China, seriously injured on bailout, and made a Chinese POW. He was freed two years after the war along with seven others when Henry Kissinger made a special mission to China to obtain their release.

Apparently some Swiss neutrals, on a train in China heading for the truce talks at Panmunjom, had seen the contrails in the sky and had stopped to watch the show. They had seen Heller go down and had also seen the two MiGs shot down by Herrick and Overton.

Next morning D. D. was called to meet with his wing commander and a colonel from 5th Air Force HQ. The visitor asked D. D. one question. "Were you over the Yalu yesterday?"

D. D. might have quibbled, saying he wasn't sure, or that he was in hot pursuit, or argued that wherever he was, he was No. 4 in a flight of four and only following his leaders. Instead, the honorable Overton merely answered, "Yes sir."

For some time, F-86 pilots, angry over the MiGs' unfair Manchurian sanctuary, had flown across the Yalu. The orders forbidding this had been largely ignored, and the wing commander, who had himself crossed over on occasion (D. D. had seen him), had condoned it. However, there was concern higher up that this particular incident might embarrass the UN negotiators at Panmunjom. A scapegoat was needed, and apparently D. D. was selected.

D. D. never knew what the wing commander told the people at headquarters, or what they told him. All he knew was that next day he was called in, reprimanded, and told he was being grounded and sent home. He would lose his spot captaincy, revert to the grade of first lieutenant, and would receive no awards or decorations for his Korean service. Back in the States, he was assigned to an airbase in Maine that had no planes. It was a disillusioning conclusion to what had been a remarkable tour of duty. A few months later, jet ace D. D. Overton resigned his commission.

The peace talks dragged on, with many stumbling blocks along the way. Perhaps the greatest barrier to a settlement was the question of POW repatriation. In January of 1952, the UN team had said no prisoner should be returned to Communist control against his will. Then, three months later, when a poll found that of 132,000 military POWs, only 70,000 wanted repatriation, the enraged Communist negotiators walked out of Panmunjom.

The talks were recessed more or less indefinitely, and the Red propaganda machine went into high gear, hurling charges that the United States was using germ warfare, mistreating POWs, and bargaining in bad faith.

In the spring of 1953, following the inauguration of Dwight Eisenhower, the Communist position softened a bit on the prisoner issue. An agreement was reached for an exchange of sick and wounded POWs, and Operation Little Switch took place between 20 April and 3 May.

While Little Switch was going on, senior negotiators resumed their talks at Panmunjom. Once again POW repatriation was the main topic. At last, on 27 June, the POW matter and other issues having been more or less resolved, the armistice agreement was signed. Shortly thereafter, Gen. Mark Clark, the UN commander, cautioned that the armistice was only a military agreement to stop the shooting so the opposing sides could seek a political solution to the conflict.

With the guns now silent, Operation Big Switch, the POW exchange, was soon underway. Only two '49ers, Tom Byrd and John Hastings, were among the 3,600 Americans released to come home.

The shooting had stopped, but for me and others, memories of Korea persisted. Once at Fort Dix, I dreamed I was at a formal banquet when a few tables away, with his back to me, I saw Les Kirkpatrick. Excitedly, I rushed to him. "Kirk," I called out, "I thought you were killed!"

He turned, and suddenly he looked as I had last seen him, dirty faced, haggard, dressed in combat fatigues. There was a bullet hole in his forehead. "I was," he said softly. I woke up shaking.

Lew Baumann, one of my neighbors at Dix, said he once woke in the middle of the night, shouting commands and swearing a blue streak. His wife Pat said he seemed to be reliving some experience from Korea. Later, when out on bivouac, Lew cautioned his first sergeant that he might hear him moaning or shouting commands during the night. "If that happens," Lew said, "don't think I've flipped out. Just wake me up." Off and on, he said, the Korean nightmares persisted for years, even when he was a lieutenant colonel in Vietnam.

Some of the memories, of course, were good ones. Jack Madison recalled a day in the middle of 1951 when his company was deployed on a certain mountain top, when it came to him that here he was, twenty-three years old, and responsible for about four hundred people on that hill—his own rifle company, various attachments from the heavy weapons company, aid men, artillery observer parties, and so forth. It would have taken any higher-up several hours to climb to his position, so in effect he was on his own, responsible for all those men in a life and death situation. It was a heavy burden, but one he accepted, and suddenly he felt a surge of pride in what he and other '49ers were accomplishing.

One of my own good memories is of a day on Governors Island, when Jeanne and I met one of my heroes, Gen. Omar Bradley. (I wondered—did the general remember that brash visit from Doug Bush, the young officer eager to join the Air Force?) The *New York Times* article reporting the event, at which five of us received the Silver Star, included a paragraph which read: "A surprise member of the reviewing party was Veronica Maihafer, 2½ years old, who lined up beside General Bradley to see her father decorated and who climbed on the general's knees after the ceremony."

Two other moments come to mind. In late 1953, by which time I had returned to West Point as an instructor, I answered a knock on

Governors Island, New York, 1952. Ceremony at which Harry Maihafer was awarded the Silver Star. Left to right: *Gen. Omar Bradley; Veronica Maihafer, age 2½; Harry Maihafer; Jeanne Maihafer.*

my quarters door, and there was John Hastings, a fellow veteran of the 24th Division and a survivor of five different North Korean POW camps. We hugged a long time before we even spoke.

Another memory comes from a class reunion at West Point many years later. Following a memorial service for those who had joined "the Long Gray Line," we visited '49er graves in the Post cemetery. At each gravesite, a classmate was called on to lay a wreath and to say a few words. At Tom Hardaway's grave, I was the man selected. It was an honor to be considered Tom's special friend.

And now, almost forty years later, having revisited the sacrifices and the suffering through the memories of my classmates, I must ask the same question the veterans of all the wars throughout history must also have asked themselves—was it worth it?

Before trying to answer, however, let me explore some of the common threads running through our '49er reminiscences. Without exception, every '49er contacted praised the senior noncoms who served as our friends and teachers. Similarly, I encountered many heartwarming tributes paid '49ers by those same veteran sergeants.

Conversely, many of us ran into resentment from a few junior officers, some of whom said openly they "hated West Pointers." Often these were captains who had served in World War II and who resented, perhaps with some justification, West Pointers being considered "special cases." Whatever the reason, it was something none of us expected and all of us tried to ignore.

Korea was a time of growth and maturation, when we came to know certain unhappy truths—that our countrymen could be lukewarm in their support, that certain bosses might be overly concerned with their personal careers, and that senior commanders might often blunder. Fortunately, despite the negatives, our values, and our belief in "Duty, Honor, Country," remained intact. When our friends were killed, many of us cried out, "Korea's not worth it!" And yet, each of us understood Matthew Ridgway when he spoke of "service to our loved ones and our Nation in beating back a world menace which free men cannot tolerate."

Similarly, no one felt cynical when reading what Bill Penington wrote shortly before his death: "If anything should happen to me, realize, as I do, that neither mine nor the other daily sacrifices being made in Korea are for any but a very worthy and important cause."

So we return to the question of whether Korea was worth the cost. Personally, I believe it was. South Korea today is a prosperous ally and vigorous trading partner, a sharp contrast to the ugly, impoverished dictatorship to its north. We can only speculate on what might have been, either in South Korea or elsewhere, had the United States, and the United Nations, not taken a firm stand against Communist aggression.

Also on the plus side, '49ers who served in that "forgotten war" learned things about leadership, sacrifice, and caring for others, which stayed with us over the years, helped us in both military and civil life, and, I like to think, helped our nation as well. Reflecting on my classmates' experiences in Korea, I can't help feeling proud. I'm proud of those who were killed and proud of those who survived. As for the later years, I'm proud of those who went on to distinguished military careers, many of whom, like Joe Kingston and Clay Buckingham, became general officers; proud of those in civilian life who became teachers, attorneys, civic leaders, or, like Dolph Overton and Jack McDonald, company presidents.

And let me finally thank those who contributed to this memoir and also apologize to the many '49ers who served bravely in Korea and whose stories, because of a lack of definite information, are not contained in this book. Finally, this story would not be complete without paying tribute to the West Point Class of '50, our esteemed Korean War comrades, many of whom entered combat directly from graduation leave. Seldom have two Academy classes been linked so closely by shared experience and mutual respect.

Appendix A.

It's Happening on Your Own Front Lawn
By Robert T. Fallon
1st Lieutenant, 17th Infantry Combat Team

Author's Note: Bob Fallon, after being severely wounded, eventually ended up in Washington as a patient at Walter Reed Army Hospital. While there, he wrote "It's Happening on Your Own Front Lawn", an essay which appeared in many newspapers and magazines, including the *Saturday Evening Post*, the *Reader's Digest*, the *Washington Star*, and the *Richmond News Leader*.

I want to tell you something about a war.

I want you to imagine for a moment that it is a very cold, wet wintry evening at about 10 o'clock. You have been sitting comfortably by your fireside reading the evening paper. It's been a pleasant day, dismal outside, but warm and restful by the fire. You decide to step out on the porch for a breath of air before turning in. I'm sure you've done it often. But on this particular evening, a strange sight greets you.

There's a great hole right in the middle of your front lawn, and the dirt has been thrown up all around it, outlined sharply against the white, even snow. Squatting in the hole is a hunched figure.

Let me tell you something about him.

He's been in this area now for about three weeks, living in a dozen holes just like this one on your front lawn. The most apparent thing about him is that he is cold, and that's because out on your lawn it's about 20 degrees colder than where you're standing. Every now and then he'll grab his shovel and dig a little deeper in the hole just to keep warm. That's the only way he has, because he'll be seen if he builds a fire, and he may bring mortar fire into your living room.

He's been cold for a long time—and wet. He can't feel his feet, and he's getting worried because he's afraid they might be frostbitten. It's going to be a long night, and it's going to get colder.

He's very dirty. The grease from a hundred "C" rations is frozen to his parka and gloves, coating the two weeks' beard which covers his face. Soot from the small fires he dares to make during the day is all over his pants and boots.

But he's dirty all the way through. He hasn't changed his underclothes in over a month and he doesn't intend to for some time to come. It's too cold to go down that far. You can smell him, and it's bad.

He's pretty hungry, too. They didn't get his rations up to him until after dark and he couldn't build a fire to thaw them out. He'll have to wait until morning. A cup of hot coffee would sure taste good. He looks old with that beard and sort of hunched over posture. But he's only about 19, though not like any 19-year-old you've ever seen.

You may wonder what he's thinking about as he sits there during those long solitary hours. Well, it's not much. Just how cold it is and again how nice that coffee would be. Maybe every now and then he thinks of home, but that's a long ways off and the cold, his feet and his hunger are much more immediate. You'd be surprised how those three things can fill your mind.

You notice that he's cut a hole through your hedge and his rifle is sitting on the pile of dirt pointing in readiness through the opening. That's another thing he's thinking: When are they coming again? He gets a little scared out there all alone. He'd like to go over and talk to his buddy in a similar hole about two houses up, but it's not a good idea to go crawling around at night. He wishes they weren't so far apart but it seems they always have a big sector to cover with never enough men to cover it. It doesn't help being so far apart.

What would you like to do with this man? Ask him to your fireside, get him a cup of coffee? Would you like to loan him your razor and let him take a hot shower? Give him a bed to sleep in instead of the dirt and cold of his fox hole? Sure you would! You wouldn't think twice about it. But I'm afraid you can't. There's some one on that hill over there who wants to get into your front door, and the man was told by his platoon leader that he's supposed to take care of your house and the one next door. So he can't come in and you find that you can't reach him. He's very far away.

But you come out in the morning and he's still there, huddled over his little fire, thawing out his hands and his rations, trying to get the feeling back into his feet. By this time the hole is pretty deep from all the digging and he's cut down a little more of your hedge.

He's there again when you come home from work. While you are greeted by a comfortable fire in a living room, the soldier is getting ready for another cold night.

I have told you about this soldier, and placed him on your front lawn, because I want you to realize that every desolate hill that soldier defends in that far-off land is in reality your front door. There are people who want to get in to do you harm, and it's his job to keep them away. He's going to do his job and he's not going to ask you to do it for him. If he has to sit on your front lawn in the cold, that's just the way things go. He's not going to begrudge you the comforts of your fireside or your dinner table, but he'll be mighty bitter if he finds out that you're not doing your part of the job.

What is "your job"? Well, it's not really important what I happen to think "your job" may be. But I think it is important that you find out soon what it is and start doing it, for whatever it is, it's a vital part of a country's struggle for existence. Perhaps it would be more clear to you what your job is if you returned home tonight to find that hunched, shivering figure sitting in a hole on your lawn.

Appendix B

KOREAN WAR SERVICE, USMA '49

KIA — Killed in Action
DOW — Died of Wounds
D-POW — Died while Prisoner of War
MIA — Missing in Action
KW — Korean War Service

ENGINEERS

Brown, William C., KW 50–52
Buffington, Ralph M., 14 EC Bn 24 Div, DOW 8-12-50
Cox, Cleatus J., 802 EA Bn Oki, KW 50–52
Donohoe, Patrick J., 65 EC Bn 25 Div, KW 50
Finnegan, Marcus B., 13 ED Bn 7 Div, KW 50–51
Frech, David F., 65 EC Bn 25 Div, KW 50–51
Fullerton, Avery S., 65 EC Bn 25 Div, KW 50–51
Gallagher, Frederick S., 93 & 10 EC Bns, KW 50–52
Griffith, Harry A., 839 EA Bn, KW 51–52
Hindman, Edward R., 93 & 65 EC Bns, KW 50–52
Kurtz, Maurice K., Jr., 3 EC Bn 24 Div, KW 50–52
McIntyre, Kenneth E., 802 EA Bn 5AF, KW 50–52
Moore, William T., 14 EC Bn, KW 50–51
Neil, James M., 931 EA Gp Oki & KW, 50–52
Nunnally, Stephens W., 1 Cav Div, KW 50–51
Powers, Terence A., CE-TC, 14 EC Bn KW 50–51
Rank, William A., 1 Cav Div, KW 50
Schmidt, Norbert O., 65 EC Bn 25 Div, KW 50
Schulz, Gerhard W., KW 50–52
Strohecker, Howard L., 93 & 13 EC Bns, 2E Sp Bde, KW 51–52
Stukhart, George Jr., 2 LogCmd & 2EC Bn, KW 50–52

Suttle, Albert B. Jr., CE-TC, 839 EA Bn Okinawa, KW 50–52
Townsley, Edwin S., 93 EC Bn Oki-KW 50–51, 65 EC Bn 25 Div, KW 51
Wagner, Richard H., 8 EC Bn 1 Cav Div, KW 50–51
Wolak, Francis A., 93 & 10 EC Bns, KW 50–52

AIR FORCE

Armstrong, John W., Tdy 27 FE Wg, KW 50–51 (KIA Vietnam 67)
Banister, Arthur W., 49 FBWg, KW 52
Barnes, David P., 27 FE Gp, MIA 4-22-51, D-POW 6-20-51
Bowman, Richard C., 729 Bb Sq, 452 Bb Wg, KW 51
Brandt, Schuyler B., KW 52
Brooksher, Dan A., 677 TR Gp, KW 51–52
Bullock, Thomas F., 37 Night Intruder Sq, KW 51–52
Bush, William Douglas Jr., 335 Ftr Sq, KIA 3-26-51
Byrne, Charles A., 67 TR Gp, KW 51
Cameron, Mortimer B., Jr., 15 TR Sq, KW 50–51
Campbell, Edward J., 4 FI Wg, KW 51–52
Cleveland, Charles G., 334 FI Sq, KW 52
Crawford, Thomas M., Jr., 6148 TC SQ, KW 52–53
Crites, Carl R., 17 Bb Gp 5 AF, KW 52
Culbertson, Alexander B., WxO Marine Air Gp 12, KW 51–52
Davis, Thomas G., 335 FI Sq, KW 50
Dederich, Frederick W., 3 Bb Gp, KW 52–53
Dougherty, Ralph E., FtrPlt, KW 52–53
Ennis, Robert B., 3 Bb Wg, KW 52
Gardner, William A. Jr., 3 Bb Wg, KW 52–53
Goering, Albert H., Tdy KW 52
Greenleaf, Abbott C., KW 51–52
Gustafson, William W., Sup Sq, 20 AF, Oki, KW 52–53
Guthrie, Joseph A., Jr., TC Sq, KW 52–53
Hansen, Robert A., 30 Wx Sq, KW 51–52
Hartinger, James V., 474 FB Wg, KW 53
Hawn, John P., KW 51–52
Hendrickson, David, 8 FB Gp 5AF, KW 51–52
Howell, Robert T., TC Sq, KW 52–53
Hunnicutt, Julian P., 45 TR Sq, KW 51–52
Ike, John E., KW 51–52
Katz, Norman F., 51 FI Gp, KW 51–52
Kramer, Milton A., 8 BbSq 3 Bb Wg, KW 52
Krimendahl, David C., KW 52
Leisy, Robert E., KW 52–53

Levings, Nelson T., Jr., 474 FB Gp, KW 52
Littell, Robert O., 49 FB Gp, KW 52
McCarthy, John N., 315 Air Div, KW 52–53
McMurry, William F., D-Korea air acdt 4-19-52
McNamee, Michael W., 307 Bb Wg Oki, KW 51
Makinney, Robert L., 334 Ftr Sp 4 Ftr Wg, KW 51–52
Mechling, Eugene B., Jr., 49 FB Wg, KW 51–52
Mueller, Wilbur J., 343BbSw98 Bb Gp, KIA 6-1-61
Norby, Wayne A., 30 Wx Sq, KW 51–52
O'Brien, Phillip R., Jr., 16 FI Sq, 51 FI Wg, KW 51–52
Orem, Robert L., 6149 TC GP, KW 52–53
Overton, Dolphin D. 3rd, 16 FI Sq, 51 FI Wg, KW 51–53
Owen, Robert E., KW 52–53
Pafe, Basil, 307 Bb Wg, KW 51–52
Paull, William T., 305 Bb Wg, KW 52
Pursley, Robert E., 8 Bb Sq, 3 Bb Wg, KW 52–53
Reed, John C., 17 Bb Wg, KW 52
Saxon, John H., Jr., KW 51–52
Sayler, John M., Air Instal O, KW 50–51
Schoeneman, Richard H., 16 Ftr Sq, 51 FI Wg, KW 51–52
Spillers, William H., Jr., 90 Bb Sq, KW 51–52
Stephenson, Floyd A., Jr., FESq 27, KIA 12-13-50
Stillson, James R., 98 Bb Wg Japan, KW 53
Toth, Richard E., 307 Bb Wg Oki, KW 53
Trieschmann, William F., 91 SR Sq, Tdy KW 53
Walker, Winston G., 98 Bb Wg, KW 52
Walter, John A. III, 3 Bb Gp, KW 51–52
Weart, Douglas S., 315 TC Wg, KW 52–53
Wentsch, George M., 4 TC Sq 315 Air Div, KW 50–51
Winter, Arnold, 343 StR SQ, KW 50
Wogan, John B., Jr., TC Sq FEC, KW 50–52
Woodson, John D., TRWg, KW 50–51
Zimmerman, Elsworth J., 30 Wx Sq, KW 51–52

INFANTRY

Abele, Louis E., 45 Div, KW 52–53
Adams, Charles M., 187 Air RCT, Jap-KW 51–53
Anderegg, Harold R., 7 Cav 1 Cav Div, KW 50–51
Anders, Curtis L., 32 Inf 7 Div, KW 50–51
Anderson, Alfred J., 31 Inf 7 Div, KW 50–51
Arnette, John Q., 21 Inf 24 Div, KW 50–51

Barber, Samuel L., Jr., 7 Div, KW 51
Baumann, Louis R., 32 Inf 7 Div, KW 50–51
Bell, Clyde B., Jr., 9 Inf 2 Div, KW 53
Bender, John A., 16 Rcn Co 1 Cav Div, KW 50–51
Black, Robert W., 15 Inf 3 Div, KW 52
Bolte, David E., 8 Cav 1 Cav Div, KW 50
Brian, A. Beecher, 5 Cav 1 Cav Div, KW 50–51
Brown, Alan G., 5 Cav 1 Cav Div, KW 50
Bunn, Charles N., Rgr Co 25 Div, KW 50–51
Byrd, Roy T., 38 Inf 2 Div, KW 50–51 (POW 51–53)
Callaway, Howard H., 17 Inf 7 Div, KW 50
Cavalcante, Anthony, Jr., 187 RCT, Jap & KW 51–53
Cave, Edmund H., 65 Inf 3 Div, KW 50–51
Coursen, Samuel S., 5 Cav 1 Cav Div, KIA 10-12-50
Cummings, Barnard, Jr., 25 Div Rgr Co, KIA 11-26-50
Davis, Courtenay C., Jr., 5 Cav 1 Cav Div, KIA 9-13-50
Denham, Ernest W., Jr., 21 Inf 24 Div, KW 51
Dunphy, Richard T., 7 Div, KW 50–51
Eagers, Joseph A., 25 Div, KW 50
Eaton, Frederic N., 7 Cav 1 Cav Div, KIA 9-2-50
English, Allen J., Jr., 17 Inf 7 Div, KW 50–51
Fallon, Robert T., 17 Inf 7 Div, KW 50
Fatum, John J., 7 Cav 1 Cav Div, KW 50–51
Fife, Roger L., 8 Cav 1 Cav Div, KIA 9-22-50
Forrest, John F., 5 Cav 1 Cav Div, 50–51
Gerometta, Arthur L., 8 Cav 1 Cav Div, KW 50–51
Hardaway, Thomas G., 21 Inf 24 Div, KIA 9-8-50
Hastings, John H., 19 Inf 24 Div, KW 50 (POW 50–53)
Hayes, John G., 5 RCT 24 Div, KW 50
Hickey, Pennell J., 7 Cav 1 Cav Div, KW 50–51
Hodes, John T., 1 Cav Div, KW 50–51
Hoffman, William H., 7 Cav 1 Cav Div, KW 50–51
Hopkins, Norman B., Jr., 5 Cav 1 Cav Div, KW 50–51
Jensen, Reed G., 17 Inf 7 Div, KW 50
Johnson, Robert J., Inf-Ord, 17 Inf 7 Div, KW 50–51
Johnson, Ross L., 5 Cav 1 Cav Div, KW 50–51
Kelly, Roger J., 19 Inf 24 Div, D-Pusan Hosp 9-28-50
Kempen, William S. Jr., 32 Inf 7 Div, KIA 11-28-50
Kendree, Ulmont R., 8 Cav 1 Cav Div, KW 50–51
Kingston, Joseph B., 32 Inf 7 Div, KW 50–51
Kirkpatrick, Leslie W., 19 Inf 24 Div, KIA 5-11-50
Kuhlman, Roger R., 5 Cav 1 Cav Div, KIA 9-12-50

Lauer, Jerry B., 7 Div, KW 51
Lindeman, Arthur H., Jr., 7 Cav, KW 50
Long, Homer S., Jr., 5 Cav 1 Cav Div, KW 50–51
Lynch, Robert O., 5 Cav 1 Cav Div, KW 50–51
Mackert, John R., 24 Div, KW 51–52
Madison, John H., Jr., 32 Inf 7 Div, KW 50–51
Magruder, Munro, 8 Cav 1 Cav Div, KIA 9-3-50
Maihafer, Harry J., 21 Inf & Hq 24 Div, KW 50–51
Marder, Eugene, 5 Cav 1 Cav Div, KW 50
Marshburn, Herbert E., Jr., 32 Inf 7 Div, KIA 12-3-50
Marslender, William M., 7 Cav 1 Cav Div, KW 50–51
Messinger, Lucien E. III, 8 Cav 1 Cav Div & PsyWar 8 AR, KW 50–51
Metzger, J. Hayes, 23 Inf 2 Div, KW 52
Meyerson, Dean W., 8 Cav 1 Cav Div, KW 50–51
Miller, Kenneth W., 8 Cav & 2 Div, KW 50–52
Miller, Robert C., 65 Inf 3 Div, KW 50
Morton, Richard L., Inf-TC, 7 Cav 1 Cav Div, KW 50–51
Newman, Cecil E., 5 Cav 1 Cav Div, KIA 8-15-50
Norman, William C., 31 Inf 7 Div, KW 51–52
Odell, Fenton M., 8 Cav 1 Cav Div, KIA 9-2-50
Ogden, Lawrence J., 7 & 8 Cav & Hq 8 Ar, KW 50–52
Orton, George S., 17 Inf 7 Div, KW 50–51
Penington, William R., 32 Inf 7 Div, KIA 3-11-51
Puckett, Ralph, Jr., 8 Ar Ranger Co, KW 50
Ragucci, John J., 19 Inf 24 Div. KIA 1-1-51
Ritchie, Robert B., 5 RCT 24 Div, DOW Korea 4-31-51
Rountree, Billy Joe, 24 Inf 25 Div, KW 50–51
St. Clair, Joseph P., 3 Div, KW 50–51
Sanders, Robert C., 65 Inf 3 Div, KW 50–51
Scholtz, James H., 5 Cav 1 Cav Div, KW 50–51
Smith, Wayne C., Jr., 9 Inf 2 Div, KW 52
Steffy, Joseph B., Jr., 3 Div, KW 50–51
Street, St. Clair, Jr., 65 Inf 3 Div, KW 52
Swett, Trevor W., Jr., 24 Inf 25 Div, KW 50
Tallman, Richard J., 3 Div, KW 51–52 (KIA Vietnam 72)
Terrien, Paul D., 17 Inf 7 Div, KW 50–51
Thomas, Jack D., 32 Inf 7 Div, KW 50–51
Tobin, Richard E., 7 Cav 1 Cav Div, KW 50–51
Toomey, Joseph D., Jr., 5 Cav 1 Cav Div, KW 50, D-POW 2-28-51
Tow, George W., 5 Cav 1 Cav Div, KIA 9-17-50
Tracy, George W., 17 Inf 7 Div & Hq X Corps, KW 51–52
Turley, Joseph M., 19 Inf 24 Div, KW 50–51

Underwood, Arthur R., 65 Inf 3 Div, KW 50–52
Vollmer, John P., 17 Inf 7 Div, KW 50–51
Wadsworth, William M., 9 Inf 2 Div, D-Jap wds 12-3-50
Walz, Charles, 35 Inf 25 Div, KW 50–51
Ware, Harry W., Jr., 17 Inf 7 div, D-Korea wds 11-5-50
White, Stephen J., 187 RCT, KW 50–51
Wightman, John D., 8 Cav 1 Cav Div, KW 50–52
Wilbur, William H., Jr., 8 Cav 1 Cav Div, DOW 9-6-50
Williams, Murray W., 23 Inf 2 Div, KW 52–53
Zickel, Lewis E., 5 Cav 1 Cav Div, KW 50–51

USMC

Crall, George M., USMC, KW 50–52

ARTILLERY

Allen, Boyde W., Jr., 187 Abn RCT, KW 50–51
Balmer, Jesmond D., Jr., 187 Abn RCT, KW 50–51
Bryant, Goble W., 11 FA Bn & Hq 24 Div, KW 51–52
Burckart, John C., 76 AA Bn, KW 50–52
Bush, Louis S., 7 Cav 1 Cav Div, KW 50
Cheves, Gilbert X., KW 50
Coghlan, James J., Jr., 187 RCT, KW 50–51
Craig, Richard S., 21 AA Bn, KW 50–51
Dalrymple, Robert K., 2 Cml Bn 7 Div, KW 51–52
Day, Seth S., 1 Cav Div, KW 50–51
de Correvont, Leon L., 2 Div, KW 51–52
Fitzgerald, Richard A., 82 FA Bn 1 Cav Div, 50–51
Freeman, David G., 187 RCT, KW 50–52
Giddings, Joseph A., Jr., 57 FA Bn 7 Div, KIA 11-30-50
Goessling, Ward C., Jr., 187 Abn RCT, KW 50–51
Gower, Donald N., 48 FA Bn 7 Div, KW 50–51
Hayne, Jack R., 75 & 865 AA Bns, KW 50–52
Heckman, Harvey T., 1 Cav Div, 51–52
Hoot, Herbert L., 82 FA Bn 1 Cav Div, KW 50–51
Kingdom, Arthur J., HQ 8 Ar & 99 FA Bn 1 Cav Div, KW 50–51
Lee, Charles B., 82 FA Bn 1 Cav Div, KW 50–51
Lochhead, Earl J., 52 FA Bn 24 Div, KW 50–51
McDonald, John V., 99 FA Bn 1 Cav Div, 50–51
Marley, John T., 77 FA Bn 1 Cav Div, KW 50
Moran, Clayton L., 48 FA Bn 7 Div, KW 50–51

Paden, Jerome J., 61 FA Bn 1 Cav Div, D-Jap wds 9-20-50
Roberts, Ernst E., 1 Cav Div, KW 50–51
Rosen, Bernard S., 77 FA Bn 1 Cav Div, KW 50
Ross, Edgar B., Jr., 555 FA Bn, KW 50
Ryan, John E., AA Bn 24 Div, KW 51
Sabel, Bernard C., 3 Div, KW 50–51
Sarsfield, Francis L., 1 Cav Div Arty, KW 50–51
Sickafoose, Keith E., 57 FA Bn 7 Div, KW 50–51
Smith, Simeon M., Jr., 99 & 82 FA bns 1 Cav Div, KW 50–51
Springer, Robert M., Jr., 99 FA Bn 1 Cav Div, KW 50
Turner, Albert F., 1 Cav Div, KW 50–51
Whitmarsh, James A., Jr., 26 AA Bn & Div Arty 24 Div, KW 50–51
Wood, J. Carver, Jr., 82 FA Bn 1 Cav Div, KW 50

SIGNAL CORPS

Howard, Edward B., 25 Div Sig Co, KW 50–51
Lamar, Kirby, 25 Sig Co 25 Div, KW 52–53
Lowrey, Willis H., 101 Sig Bn, KW 52–53
Monahan, Lawrence P., Jr., 7 Sig Co 7 Div, 50–51
Nigro, George A., 32, 31, & 17 Inf, 7 Div, 50–52
O'Brien, Robert T., 7 Div, KW 50–51

CHEMICAL CORPS

Vargovick, William S., 57 FA Bn 7 Div, KW 50–51
Yacker, Everett J., 65 Inf 3 Div, KW 50–52

ARMOR

Buckingham, Clay T., 64 Tk Bn 3 Div, KW 50–52
Gess, Robert H., 17 Inf 7 Div, KW 50
McBeath, Cosby Jr., 19 Inf 24 Div, KW 50–51

ORDNANCE

McCarron, Dean J., AA Units & 17 Ord Maint Co, KW 50–52

QUARTERMASTER

Deem, Fred B. Jr., KW 50–52
Martin, Stuart F., 21 Inf & 6 Med Tk Bn 24 Div, KW 50–51

KILLED IN AIRCRAFT TRAINING ACCIDENTS
DURING KW PERIOD

Gabel, Donald L., D-Williams AFB, air acdt, 7-28-50
Horton, Alan J., D-Patterson AFB, 1-15-52
Jenkins, John A., D nr Las Vegas, NV, air acdt, 7-7-50
Latimer, John B., D-Alaska, air acdt 8-23-51
McDaniel, James R., D-Williams AFB, AZ, air acdt, 8-16-51
Moore, Wayne S., Jr., D-nr Chandler, AZ, air acdt 6-29-50
Trubin, Chester, D-Germany, Air Acdt, 6-16-52

Index

From the Hudson to the Yalu was composed into type on a Compu-graphic digital phototypesetter in ten point Trump Medieval with two points of spacing between the lines. Trump Medieval was also selected for display. The book was designed by Jim Billingsley, type-set by Metricomp, Inc., printed offset by Thomson-Shore, Inc., and bound by John H. Dekker & Sons, Inc. The paper on which this book is printed carries acid-free characteristics for an effective life of at least three hundred years.

TEXAS A&M UNIVERSITY PRESS : COLLEGE STATION